THE BEST OF
THOROUGHBRED
HANDICAPPING

THE BEST OF
THOROUGHBRED
HANDICAPPING

Handicapping Advice from
Today's Leading Experts

JAMES QUINN

CASINO PRESS • NEW YORK

THE BEST OF THOROUGHBRED HANDICAPPING

For information, contact
CASINO PRESS, INC.,
128 East 56th Street,
New York, New York 10022

ISBN: 87019-028-8

10   9   8   7   6   5   4   3   2   1

To Frederick S. Davis

Table of Contents

A complete list of
THE WORLD'S FINEST LIBRARY OF GAMING BOOKS
can be found on pages 237 - 238.

Acknowledgments

I am indebted to the authors whose work has been represented in these 38 essays. Collectively, their contributions have absolutely transformed the study and practice of the great game of handicapping. That which formerly has been considered dubious and oftentimes scandalous today enjoys a basis in scholarship and even science. It has been no small feat.

Whether racegoers will become loyal participants in the pari-mutuel wagering games offered by racetracks depends ultimately on their ability to handicap intelligently and effectively. The sources of instruction illustrated here are offered to handicappers and racegoers everywhere as the best of their time. For students of the game, these authors also deserve credit for making these the most interesting and exciting of times.

Alphabetically, I wish to acknowledge Tom Ainslie, Andy Beyer, Mark Cramer, Steven Davidowitz, Fred Davis, Burton Fabricand, Milt Gaines, Gordon Jones, Henry Kuck, Bonnie Ledbetter, Huey Mahl, John Meyer, William Quirin, Steven A. Roman, William L. Scott, and James Selvidge.
Also, from another time, Robert Saunders Dowst.

Moreover, many excellent handicappers and students of the art nowadays provide local services and products that can be fairly characterized as reflecting no less than the latest and best in information and knowhow. Two that have influenced my thinking and in that way have contributed nicely to this recollection are Ron Cox, of San Francisco, and Scott McMannis, of Chicago. To them and their colleagues at North American racetracks large and small, my firm salute.

—James Quinn
Los Angeles, Ca.

THE BEST OF
THOROUGHBRED
HANDICAPPING

PERSPECTIVES

The first of its kind, this practical-technical and thoroughly comprehensive review of the literature of handicapping could not have been written as recently as fifteen years ago. The field by 1967 had continued virtually barren of the kind of literary product that invites a serious recollection and critique.

The published voices of intellectually substantial handicapping authors Colonel E. R. Bradley, Robert Dowst, Ray Taulbot, Robert Rowe, and few others represented from 1935 through 1964 only occasional and largely lost reverberations in a vast and untamed wilderness. Of handicapping instruction and its market, to the extent either was recognized to exist at all the instruction was cast as dubious to scandalous and the market was thought to consist of dreamers, drifters, and hardcore gamblers.

So pervasive were the stereotypes they became rigidly institutionalized. This assured that truly scholarly efforts to illuminate the theory and practice of the great game of handicapping would be met among decent people with a massive skepticism and resistance.

The penetrating aroma of mischief served as well to cloud the better judgment of those book publishers and racetrack operators susceptible to the widely-dispersed tendencies to play it safe and to run scared. In consequence, handicapping instruction and the literature that suffuses it with knowledge, evidence, and wisdom did not seriously accumulate.

Those days have ended.

In the period encompassed by this anthology, from 1965 to 1984, the literature of handicapping has grown into its coming of age, and indeed has greatly matured. The period has absolutely luxuriated in the book publications of several major authors, numerous important others, and the kinds of scholarly contributions that were unprecedented just a while ago. The scientific method has wedged its way into the study of handicapping, lending its rigor, and demanding that future claims of success unsupported by facts cannot be held as tenable. Owing to the best probability studies yet conducted in this field, the art of handicapping enjoys today a scientific basis at last. Those findings are generously sprinkled throughout these pages.

As with any of its kind, this collection has been necessarily selective, resulting in 38 essays its author believes represent the brightest kaleidoscope in the current literature about fundamental handicapping and effective racetrack money management. The essays survey 18 authors and 29 books or articles. No doubt some meritorious books have been left out. In most cases disregard for meaningful work is more apparent than real. Where substance has overlapped as between authors, priority was afforded those books that have enjoyed national distribution and impact, and therefore have achieved stronger identity among larger numbers of handicappers, such that points of departure and frames of reference might be more commonly recognized and shared.

Other criteria of selection deserve explication. In concert with sticking to the facts, assertions as to the effectiveness or usefullness of ideas, techniques, or methods were required to display their verification, either statistical support or empirical support, the latter deriving from systematic field studies that are properly focused, lengthy, representative of the racing calendar, free of subjective bias, and factually-based in the reporting of findings. Where exceptions have been admitted, these have been qualified. Moreover, descriptive studies were required to remain consistent with the statistical evidence supplied by more rigorous research. Where the two conflicted, the hard stuff carried the point.

Priority was awarded too to information attending to fundamental kinds of questions or problems. The wider the scope of a text, or the broader the problem area under study, the likelier the contribution has been included here. Related to this was an expedient capitulation to that which might be more practical for, useful to, or applicable by the majority of handicappers at most tracks. Well-defined practices, techniques, or methods, these were especially emphasized.

Alternatively, there is wonderful merit to the argument that nothing is so practical as a pertinent idea properly applied. Important ideas about handicapping and money management find full expression in these pages. Where ideas dominate, a concentrated attempt to translate these into appropriate practices has been made, either by citing the author's application, if available, or, if not, by inventing a tenable alternative.

The matter of exposition was also considered important. Research and its resulting knowledge are pragmatic only to the extent the ideas have been communicated with clear, logically arranged, and civilized prose. Where exposition has been ambiguous, confusing, exaggerated, or contradictory, its message has been sacrificed.

A danger with a review of literature is to place excessive stress on interpretation or judgment, the latter surely. Put into context, the facts speak best when they speak for themselves. Great attention was paid therefore to allowing handicapping authors to retain their personal interpretations and evaluations. Where secondary interpretation has been provided, naturally I stand responsible for misinterpretations or misguided judgments. Where comment on factual presentations that would be anything less than positive needed to be engaged at all, I chose instead to avoid the clash of issues.

On that point the practitioner's guide to the handicapping literature is intended as a guide to that which has been good to excellent. The purpose will have been achieved if readers discover or rediscover here the best of familiar authors Tom Ainslie, Andy Beyer, William Quirin, Steve Davidowitz, Fred Davis, Huey Mahl, Gordon Jones, and James Selvidge, plus the best from Henry Kuck, John Meyer, Bonnie Ledbetter, William L. Scott, James Quinn, Burton Fabricand, Milt Gaines, Steven Roman, and Mark Cramer. There is too a modernized reacquaintance with a friendly ghost from handicapping's past, Robert Saunders Dowst.

Finally, before beginning, a caution on the matter of money management and its literature. The approaches entertained here apply best to seasonal play. Where handicapping proficiency warrants, the profits they are designed to yield are of the sort that accomplished handicappers can duplicate annually. The methods are not recommended to promote the success of recreational handicapping. That involves the attempt to make money at the races in an entertaining way, and does not often succeed. Recreational handicapping and betting includes whatever practices one enjoys, a not unimportant consideration at the track. However, the methods of money management intended for profit-making demand more deliberate considerations than those.

At the same time it so happens the inevitable opinion promoted by veteran racegoers that as soon as people become practiced handicappers their level of financial success depends on how well they manage their money is desperately wrong. It confuses money management with program management more broadly, and with self-control. Effective money management at the races is cut and dried. The behavior associated with its implementation is automatic. Nothing at the track is more easily applied than an operationally-defined, demonstrably-effective method of managing money, and certainly not a skill as multivarious and complex as handicapping. If the methods found here do not work for handicappers, the explanation is almost certainly a shortage of handicapping skill.

Taken in its entirety, if the literature of handicapping suggests anything approaching certitude about playing the horses, it might be this. Where handicapping knowledge and skill has risen to that certain threshhold that begs success, the application of money management procedures that maximize profits at that level of proficiency will certify financial gain. The ultimate burden rests, as always, with improving one's knowledge and skill in handicapping.

These fine pearls from the literature are intended to help handicappers everywhere accomplish precisely that.

SPEED POINTS

Developed ingeniously and tested successfully by William Quirin, Professor of Mathematics, Adelphi University, New York, and a major contemporary figure in handicapping instruction, the technique explained and illustrated below, of assigning speed points to horses, is the best known predictor of which horses are likely to control or contest the early pace.

How important is early speed? Consider the facts:

1. Horses that run 1st, 2nd, or 3rd at the first call positions in the past performances win five of every nine races at all major tracks.

2. Horses that run 1st, 2nd, or 3rd at the first call positions win far more than their fair share of all races (179 percent) and as a group throw a profit of approximately 28 percent on the invested dollar when bet to win.

3. Though early speed horses perform best in sprints, the above statistics hold relatively stable at all distances.

4. Horses able to get a clear early lead at the first call (one length or better) are among the best bets at racetracks when sent off at odds of 10-1 or lower. These win almost three times their rightful share of races, and return an astonishing 80 percent on the dollar. As a group, these frontrunners represent perhaps the most consistent overlays in racing. Taking pains to predict which horses might earn the early lead seems well worth the effort.

The practice of assigning speed points relies on the first call positions of horses in *Daily Racing Form's* past performance tables.

For sprints, or races around one turn, the first call position occurs after the horses have raced for one-quarter mile.

Speed points are assigned and totalled for three recent

qualifying races, but never referring back to more than the latest five races. Three races are used because a series of performances represent a far better predictor of what should happen today than does any single race.

Here are the rules and some illustrations:

For horses in sprints, award speed points as follows:

1 point	for any sprint in which the horse ran 1-2-3 at the first call.

and

1 point	for any sprint in which the horse ran within two lengths at the first call
0 points	for any other sprint performance
0 points	for any route performance, **unless** the horse ran within one length of the lead at the first call, in which case the race is passed (receives a bye).

Exception: at seven furlongs, a horse is eligible for two points only if it **led** at the first call; if the horse were merely 2nd or 3rd, or within two lengths, it gets just one point.

Each horse starts with "1" speed point and the total for its three "rated" races is added to "1". At that point, horses will be assigned between 1 and 7 speed points.

To get a bonus point, for a total 8, the horse must have **led** or raced **within a neck** of the leader in each rated race.

Examples:

William Quirin, "Winning at the Races: Computer Discoveries in Thoroughbred Handicapping," *William Morrow and Company*, Inc., New York, 1979, Ch. 2, pp. 32-37.

Arrant Drive, 5th and 5½ behind at the first call Nov 8 gets no speed points for that race.

It earns two points Oct. 31.

Oct. 16 it gets no points for position, but 1 for being within two lengths of the lead.

Total speed points equals 3 plus the original 1, for 4.

Milt the Tilt — B. g. 6, by Creme dela Creme—Bright Match, by Nashua

Own.—Fourzon H — 119 — Br.—B C Farm (Ky) — Tr.—Moffatt Alex — $12,500 — 1981 6 3 1 0 $11,386 — 1980 1 0 0 0

13Nov81-1Hol	6f	:22	:45	1:10^{1}ft	*2	118	3^{4}	2$^{3\frac12}$	2^{3}	2$^{1\frac12}$	Pincay L Jr^{8}	12500	84	Parkinthedark, MilttheTilt,Rooney	12
31Oct81-7LA	6f	:22^{1}	:45^{4}	1:11^{4}ft	*3-2	120	3$^{\frac12}$	3^{4}	3$^{2\frac12}$	1$^{\frac34}$	Navarro V G^{1}	c7500	86	MilttheTilt,ArrntDriv,Disingnucus	10
26Sep81-9AC	6f	:22^{1}	:44^{2}	1:09^{1}ft	2½	120	1^{hd}	2^{hd}	2$^{1\frac12}$	4^{5}	Navarro V G^{3}	Alw	88	NovaPark,Knight'sValor,Financiero	6
12Sep81-10AC	6f	:22^{2}	:44^{3}	1:08^{3}ft	2	114	1$^{1\frac12}$	1^{1}	1^{1}	1$^{2\frac12}$	Navarro V G^{3}	Alw	96	Milt theTilt,Nanimo,SanMarinoPals	8
30Aug81-4AC	6f	:22^{2}	:44^{4}	1:09 ft	2¾	120	1^{hd}	1^{1}	1^{2}	1^{5}	Zubieta F^{6}	5000	94	Milt the Tilt,Kerave,LayOnMacduff	7
15Aug81-2AC	6f	:22	:44^{4}	1:10^{4}ft	*8-5	120	1^{hd}	2^{2}	2^{2}	5$^{3\frac12}$	Zubieta F^{5}	5000	81	SirJ.J.,LayOnMacduff,Struttin'Billy	7
3Apr80-1SA	6f	:21^{4}	:44^{4}	1:09^{3}ft	9½	115	2^{hd}	3^{4}	7^{11}	8^{18}	Baltazar C^{6}	c9000	73	King Elect, Jim Burke, No Bias	9

Nov 10 Hol 3f ft :35^{4} h   Oct 26 AC 5f ft :59^{4} h   ●Oct 18 AC 6f ft 1:10^{4} h   ●Oct 13 AC 4f ft :48^{4} h

Milt the Tilt earned 1 point for its 3rd place Nov. 13. It earned two points Oct. 31, racing 3rd and within 2 lengths. It earned two more points Sept. 26 at Caliente. Total: 6 speed points.

Fancy Guy — B. g. 4, by Gin Tour—Extravagant Lady, by Bold Combatant

Own.—Murdock-Wiseman-Wright — 116 — Br.—Nicholson J W (Cal) — Tr.—Wright Robert — $12,500 — 1981 12 0 3 2 $13,675 — 1980 16 3 1 1 $14,135

20Nov81-2Hol	6½f	:22	:45	1:16^{2}ft	34	117	5$^{2\frac34}$	5$^{5\frac14}$	6^{10}	7^{13}	Spencer S J^{3}		16000	75	Decoded,SpottedLion,OmahaMike	11
9Nov81-7LA	7f	:22	:45^{2}	1:25 ft	13	114	4^{3}	4$^{3\frac12}$	3^{3}	3$^{3\frac12}$	Spencer S J^{2}		16000	80	RottnScott,Toondr'sBrthr,FncyGy	10
13May81-2Hol	1$\frac{1}{16}$:46^{4}	1:12^{1}		1:44^{2}ft	18	116	1^{1}	4$^{1\frac12}$	7^{10}	10^{16}	Lipham T^{2}		12500	57	BendIntheRod,AlphPower,OldAce	11
24Apr81-2Hol	1$\frac{1}{16}$:47^{1}	1:12^{1}		1:45 ft	5½	116	1^{1}	1^{hd}	2^{3}	2^{6}	Castaneda M^{4}		c10000	64	Sky Mission,FancyGuy,MainGa'lant	7
4Apr81-1SA	6f	:21^{3}	:44^{2}	1:09^{3}ft	9¼	116	7$^{5\frac14}$	7$^{8\frac12}$	7$^{8\frac14}$	7^{11}	CastanedaM^{4}	Ⓢ	16000	80	BondRullh,KngTutnkhmun,VlntnLw	8
28Mar81-9SA	1$\frac{1}{16}$:46	1:10^{3}		1:43^{3}ft	15	116	3^{1}	—	—	—	McHargue DG^{1}		20000	—	DrStork,PlasticFntstic,TheMethod	10
28Mar81—Eased																
13Mar81-2SA	1	:46	1:11	1:36^{2}ft	6¼	116	1$^{4\frac12}$	1$^{1\frac12}$	1$^{1\frac12}$	2^{2}	Lipham T^{2}		c12500	85	BendIntheRod,FncyGuy,TrondSng	10
21Feb81-1SA	6½f	:21^{4}	:44^{4}	1:15^{3}ft	8	115	4^{1}	2^{hd}	3$^{\frac12}$	4^{8}	Lipham T^{1}		16000	84	TkDdAim,ThMthod,MonsignorWlsh	7
13Feb81-2SA	6f	:21^{3}	:44^{2}	1:08^{4}ft	7	115	5$^{1\frac14}$	4$^{3\frac12}$	5$^{4\frac34}$	5$^{6\frac12}$	CastanedaM^{8}	Ⓢ	16000	88	Another Toast, Clancy, Otias	9
6Feb81-3SA	6½f	:22	:44^{3}	1:16^{4}ft	2¾	115	2^{hd}	3^{1}	3^{nk}	2no	Castaneda M^{7}		c12500	86	Bold Talent, Fancy Guy, Wheat	7

●Nov 18 Hol 4f ft :46^{4} h   Nov 4 Hol tr.t 3f ft :37^{3} hg   ●Oct 27 Hol tr.t 4f ft :51^{1} h

Fancy Guy earned nothing Nov. 20. It gets nothing for Nov. 9 either. Its front-running routes of May 13 and Apr. 24 draw byes. It gets nothing for the Apr. 4 sprint. Total: 1

Red Current — Ch. c. 2, by Little Current—Hello Theo, by Pronto

Own.—Heerensperger Mr-Mrs D J — 118 — Br.—StonereathFm&VanDenBerg (Ky) — Tr.—Smith Marion L — 1981 6 1 2 0 $14,925

31Oct81-10LA	7f	:22	:45^{3}	1:24^{1}ft	28	115	2^{1}	4$^{4\frac12}$	5^{11}	5^{12}	Nicolo P^{6}	Juaneno	76	Tropic Ruler, BisonBay,SafeAtFirst	6
14Oct81-8SA	1$\frac{1}{16}$:46^{2}	1:11^{3}		1:43^{3}ft	15	117	3^{1}	6$^{4\frac12}$	7^{12}	7^{20}	McCrrCJ^{4}	El Rio Rey	63	PrincSpllbound,Muttrag,SpdBrekr	10
27Sep81-9Lga	1$\frac{1}{16}$:47^{1}	1:12^{3}		1:45^{3}sy	*2¾	113	3^{4}	3^{4}	4^{8}	2^{11}	Nicolo P^{9}	Juvenile	60	FlyngJudgmnt,RdCrrnt,NghtT[illegible]	9
13Sep81-5Lga	6½f	:22^{1}	:45^{2}	1:16^{1}ft	3	110	2^{1}	1$^{1\frac12}$	1^{hd}	1$^{2\frac12}$	Nicolo P^{8}	Alw	88	RedCurrent,ImaSizzler,Jcket'sSong	8
29Aug81-5Lga	6f	:21^{3}	:45^{3}	1:12 ft	7	120	4$^{4\frac12}$	3$^{5\frac12}$	3$^{3\frac12}$	2$^{1\frac12}$	Loseth C^{5}	Mdn	74	MstrHold'm,RdCurrnt,JollyDrmmr	11
1Aug81-4Lga	5½f	:22^{2}	:46^{3}	1:06^{1}ft	*2¼	120	5^{3}	8^{11}	7$^{9\frac34}$	4$^{6\frac14}$	Sorenson D^{3}	Mdn	75	Stroombelekee, IronAl,SyrianWay	11

Nov 24 Hol 5f ft 1:00^{4} h   Nov 16 Hol 5f ft 1:00^{4} h   Nov 10 Hol 5f ft 1:00^{4} h   Oct 21 Hol tr.t 4f ft :51 h

Red Current earns 1 point for its 7f quarter Oct. 31, when it was a length behind, but gets nothing for racing 2nd at 7f. It gets a bye for the Oct. 14 route for racing within a length at the half-mile call, but earns nothing for the Sept. 27 route. It earns two points Sept. 13. Total: 4

Matching

Matching							Ro. f. 3, by What Luck—Dancing Straw, by Dancing Dervish								
							Br.—Henderson S F (Ky)						1981 9 4 3 0	$71,800	
Own.—Henderson S F						121	Tr.—Taliaferro Charles L						1980 5 1 1 1	$5,455	
15Nov81-7Hol	6f	:22	:444	1:09 ft	9-5	120	21½	21½	2hd	12	Baltazar C4	ⒻAlw	92	Matching,ImperialLass,She'sSwope	6
1Nov81-10LA	6f	:214	:45	1:093ft	*6-5	117	1½	12	12	12¾	BaltazarC7	ⒻMsn Vjo	97	Mtching,OlympicMomnt,DynmcLdy	8
23Oct81-7SA	6f	:213	:441	1:082ft	9¼	118	2hd	2½	2hd	2no	Baltazar C3	ⒻAlw	96	ExcitableLdy,Mtching,InTrueForm	6
12Oct81-5SA	6f	:22	:451	1:102ft	*1	113	21½	32	65¼	87¾	Baltazar C4	ⒻAlw	78	Home Last,TrackJester,Jet'sDelta	10
7Sep81-5Dmr	6f	:214	:443	1:093ft	2¼	116	2hd	2hd	2hd	21½	Baltazar C1	ⒻAlw	88	La Pistola, Matching, Track Jester	5
29Aug81-7Dmr	6f	:214	:443	1:10 ft	*8-5	117	2hd	2½	12	12	Baltazar C8	ⒻAlw	88	Matching,DynamicLady,Raj'sSong	10
19Aug81-5Dmr	6f	:22	:45	1:102ft	3¾	113	21½	22½	2hd	13	Baltazar C7	ⒻAlw	86	Mtching,Belleo'Dmscus,LytLnding	10
2Aug81-5Dmr	6f	:22	:451	1:101ft	97	114	1hd	1hd	12	22½	Baltazar C3	ⒻAlw	85	NorthrnFbl,Mtchng,ConkyJohnstn	11
18Jly81-5Hol	6f	:212	:443	1:104ft	39	114	65	79¾	1012	109¾	Baltazar C3	ⒻAlw	73	Shy Bidder, On Cue, True Maiden	11
16Aug80-7Rui	6f	:23	:463	1:173sl	3	116	32½	31½	34	49½	Bickel R4	Fut Trl	60	BlueGzi,NoMnners,ImpressivWinnr	9
Nov 25 Hol 3f ft :353 h				Nov 21 Hol 4f ft :491 h					Nov 14 Hol 3f ft :354 h				Nov 10 SA 4f ft :482 h		

Matching earns two speed points for each of its last three sprints. Does it qualify for the bonus point? No. It did not race within a neck of the lead Nov. 15.

For horses in routes, award speed points as follows:

1 point	for any route in which the horse ran 1-2-3 at the first call
and	
1 point	for any route in which the horse ran within three lengths of the leader at the first call
0 points	for any other route performance
1 point	for any sprint in which the horse ran 1-2-3 or within three lengths at the first call
and/or	
1 point	for any sprint in which the horse ran within six lengths of the leader at the first call
Note:	Any sprint in which the horse was neither 1-2-3 nor within six lengths of the lead at the first call is passed (given a bye), and the handicapper refers back to the next most recent race, never going back more than five races.

As with sprints, each horse is awarded "1" point to start, and at this point has earned from 1 to 7 speed points. For routes, the bonus point goes to any horse earning a 7 that was on the lead or within one length in each of its rated races.

Nell's Briquette

Nell's Briquette							Dk. b. or br. f. 3, by Lanyon—Double's Nell, by Nodouble								
							Br.—GlenMdwFm–RchoMissnVjo (Cal)						1981 9 2 2 1	$135,470	
Own.—Triple L Stables Inc						120	Tr.—Rettele Loren						1980 6 5 1 0	$94,865	
23Aug81-8Bel	6f	:222	:452	1:093ft	15	115	42	55½	55½	69½	McHrDG8	ⒻGrFightH	85	IslndChrm,ChrokFrolic,HighstRgrd	6
2Aug81-9AP	1⅛	:46	1:104	1:493ft	*3-2	121	1hd	1hd	54½	820	Day P3	ⒻArl Oaks	63	SweetestChnt,FncyNskr,Contrefire	9
24Jly81-8Aks	1⅛	:462	1:094	1:493ft	*3-5e	123	1hd	1½	1hd	2hd	Jones K5	ⒻAks Oaks	89	Bersid, Nell'sBriquette,DoneWrong	8
15May81-8Pim	1 1/16	:47	1:113	1:441sy	4¼	121	1½	1hd	2½	45½	PssrWJ4	ⒻBlkEydSs	78	DmeMysterieuse,WywrdLss,RefPriz	7
1May81-8CD	1 1/16	:484	1:13	1:434ft	5	121	1½	32	611	621	Lively J5	ⒻKy Oaks	68	HeavenlyCause,DelRose,WywrdLss	6
4Apr81-9OP	1 1/16	:471	1:122	1:434ft	2¼	121	11	2hd	2hd	2hd	ShomkrW1	ⒻFantasy	89	HevenlyCus,Nll'sBriqutt,WywrdLss	9
21Mar81-8SA	1 1/16	:462	1:104	1:424gd	4	115	12	12	15	1¾	ShmrW3	ⒻSta Susna	87	Nell'sBriquette,BeeScout,IcPrincss	8
14Feb81-8SA	7f	:211	:433	1:222ft	9-5	121	1½	1½	12½	31¼	ShmrW8	ⒻSnta Ynez	87	PstForgtting,RosDoon,Nll'sBrqutt	11
28Jan81-8SA	6f	:213	:45	1:11 gd	3¼	121	1½	12½	14½	13¼	ShmkrW7	ⒻPasadena	84	Nll'sBriqutt,RosiDoon,PstForgtting	7
31Dec80-8SA	7f	:212	:434	1:214ft	*3-5	119	2hd	1½	1½	1no	ShrW5	ⒻⓈCal Brdrs	91	Nll'sBrqtt,OlympcMomnt,Doonstr	11
Nov 24 SA 4f ft :47 h				Nov 18 SA 4f ft :471 h											

Nell's Briquette earns 1 point Sept. 23, for racing within 6 lengths of the sprint lead. It gets 2 points Aug. 22, again July 24. Total: 5 plus the original 1, or 6.

Mercator

(Mercator past-performance chart)

Mercator gets two points Nov. 5, two more Oct. 28. The Oct. 16 sprint gets a bye. Mercator earned no points Sept. 25. Total: 5

The Method *

(The Method past-performance chart)

The Nov. 13 sprint represents a bye.

The Method earned two points October 5. It earned two points in the Sept. 25 sprint, for racing 3rd and within 6 lengths. It earned another two sprinting September 20. Total: 7

Regarding **interpretation and use**, handicappers should honor these guidelines:

1. A horse with 4 speed points or more is said to have early speed dependability. That is, such a horse is most likely to be among the early leaders.

2. Horses that have at least 4 speed points and stand alone as the highest speed point horse in the field win frequently enough to return about a 4 percent profit on the dollar. In three of four races one horse stands alone as having the highest speed point total.

3. Horses with at least 4 speed points and at least 2 points advantage over their nearest rivals do better. These kind win almost twice their rightful share of the races, and return a 10 per cent profit.

4. A horse having 8 speed points is most likely to battle the early pace or to set the pace alone. If no other horse has a high speed point figure, its chances of winning increase terrifically. But if the race contains a 7 or 6 or both, an early speed duel is likely, and this will decrease the high figure horse's chances.

5. The best way to estimate the high speed point horse's relative chances is to calculate its speed point **percentage**. Simply add each horse's speed points and divide the sum into each of the three top figure horses. Suppose the speed points in an 8-horse field are 4-2-7-4-1-4-5-2. The sum of speed points is 29. The top three figure horses have a speed point percentage equal to $7 \div 29$, $5 \div 29$, and $4 \div 29$, or 24%, 17%, and 13%. Studies indicate horses having speed point percentages of 30% or greater are most likely to dominate the early pace.

The horses below competed at the mile, a route. Their speed points have been totalled and written to the right below their names.

See if you can get the same totals for each horse.

Tiempo ✳ Dk. b. or br. h. 5, by Pontoise—Happy Apple Ann, by Right Reason
Br.—Taub L (NY) 1981 12 0 2 1 $19,516
Own.—Taub A **5** **105** Tr.—Hunt Leonard H 1980 11 1 0 2 $28,500
Turf 3 0 0 0 $1,800

12Nov81-9Aqu	7f :23² :47 1:24¹ft	9 108	4¹¹ 4² 57¹ 67¹	Samyn J L²	Ⓢ HcpO 72	AdrndckHlm,Km'sChnc,WmbrnCstl 9
12Oct81-5Bel	7f :23¹ :46² 1:24¹ft	*8-5 117	3² 1¹ 2¹ 23¹	Venezia M⁵	Ⓢ 75000 78	Roman Chef, Tiempo, Slip 6
23Sep81-1Bel	6f :23¹ :46¹ 1:10²ft	10 112	4¹¹ 2¹ 2² 2¹	Venezia M⁵	Ⓢ 75000 89	Furrow, Tiempo, Rosin The Bow 6
6Sep81-9Bel	7f :23³ :46⁴ 1:23⁴ft	15 106	11¹ 2ʰᵈ 79¹ 7¹³	Molina V H¹	Ⓢ HcpO 70	DedictedRullh,SirAck,SheerSurvivl 7
30Aug81-3Bel	1 :46⁴ 1:11² 1:37¹ft	8¹ 122	62¹ 62¹ 73¹ 7⁴	AsmssnCB³	Ⓢ 100000 78	Newsman, Slip, Roman Chef 7
21Aug81-8Sar	1⅟₁₆ ①:46²1:10 1:41 fm	27 106	6³ 6⁵ 89¹10¹¹	MglrR⁴	⒮ W. Point H 81	Naskra'sBreeze,THoTom,Adlibber 12
14Aug81-4Sar	6¹f :22² :45³ 1:17¹ft	15 1125	6³ 54¹ 32¹ 31¹	Migliore R³	Ⓢ Alw 84	Rosin The Bow, Slip, Tiempo 10
31Jly81-8Sar	6¹f :22⁴ :45⁴ 1:16¹ft	17 1105	5² 3¹ 52¹ 56¹	Migliore R⁵	Ⓢ Alw 84	DdctdRullh,Km'sChnc,WmbornCstl 6
Nov 24 Bel tr.t 3f ft :36⁴ b		Nov 20 Bel tr.t 4f ft :50¹ b		Nov 10 Bel tr.t 3f ft :37² b		Nov 5 Bel 4f ft :49³ b

Newsman B. h. 5, by Nalees Man—News Bearer, by Prince John
Br.—Bird & Moseley (NY) 1981 7 2 0 0 $55,560
Own.—Ardboe Stable **3** **113** Tr.—Kelly Thomas J 1980 8 4 1 2 $87,364
Turf 2 0 0 1 $4,440

12Nov81-9Aqu	7f :23² :47 1:24¹ft	4¹ 116	98¹ 98¹ 88¹ 57¹	Velasquez J⁵	Ⓢ HcpO 73	AdrndckHlm,Km'sChnc,WmbrnCstl 9
50ct81-8Bel	1⅟₁₆ :47² 1:11³ 1:49¹ft	2¹ 116	53¹ 79¹ 43¹ 48¹	Viszan J²	Ⓢ B F Bongard 72	Accptr'sHp,AdrndckHlm,DdctdRllh 7
16Sep81-8Bel	1 :45⁴ 1:10² 1:36³sy	4 113	5⁸ 4³ 2¹ 12¹	VisquzJ⁴	Ⓢ Hudson H 85	Newsman, Sir Ack,DedicatedRullah 5
30Aug81-3Bel	1 :46⁴ 1:11² 1:37¹ft	3 122	2ʰᵈ 3ⁿᵏ 2ʰᵈ 1ʰᵈ	VelasquezJ²	Ⓢ 100000 82	Newsman, Slip, Roman Chef 7
21Aug81-8Sar	1⅟₁₆ ①:46²1:10 1:41 fm	26 112	11¹³10⁹¹10¹⁰ 9⁹	VlsqzJ⁹	Ⓢ W. Point H 83	Naskra'sBreeze,THoTom,Adlibber 12
14Aug81-4Sar	6¹f :22² :45³ 1:17¹ft	*2 117	7⁸ 78¹ 7⁶ 7³	Velasquez J⁶	Ⓢ Alw 83	Rosin The Bow, Slip, Tiempo 10
31Jly81-8Sar	6¹f :22⁴ :45⁴ 1:16¹ft	7¹ 115	3¹ 4¹ 4² 4⁵	Velasquez J⁶	Ⓢ Alw 86	DdctdRullh,Km'sChnc,WmbornCstl 6
11Jly80-5Bel	1⅟₁₆ :48¹ 1:13 1:50¹ft	*7-5 115	31¹ 3¹ 3ʰᵈ 2ⁿᵒ	Velasquez J⁶	Ⓢ HcpO 76	Kim's Chance, Newsman, Furrow 6
Nov 19 Bel 3f ft :36 b		Nov 10 Bel tr.t 3f ft :37 h		Nov 4 Bel 5f ft :59⁴ h		Oct 25 Bel tr.t 6f ft 1:20 b

North Country Blue

Gr. g. 4, by Turn to Mars—Paula Jean, by O'Hara
Br.—LochwinnockBloodstockLtd (NY) 1981 29 5 5 2 $110,600
Own.—Garren M M 5 111 Tr.—Puentes Gilbert 1980 7 1 2 3 $32,200
Turf 4 0 0 2 $7,200

12Nov81-9Aqu 7f :232 :47 1:241ft 6½ 113 86½ 86½ 45½ 42½ MacBeth D7 [S]HcpO 77 AdrndckHlm,Km'sChnc,WmbrnCstl 9
2Nov81-5Aqu 7f :224 :454 1:232ft *6-5 119 66 66 31 1½ Velasquez J3 [S]Alw 84 NorthCountryBlu,ShrSrvvl,FrlssLdr 7
23Oct81-6Aqu 6f :23 :462 1:111ft 7¾ 117 69 69 65½ 31¼ Velasquez J1 [S]Alw 84 KnghtlSpcd,EdOfWsdm,NrthCntrBl 6
16Oct81-1Aqu 6f :232 :47 1:112ft 4¼ 112 31½ 33 34 32½ VelasquezJ3 [S] 125000 81 ProdNorthrn,Frrow,NorthContryBl 5
8Oct81-5Bel 7f :234 :473 1:251ft 4½ 117 63¾ 53¾ 12 14¼ Velasquez J2 [S]Alw 76 NrthCntrBl,EdgOfWsdm,KnhtlSpcd 7
27Sep81-4Bel 6f :222 :461 1:114ft 5¾ 117 912 79 75¾ 42¼ Velasquez J4 [S]Alw 80 EdgOfWsdom,ProdNrthrn,ShrSrvvl 9
17Sep81-3Bel 1 1/16 :47 1:114 1:43 m *1 117 33½ 32 43 46¾ MacBeth D5 [S]Alw 80 AdmirlByrd,NeedAPenny,BnglLncr 8
4Sep81-5Bel 1 :461 1:11 1:37 ft 5 117 33 31½ 22½ 21½ MacBeth D4 [S]Alw 81 FrlssLdr,NorthCountryBl,SlckRson 8
Nov 19 Bel tr.t 5f ft 1:02 h Nov 9 Bel tr.t 5f ft 1:024 b Oct 29 Bel tr.t 5f ft 1:05 b Oct 4 Bel tr.t 5f ft 1:033 b

Publisher

Ro. g. 3, by Moving Target—Exclusive Christy, by Exclusive Native
Br.—Wehle R G (NY) 1981 12 2 0 2 $27,977
Own.—Wehle R G 4 107 Tr.—Martin Frank 1980 7 4 1 0 $36,932

7Nov81-5Aqu 1 :464 1:114 1:372ft 14 1095 710 814 820 819 Molina V H1 80000 60 Main Stem, Axe TheFool,RahwayII 8
16Oct81-1Aqu 6f :232 :47 1:112ft 9 114 54½ 53¾ 44¼ 43 AsmssnCB2 [S] 125000 81 ProdNorthrn,Frrow,NorthContryBl 5
27Sep81-8FL 1 1/16 :482 1:131 1:491sy *9-5e 112 32 34 32 43 Cordero A E2 HcpO 69 HospitalShip,DancingTrget,CptinPt 6
7Sep81-9FL 1 1/16 :481 1:132 1:461hy 8¾ 115 77 46½ 48½ 618 LizG5 [S]Gensee Vly H 69 Accipiter'sHope,SeBourne,CptinPt 8
16Aug81-8FL 170 :48 1:133 1:46 sy *4-5 111 45 33½ 32 42½ Rincon R2 [S]Alw 68 HrlequinBlues,PtomcStr,GreenOrde 6
6Aug81-8Sar 1⅛ :464 1:114 1:503m 42 117 1113 811 65½ 45 AsssCB10 [S]DwittClnt 77 Accptr'sHop,AdrondckHolm,Prspr 13
19Jly81-9FL 1 1/16 :47 1:114 1:45 ft 9¾ 117 36 44 36 47¼ RnconR2 [S]N Y Derby 89 AdrondckHolm,THoTom,CmptrCrls 6
27Jun81-8FL 170 :48 1:123 1:422ft 4½ 113 33 32 1hd 11 Rincon R5 [S]Alw 103 Publisher, CaptainPat,D.J.'sNitecap 5
Nov 20 Bel tr.t 4f ft :49 h ●Nov 17 Bel tr.t 4f ft :472 h Nov 14 Bel tr.t 4f ft :49 h Oct 30 Bel tr.t 4f ft :49 h

Roman Chef

B. g. 6, by Roman Range—Sand Pail, by Beau Gar
Br.—Lawrence J C (NY) 1981 15 4 3 2 $32,740
Own.—Thylan H 5 108 Tr.—Schlesinger Todd D 1980 8 0 2 0 $12,080
Turf 2 0 1 0 $4,400

12Oct81-5Bel 7f :231 :462 1:241ft 9½ 114 56½ 43 1½ 13¼ AsmussnCB4 [S] 70000 81 Roman Chef, Tiempo, Slip 6
12Sep81-2Bel 7f :234 :471 1:241ft 3½ 1105 76½ 76¼ 67½ 610 Migliore R2 [S] 57500 71 BcnndEggs,EdgOfWsdm,AdmrlBrd 7
30Aug81-3Bel 1 :464 1:112 1:371ft 3¾ 1075 1hd 2hd 1hd 3¾ Migliore R1 [S] 75000 81 Newsman, Slip, Roman Chef 7
26Aug81-3Bel 1 :461 1:112 1:374ft *2 117 54¾ 32½ 54½ 46½ Maple E6 [S] 50000 72 SlickReson,Strtop'sAc,BconndEggs 7
22Jly81-2Bel 1 1/16 :462 1:111 1:422ft 12 1075 31 2hd 12 13¾ Migliore R1 [S] 50000 90 Roman Chef. Slip, Rosin The Bow 8
13Jly81-9Bel 7f :241 :474 1:243ft 5¼ 1125 2½ 21½ 43 45½ Velez J A Jr5 [S] 50000 73 Slip, Bacon and Eggs, Eddie'sLuck 7
4Jun81-3Bel 7f :23 :463 1:241m 3 1125 67½ 54¾ 33½ 21¼ Migliore R2 [S] 50000 80 Slip, Roman Chef, Eddie's Luck 9
14May81-1Bel 1 :461 1:113 1:383ft *8-5 1145 2½ 2½ 2½ 2½ Migliore R5 [S] 50000 74 Slip, Roman Chef, All Guns 6
Nov 11 Bel tr.t 4f ft :51 b Oct 23 Bel tr.t 4f ft :514 b Oct 6 Bel tr.t 5f ft 1:02 h

Naskra's Breeze

B. g. 4, by Naskra—Topical Heat, by Tropical Breeze
Br.—Davis C C (NY) 1981 8 2 1 2 $107,951
Own.—Broadmoor Stable 3 117 Tr.—Johnson Philip G 1980 12 5 3 1 $112,832
Turf 5 3 0 1 $118,135

3Nov81-6Aqu 1⅜ (T):492 1:394 2:182gd 3 115 33 11 2hd 31½ SmnJL5 Kn'ckrb'kr H 77 Euphrosyn,OurCptinWilli,Nskr'sBrz 8
3Nov81--Run in two divisions sixth & eighth races.
17Oct81-6Med 1 1/16 (T):472 1:104 1:41 fm *2½ 117 96¼ 87¼ 59 56½ SmnJL2 Jersey Blu H 90 Acaroid, War of Words, DataSwap 10
9Sep81-8Bel 1 1/16 (T):474 1:131 1:452sf 8¾ 112 64½ 1hd 16 111 SmynJL9 Britn Bch H 69 Nskr'sBreeze,Mnguin,RestlessThief 9
21Aug81-8Sar 1 1/16 (T):462 1:10 1:41 fm 12 117 95 76 53 1nk SnJL12 [S]W. Point H 92 Naskra'sBreeze,THoTom,Adlibber 12
10Aug81-9Sar 1 [T]:473 1:121 1:37 fm 3 116 67½ 53 2½ 1½ Samyn J L3 [S]HcpO 91 Nskr'sBrz,SrAck,NorthCountryBlu 10
10Aug81--Disqualified from purse money.
20Jly81-8Bel 1 :452 1:093 1:35 sy 19 117 45½ 44¼ 45 33¼ SJL1 [S]Evan Shipman 90 Fio Rito, Sir Ack, Naskra's Breeze 7
29Jun81-7Bel 6f :231 :463 1:11 ft 2½ 122 44½ 43½ 43 2½ Samyn J L2 [S] 75000 86 Prosper,Nskr'sBreeze,RosinThBow 6
19Jun81-5Bel 7f :231 :461 1:232ft 11 117 52½ 44 53¾ 51¾ Samyn J L3 [S]Alw 83 AdirondckHolm,SirAck,RosnThBow 6
Nov 19 Bel tr.t 4f ft :48 h Nov 13 Bel tr.t 4f ft :51 b Oct 30 Bel tr.t 4f ft :481 h Oct 25 Bel tr.t 4f ft :482 h

For horses whose past performance tables do not yet contain five races, Quirin has projected speed point totals from points already earned. Consult this table:

	Points					
Career Starts	**0**	**1**	**2**	**3**	**4**	
one start	0	3	5	x	x	**Projected Points**
two starts	0	1	3	4	5	

The zeros are included because in Quirin's original technique horses that earned no speed points beyond the one given, and did not beat at least half the field to the first call in any of their three rated races, were penalized by having the original point taken away.

OPTIMAL BETTING

In a beautifully concise and possibly perfect technical paper on money management delivered in 1979, the redoubtable Huey Mahl took bettors of games by the hand, escorted them to the mountaintop, and there explained the facts of life in language so clear and persuasive that anyone who listened and learned the truth need never be troubled again. Handicappers sufficiently skilled in their art that they are capable of making seasonal profits by betting on horses can take it as gospel that the source of their greatest possible prosperity is Mahl. The method of the man is called Optimal Betting, and it is exactly that.

Handicappers in consultation with Mahl will at last find answers to all the eternal questions. They can consider themselves for now and evermore enlightened on the following:

1. What exactly is the nature of a gamble?

2. Whether to bet at all, or how to determine whether they can expect positive results?

3. How to bet, or how to maximize the utilization of capital?

4. How much to bet, or how to relate the size of the bet to their advantage in the game?

5. How not to bet, or how to turn advantage into disadvantage, and certain profits into certain losses?

6. How to use a simple mathematical formula to determine the optimal size of the bet?

As Mahl tells, a gamble consists of three elements: the event, the proposition, and the bet. The handicapper's **event** is the horse race. Nobody bets on that. Handicappers bet on the **propositions** offered by other handicappers, not so dissimilar from neighborhood bar bets, specifically on the odds spreads that reflect all the players' opinions regarding the winning chances of each horse. Because the proposition is framed by the public, fallible and possibly badly informed people, bettors sometimes encounter propositions that offer a **positive expectancy.** That is, bets on certain kinds of propositions have been known historically by the bettor to achieve positive results. Winning bettors bet on propositions whose outcomes they know to be ultimately and necessarily positive. To this incredibly important point we shall return immediately.

First, Mahl considers the actual bet. **It is the single aspect of the gamble over which the bettor exercises complete control, or relative lack of same. The prime considerations are method and size. The flat bet (same amount each bet) turns out to serve a critical function. It determines whether the bettor has a positive expectancy. Handicappers need to know first of all whether a season's selections win or lose money. They also need to know the average mutuel on winning bets. Flat bets, of a season's duration, tell handicappers whether they are playing a losing game. Those that are best retreat to a study of handicapping, and postpone the wrestling with money management methods. None that count will matter anyhow, unless flat bets first determine a positive expectancy.**

Handicappers discovering a positive expectancy with flat bets have satisfactory basis for assuming profits over time, the critical point previously remarked, but should consider whether that method gets the most from their money. Mahl says no. He hastens to comment on the variation of flat betting referred to as unit betting, whereby handicappers bet more on some bets than on others, either when pressing good luck or having high confidence in the expected outcome. This works well enough when winning streaks occur, but as Mahl explains, unit betting has a great capacity for converting a positive expectancy into loss. If handicappers lose the big ones and win the little ones, to use Mahl's metaphor, they are deep in mashed potatoes again.

Huey Mahl, *Money Management*, a technical paper delivered in symposium at the SportsTyme Handicapping Seminar, Dunes Hotel, Las Vegas, Nevada, Dec. 12-13, 1979, *GBC Press*, Las Vegas, Nevada, 1979.

Flat betting is also held to be ultra-conservative. It takes quite a season to make any real money with that method. And the question and answer remain. Are flat bets the best way to appreciate a bankroll? No. At some point beyond the expectancy that signals positive results, handicappers are urged to entertain money management methods capable of maximizing results.

There is really only one. Optimal betting. Optimal betting holds that the bettor gets maximum appreciation on investment only by sizing the bet as a **percentage of bankroll equal to the bettor's advantage over the game.** Mahl provides the formula that determines the bettor's advantage, and therefore the percent of capital to be bet. Handicappers will arrive at that great divide momentarily.

First, the rationale for the method and Mahl's explanation of the occasional reverent references among punters to the Kelly Criterion. It came to pass that J. L. Kelly, Jr., a mathematician with Bell Telephone in the fifties, solved a greatly technical communications problem by using complex calculus formulae he published in a treatise entitled "A New Interpretation of Information Rates." How Mahl came to prosper by the article is strictly coincidental, as Kelly used gambling as the analogy for his problem-solving.

Kelly told of baseball results passing along a ticker wire into an illegal bookie parlor. A telephone man, he said, could interrupt the wire flow, intercept the transmission, and make a bet with the bookie before reconnecting the wire and transmitting the results. Kelly asked how much the telephone man should bet on the game? Since the outcome was 100 percent certainty, the telephone man should bet every penny he owned, and make a 100 percent profit. The operating principle was **maximum utilization of capital**, or optimal betting, the putting of money to work in the most effective manner.

Next Kelly assumed the possibility of a transmission error. If the telephone man intercepted the wire once a week, how much should be bet each time? To frame the question differently, since the outcome was now something less than 100 percent certainty, how to determine the size of bet or percentage of bankroll the telephone man could afford each week, and still achieve optimal results in terms of bankroll appreciation?

Mahl perceived that in each case Kelly was betting on a sure thing. The single difference was the difference between 100 percent profit maximization (based on certainty) and something less than 100 percent profit maximization (based on some advantage less than certainty). What Kelly and his calculus went on to prove Huey Mahl translated into the first axiom of betting. For optimum results, the size of the bet, taken as a percentage of the bettor's bankroll, should be equivalent to the bettor's advantage over the game.

In any game having a one to one (even) proposition, Kelly showed that a bettor's advantage was equal to $P-Q$. Mahl translated the symbols to Win Percentage−Loss Percentage, a remarkably simple way to calculate your advantage over a game, as illustrated in the blackjack sample below. Blackjack counters who determined the remaining cards in a deck presented propositions that were 52% favorable to the player, 48% unfavorable, knew they enjoyed a 4% advantage. Thus, they bet 4% of their bankroll. If the bankroll were $1000, the bet each time was $40.

The graph **OPTIMAL BETTING** illustrates a feature of the method almost universally ignored or misunderstood. To wit, a bankroll grows positively and reaches a peak when the percentage bets are **equal to** the advantage. If bettors bet in percentage amounts larger than their advantage, however, the bankroll will begin to decrease, eventually to convert positive results (+) into losses (−). Even though the bettor holds an advantage over a game, if the bettor bets too much, the bettor will lose.

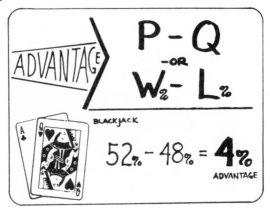

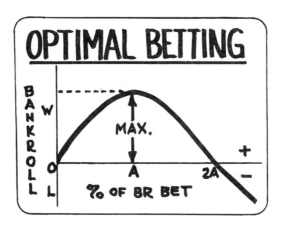

OPTIMAL BETTING

Mahl supposes a guy has a 10 percent advantage over his pals in a nightly bar bet. Thus he wins 55 percent of the time, loses 45 percent. If the guy's playing with $1000 to start, then his first bet is $100 (10% advantage), and changes thereafter only as the bankroll changes. Suppose the guy gets greedy, says Mahl, and starts to bet 20% of his bankroll. By betting twice his advantage (2A on the graph), the guy ends as a loser for sure. That indeed the greedy bettor will loss is a mathematical certainty. A crucial principle of optimal betting techniques is this: the bettor will win less if he bets more at a certain point, that point being any percentage of capital beyond the bettor's advantage over the game.

Now to handicapping, where the one to one relationship is replaced by pari-mutuel betting odds. The adjustment to the optimal betting formula is simple. It divides the loss percentage by the **average payoff to one dollar**. Thus,

$$\%\text{Advantage} = \text{Win}\% - \left(\frac{\text{Loss}\%}{\$\text{Odds}}\right) \quad , \text{ where}$$

$ means average payoff to one dollar. If handicappers can pick 40 percent winners at an average mutuel of $5.00 (odds 3-2, payoff to $1 is $1.50), they have no advantage over the game, as

$$40\% - \left(\frac{60\%}{\$1.50}\right) = 40 - 40 = 0\% \text{ Advantage.}$$

Such handicappers have no business betting the races, until they either raise their proficiency level (% winners) or average mutuel, or both. In like manner handicappers can calculate their advantage over the races, and set the size of their bets equivalent to their advantage. In practice, this requires nothing more than records indicating the seasonal win percentage and average mutuel.

Handicappers who wish to make optimal profits but do not have the performance data to plug into Mahl's formula can start today to establish their advantage. Whatever other practices are engaged, take $100 and make a series of 100 bets ($2) on prime selections. Calculate the win percentage and average win mutuel. Plug the data into the formula. That is the best available estimate of your personal advantage. Establish a betting bankroll, and begin. The size of each bet across a season equals your advantage over the game. The advantage changes (a) when handicapping knowledge improves or (b) methods of selection are systematically altered or (c) personal judgment is impaired or (d) the conditions of racing are fundamentally changed, i.e. bad weather, new track. A new baseline is needed.

Fixed percentage wagering principles and methods have long been touted by handicappers as avenues to maximizing profits when winning and minimizing losses when losing, but the conventional percents to be bet have been concerned with avoiding bankruptcy, and not with maximizing utilization of capital, and therefore not with maximizing profits. The traditional 5 percent guideline is the classic example. This serves to avoid calamity, but winning players wish instead to maximize gains. Optimal betting permits the bettor's true advantage to work towards the best possible financial return.

Estimates of advantage can be continually calculated, after perhaps each series of 100 bets. In the beginning, if estimates of advantage are not thought precise, an underestimate represents a more favorable type of error than an overestimate. The overestimate leads to betting more than the true advantage allows, which leads to ruin, as Mahl has shown. The underestimate merely assures the bettor will be winning at something less than an optimal rate of profit, a sorry but not desperate state of affairs.

The beauty of Mahl's optimal betting is that it guarantees the best of handicappers the greatest rewards. Experts capable of 40 percent winners at average odds of 5-2 enjoy a 16 percent advantage over the game. Each of their bets can be 16 percent of capital, yielding a return far greater than the flat-bet 40 cents on the dollar. If 40 percent winners average 2-1 on win bets, they can invest 10 percent of capital at each risk.

Handicappers that win 30 percent at 3-1 on average hold a 7 percent advantage. They can risk just 7 percent of capital each bet. If they bet 10 percent, they will lose.

As all know, the crowd wins 33 percent of its bets, loses 9 percent on the dollar. Its advantage is negative, a −9 percent, because its winners average 8-5 odds, or $1.60 to 1.

Optimal betting also reveals the handicapping pretenders for the varmits they are. Prophets of 50 percent winners at average odds of just 5-2 hold an insurmountable 30 percent advantage. They have the game by the throat. All they need to do is wager 30 percent of a fat bankroll each bet, and it's guaranteed goldmine. If such claims were true, these hucksters would be wasting their time hawking leaflets.

In determining advantage, handicappers benefit if they refine first estimates successively, as more data accumulates. The tendency to define advantage in terms of best results or results recently achieved leads inevitably to overestimation and therefore to the betting of more capital than true performance warrants. Once upon a time not repeated since, the writer hit 42 percent winners at Hollywood Park, average mutuel $8.40 ($3.20 to $1). The advantage was approximately 18 percent. To press an 18 percent betting advantage at Del Mar (next stop) that season, where win percentage was 29 and average mutuel $6.20 would have meant tapping out. Stable estimates, conservatively interpreted, are best estimates for Mahl's formula.

A perfectly legitimate assumption for winning handicappers not in possession of accurate and reliable estimates of their true advantage over the game borrows from well-known attainable results. Handicappers who win approximately 20 cents on the dollar invested do so by winning

half of the bets, at average odds of 7-5	advantage 15%
40% of the bets, at average odds of 2-1	advantage 10%
a third of the bets at average odds of 13-5	advantage 8%
30% of the bets, at average odds of 3-1	advantage 7%

Handicappers that do twice as well, earning profits of 40 cents on the dollar invested, do so by winning

half of the bets at average odds of 9-5	advantage 22%
40% of the bets, at average odds of 5-2	advantage 16%
a third of the bets, at average odds above 3-1	advantage 10%
30% of the bets, at average odds exceeding 7-2	advantage 9%

If handicappers feel certain they perform at slightly better than one of the above thresholds, they can assume the advantage at that threshold, and bet an equivalent percent of their capital each time. Projected profits depend upon (a) amount of starting bankroll and (b) order of winning and losing bets. All handicappers can know is they will win more than 20 or 40 cents on the dollar invested. They will win as much precisely as they are capable of winning.

A KEY TO OLDER MAIDENS

In 1974 Fred Davis demonstrated conclusively that in races for older maidens (three or older) the second-place finish last out is a powerful predictor of success next time. But first-time-starters win less than 50 per cent of their fair share of those races. Even maidens that finished third last out do much better than first starters.

Here's the results of a 300-race national sample:

| Finish | Starters | | | Winners | | |
	Number	Percent		Number	Percent	Probability
2	312	9.0		74	24.6	274%
3	287	8.2		43	14.3	172%
4-Last	2646	76.0		174	58.1	77%
No Starts	235	6.8		9	3.0	44%

(Note. The probability of winning equals simply the percentage of winners having the characteristic—finish last out—divided by the percentage of starters having the characteristic.)

These findings hold clear implications for handicappers. When considering the merits of two maidens, one that finished second last out, the other a first starter, handicappers can solve the dilemma by selecting the second-place finisher every time. Informed handicappers are playing with the percentages, not against them.

First starters win only three percent of the races for older maidens and only 44 percent of their appropriate share of these races. Inexperience defeats them, notwithstanding the lickety-split workouts they often show, or the strong trainer-jockey connections, or the fashionable breeding.

Handicappers should appreciate the second-place finish last out in races for older maidens is one of the strongest probability statistics in handicapping. The finding takes on even greater significance:

    (a) during Summer and Fall
    (b) at the route
    (c) when accompanied by a jockey change from journeyman to leader

Frederick S. Davis, "Thoroughbred Racing: Percentages and Probabilities," *Millwood Publications*, New York, 1974, Ch. 1, p. 9.

Remembering that probabilities are generalities that apply to many specific situations but not to all, two qualifications of the second-place-finish-last-out statistic are warranted:

one, be skeptical of maidens that have previously finished second, perhaps more than once, but failed to win next time. The past performances and earnings' tables of these kind will often look like the horse below:

The horses finish second or third repeatedly, but fail to win. Consistently inconsistent, Valuater's second-place finish Nov. 6 is not the strong predictor of success upcoming isolated in the Davis research. Professionals often refer to these kind as "sucker" horses. Do not be fooled. If maidens have finished second and third repeatedly in the past, without winning yet, mark them down. Studies have shown that if older maidens have not won in four-six attempts, their chances diminish next time.

two, first starters have a better chance early in the calendar year.

The point applies to major Winter racing. Earlier in the year many nicely-bred, well-connected, fast-working three-year-olds will be given their first starts. Players should respect them, particularly if nothing that has raced shows the preferred second-place finish, and in decent time.

Even when the second-place finish last out horse qualifies, if bothered by sharp-looking first starters, handicappers might decide to pass the race. First starters lose too often to offer handicappers profits, but they do better during the early months of the year. When in doubt, pass the race.

STANDARDS OF THOROUGHBRED FORM

As all know, form refers to the condition, fitness, or readiness of the horse. Form analysis is often thought the most difficult part of handicapping, as horses vary so in their conditioning needs and training patterns. In 1968 leading handicapping authority Tom Ainslie published the standards of acceptable Thoroughbred form in a book chapter that is widely accepted as the most instructive literature on form analysis ever produced. In 1978 Ainslie revised some of the standards after analyzing recent probability studies that substantiated many of the original propositions, but indicated some modifications were in order.

Ainslie identified recent action (races) and training patterns (workouts) as the prime indicators of form. He set up both negative standards horses must satisfy—or handicappers can safely eliminate them—and positive standards that can be used to award extra credit on the form factor. Below are the latest standards and several associated guidelines for evaluating the past performance tables.

In analyzing claiming races, stay close to these considerations on recent action:

1. In races at seven furlong or less, accept horses that have run **within the last calendar month,** preferably at the present track or at a sister track on the circuit.

2. In routes, horses should show a race within the last calendar month plus at least two workouts. If they have raced within two weeks and show one workout, that's acceptable. If horses have raced within a week, they need show no workouts.

3. At seven furlongs or less, horses can be accepted on form even if they have been unraced for 45 days, provided they have been working out at intervals of four or five days and have **previously won** after absences of that length or longer.

In analyzing nonclaiming races (allowance, handicap, and stakes horses), handicappers can be even more relaxed about recent action. Nonclaiming horses need not race so often to retain their sharpness. Here are two encompassing guidelines:

1. Horses that have not raced for 60 to 90 days are seldom acceptable on form **unless they have worked out frequently, recently, and with respectable clockings** (see below).

2. In allowance races, the genuine allowance horse that has raced well within the last week or two is usually a far better risk than one that has not been postward for three or four weeks or more.

Regarding workouts, for claiming horses that have been away for six weeks or longer, and are returning to sprints, look for:

1. **Frequent** workouts, including **at least one** of real speed.

2. **Longer** workouts, including one at today's race distance.

For nonclaiming horses—and claiming horse workouts of real speed—use the following time standards:

1. At most tracks a workout is more than satisfactory if the horse breezes (b) (runs without urging) at a rate of approximately **12 seconds** for each eighth of a mile (one furlong). A workout of .36b for three furlongs, or .48b for four, or 1.00b for five, is a definite sign of life. So is 1.13b for six furlongs, 1.27b for seven, and 1.42b for the mile.

2. If a breezing work of .48 is acceptable, so is .47h—the symbol (h) for "handily." Handily refers to the jockey's running his knuckles along the horse's neck in the familiar pumping motion, which encourages speed.

3. A second of credit is given for a workout that begins in the starting gate (g) rather than from the customary running start. Hence .47hg is as good as .47b.

4. If horses work out on the training track (tr.t.) the footing will be deeper and slower, to help the animals develop

---

Tom Ainslie, "Ainslie's Complete Guide to Thoroughbred Racing," *Simon and Schuster,* New York, 1968, 1979, Ch. 9, pp. 160-184.

stamina. Give a one-second credit. Thus, tr.t. .48h is as good as .48b.

5. A longer workout is always more significant than a shorter.

6. Bold-face type to identify workout times means the horse has trained the quickest at the distance that day and is usually worth noting. So is the time of any cheaper horse whose workout was clocked within a few fifths-second of the fastest time.

7. A workout around the dogs (d) is longer than one along the rail. Credit the time as approximately a second faster.

Negative standards of form often eliminate several starters, without eliminating many winners, thereby easing the remaining handicapping load.

Form eliminations consistent with the 11 guidelines below have been shown to discard the losers most of the time.

Certain performances should be inexcusable. Assuming the horse (a) ran with its own class range (b) was at a comfortable distance and (c) had no legitimate excuse, discard it on the grounds of unacceptable form if:

1. It failed to beat half its field, finishing 5th or worse in a field of seven, 6th or worse in a field of eight or nine, 7th or worse in a field of 10 or more—and earned a speed rating at least 5 points below the ones recorded in its better local races.

2. It failed to gain on the leader at any call, and finished out of the money more than six lengths behind.

3. It lost more than two and one-half lengths between the stretch call and the finish.

Exception to #3: In an improved performance, the horse showed good early speed and carried it until the pre-stretch or stretch calls.

4. It got off to a poor start, and poor starts have been one of its problems.

5. It earned an uncomplimentary chart comment, such as "Dull," "No Speed," or "Showed Nothing."

Here are another half dozen danger signals. They warrant elimination, according to Ainslie:

1. Throw out any horse that bled, ran sore, or finished lame in its last race.

2. Throw out any horse that lugged in or bore out notably in its last race.

3. Throw out any horse that is stepping up in class after a race it won while losing ground in a driving stretch run.

4. Excepting the highly consistent kind that give their best every race, throw out any horse four-years-old or older that engaged in driving finishes in each of its last two races.

Notable exceptions to #4: handicap and stakes horses from top barns, lightly-raced 3-year-old fillies of high quality, and 3-year-old colts and geldings of almost any grade.

5. Throw out any horse aged five or older whose best effort at today's distance occurred in its last race, unless the horse is a male that demonstrated reserved speed in that race.

6. Throw out any claiming horse whose last race was a "big win" more than two weeks ago.

"Big wins" mean the horses won handily or easily, or with plenty in reserve, after staying close to the early pace. They look like this:

3 3^4 2^1 1^1 1^2 or like this:
1 1^1 $2^{1/2}$ $2^{1/2}$ $1^{1 1/2}$

DROPDOWNS IN CLAIMING RACES

Which is the better bet, claiming horses moving up in class or their counterpart, claiming horses moving down? It's the horses moving down, by a landslide!

In fact, claiming horses dropping in class by 30 per cent or more after a recent decent race represent the most powerful probability statistic yet discovered in handicapping. These horses represent approximately 2.8 per cent of the starters in claiming races, but they win almost 11 per cent of the races.

That is, horses dropping 30 per cent or more in claiming price win 378 per cent their rightful share of these races!

In general, dropdowns in claiming races represent 15 per cent of the starters, but 30 per cent of the winners. Dropdowns win twice their fair share of the claiming races. Moreover, the greater the drop in claiming price, the more likely the horses will win.

Remember to require the dropdowns show a decent recent race. A finish 1st, 2nd, or 3rd, or within three lengths of the winner, is a good race. Acceptable too is a race that shows high early speed until the pre-stretch or stretch calls. So is a race that shows a pre-stretch or stretch gain of two or more lengths while beating at least half the field.

By combining the key findings of recent probability studies and the traditional emphasis on current form, handicappers have practically arrived at knowledge as to what kind of horse represents the ideal play in claiming races.

The ideal claiming race contender combines:

1. early speed

2. improving or peaking form

3. a drop in class

Frederick S. Davis, "Thoroughbred Racing: Percentages and Probabilities, *Millwood Publications,* New York, 1974, p. 11.

BB + SR

While their methods of investment and amounts wagered may differ dramatically, all serious students of handicapping, from Dowst to Taulbot to Ainslie to the new wave writers of the seventies and eighties, agree strongly as to the merits of the following principles of money management at the track:

one, the great majority of one's capital must be allocated to win betting.

two, straight bets (to win) must be limited to overlays; that is, to horses whose real chances are better than the betting odds suggest.

three, handicappers should bet more when they are winning and less when they are losing.

four, progressive methods and due-column methods, which require heavier bets after losses until the next win bet, are ruinous.

five, the most useful way to evaluate any money management strategy is to submit it to a risk-benefit analysis. The most effective methods minimize risk while they maximize benefit (gain).

On the last point, James Selvidge, publisher, Jacada Publications, Seattle, has persuasively demonstrated the risk-benefit power of a money management method he calls BB + SR, which means base bet plus square root of profits.

The base bet recommended is $2.

Using BB + SR, a handicapper's every bet to win is equal to $2 plus the square root of any profits that have accumulated. If no profits have accumulated, the bettor's bet remains $2, the minimum risk at most tracks. As profits do accumulate, the bettor finds the amount to be added to $2 by referring to a simple square root table, which is included with this article.

Before explaining and illustrating BB + SR, let's examine its advantages, particularly as these apply to the average racetrack customer.

One of the best is that BB + SR offers the best return on money invested by the small bettor. That is, the risk factor associated with the method is as low as can be found anywhere. BB + SR is practically custom-made for the $2 bettor.

A second advantage is that the method can be used by persons who attend the track regularly, weekly, or just occasionally. That is, the method gets good results at minimal risk over a season's time, a month's time, a week's time, or even one day's play. Best results are achieved from continuous play.

The method is also a low-risk way to test handicapping "angles" as to effectiveness and rate of return.

Fourth, handicappers who play about one-third of the races during a major season and can pick as many winners as the crowd as a whole normally does (33 per cent), at average odds of 2.6 to 1 or so, can expect to earn a fine return on the amount invested. Any performance exceeding that norm returns substantial profits.

Fifth, as with any effective systematic method of money management, handicappers using BB + SR for their normal selections or for angles under study will be proceeding with discipline in their betting, thereby relieving themselves of the problems and anxieties that regularly result from unsystematic money management.

Sixth, the method is highly sensitive to longshot payoffs. When these occur, however intermittently, profit margins increase terrifically.

Since the objective of money management is to achieve the most profit for money at risk, long-term effective methods must be consistent with this purpose. The $2 base bet of BB + SR assures handicappers they will be betting at minimal risk.

For that reason the base bet should **always** remain $2, not any higher amount. Selvidge has stressed the point again and

James Selvidge, "Hold Your Horses," *Jacada Publications*, Seattle, WA, 1974, Ch. 9, pp. 104-129.

again, for many practiced handicappers cannot imagine making profits with $2 base bets. To repeat, most gain occurs from the smallest base bet, as profits depend on other profits more than risk capital, and money lost during any series of losses must be minimized. If the first five bets are lost, for example, the amount lost is $10, the absolute minimum. If the base bet were $20, the handicappers would be $100 behind already, and reinvesting a greater amount in ratio to any profits that began to accumulate. In short, the risk factor goes up.

Beyond relying on a minimum base bet, the real power of BB + SR comes from **the additive power of the square root function**. Put simply, as profits accumulate, with each succeeding bet the player is betting back a smaller percentage of the profits. As profits grow the size of the bet increases, but the percentage of capital at risk decreases. If early profit is $25, for example, the next bet is $2 plus $5 or $7, which is 28% of the profit. If later profit is $400, the next bet is $2 plus $20 or $22, which is 5½% of the profit. Handicappers betting only small percentages of profits can stay active for long periods regardless of winning and losing series. When such handicappers have started with a minimal amount at risk, they can only end by losing small amounts or by winning relatively large amounts. That's effective money management.

A major dynamic of BB + SR works wonderfully for handicappers where success is present. Selvidge has shown that handicappers capable of winning 30 per cent of their wagers at average odds of 4-1 with reasonable consistency will see their profits explode geometrically as time goes by. That's not easy, and absolutely demands superior handicapping skill, but it's worth working towards. By comparison, flat bets producing 30 per cent winners at average odds of 3-1 return a 20% profit, and that norm has long been regarded an attainable result. Handicappers that can win 30 per cent at 3-1 average odds can do considerably better than a 20% dollar return by abandoning flat bets, and using BB + SR.

Selvidge recommends that handicappers using BB + SR invest in a "flow" of bets not to exceed 15 losses. That is, the risk capital for any series of bets is $30, whether handicappers are supporting normal selections, or testing some angle they fancy. If the selections or angles do not begin to produce profits before 15 losses or such that bankrupt the risk capital, so the argument goes, the selections and angles are not worth further investment.

The argument holds well. If handicappers' selections cannot produce profits with BB + SR they are well advised to suspend play and polish their handicapping skills. If angles do not work in that run of play, they are best discarded.

The BB + SR flow is particularly well-suited to testing angles that tickle handicappers' fancy. Risk capital—to find out whether the angle is worth backing—is $30. If handicappers believe a particular trainer-jockey combination is profitable, they can test it cheaply with BB + SR, using a 15-loss flow as the criterion. If they fancy certain workout patterns, they can test those. No matter their favorite angles or patterns, these can be tested cheaply and rather surely with a $30 BB + SR flow.

The notion of "flows" allows handicappers to decide on an amount of risk capital for the season before play begins. Handicappers merely decide on the number of flows they will support. Each costs $30. If five flows are developed for the season, the largest possible loss is $150; profits might run terrifically high.

Studies indicate BB + SR flows do not work well enough for place betting, as the average payoff is inadequate to stimulate profits. More positively, Selvidge has consistently demonstrated how much better handicappers who send him their workouts would have done had they substituted BB + SR for customary methods.

Handicappers who prefer larger investments are encouraged to make five or ten "parallel" flows on selections or angles. Each parallel is a multiple of the BB + SR bet. The base bet of $2 added to the square root of profits remains the basic wager, and this amount is multiplied by the number of "parallels" handicappers have chosen to play. At five parallels, the first bet is $2 x 5 or $10. At ten parallels, the bet is $2 x 10 or $20.

At five parallels, a 15-loss BB + SR flow requires $150 of risk capital. At ten parallels, a one-flow risk capital amounts to $300. A season's risk capital for five flows at 5 parallels is $750; for five flows at ten parallels it is $1500.

Illustration

A small four-race sequence in which the first horse lost and the next three won is sufficient to represent the BB + SR method in practice:

	Base Bet	S.R.	Total Bet	Pay-Off	P/L	P/L×10
#1	$2.00	X	$2.00	LOSS	−$2.00	−$20.00
#2	$2.00	X	$2.00	$15.20	$11.20	+$112.00
#3	$2.00	$3.00	$5.00	$ 4.40	$17.20	$172.00
#4	$2.00	$6.00	$ 6.00	$ 5.00	$26.20	$262.00

Notice the square root of the **cumulative** profit is taken, not merely the profit of the previous race. The far right column indicates profit and loss totals at 10 parallels.

SQUARE ROOT TABLE

On Profit	Add	On Profit	Add	On Profit	Add
$ 0- 2	$ 1	$2862-2969	$54	$11351-11564	$107
3- 6	2	2970-3079	55	11565-11780	108
7- 12	3	3080-3191	56	11781-11998	109
13- 20	4	3192-3305	57	11999-12218	110
21- 30	5	3306-3421	58	12219-12440	111
31- 42	6	3422-3539	59	12441-12664	112
43- 56	7	3540-3659	60	12665-12890	113
57- 72	8	3660-3781	61	12891-13118	114
73- 90	9	3782-3905	62	13119-13348	115
91-110	10	3906-4030	63	13349-13580	116
111-132	11	4031-4185	64	13581-13813	117
133-156	12	4186-4288	65	13814-14049	118
157-181	13	4289-4420	66	14050-14287	119
182-208	14	4421-4554	67	14288-14527	120
209-239	15	4555-5690	68	14528-14769	121
240-271	16	4691-4828	69	14770-15012	122
272-305	17	4829-4968	70	15013-15258	123
306-341	18	4969-5112	71	15259-15505	124
342-379	19	5113-5256	72	15506-15756	125
380-419	20	5257-5402	73	15757-16008	126
420-461	21	5403-5560	74	16009-16262	127
462-505	22	5561-5700	75	16263-16518	128
506-551	23	5701-5852	76	16519-16776	129
552-599	24	5853-6006	77	16777-17036	130
600-649	25	6007-6162	78	17037-17298	131
650-701	26	6163-6321	79	17299-17562	132
702-755	27	6322-6480	80	17563-17828	133
756-811	28	6481-6641	81	17829-18095	134
812-869	29	6642-6807	82	18096-18365	135
870-929	30	6808-6975	83	18366-18637	136
930-991	31	6976-7143	84	18638-18913	137
992-1055	32	7144-7312	85	18914-19190	138
1056-1121	33	7313-7483	86	19191-19470	139
1122-1189	34	7484-7657	87	19471-19752	140
1190-1259	35	7658-7833	88	19753-20036	141
1260-1331	36	7834-8011	89	20037-20322	142
1332-1405	37	8012-8192	90	20323-20610	143
1406-1481	38	8193-8374	91	20611-20900	144
1482-1559	39	8375-8558	92	20901-21192	145
1560-1639	40	8559-8744	93	21193-21485	146
1640-1721	41	8745-8943	94	21486-21781	147
1722-1805	42	8944-9133	95	21782-22079	148
1806-1891	43	9134-9325	96	22080-22379	149
1892-1979	44	9326-9518	97	22380-22681	150
1980-2069	45	9519-9716	98	22682-22985	151
2070-2161	46	9717-9908	99	22986-23221	152
2162-2255	47	9909-10108	100	23222-23529	153
2256-2351	48	10109-10310	101	23530-23839	154
2352-2449	49	10311-10514	102	23840-24151	155
2450-2549	50	10515-10720	103	24152-24465	156
2550-2651	51	10721-10928	104	24466-24781	157
2652-2755	52	10929-11138	105	24782-25099	158
2756-2861	53	11139-11350	106	25100-25391	159

A Key Race Method With Charts

Handicappers with results charts hold a razor's edge. The charts contain the keys to unlocking class within a class. Whether it's purse comparisons for open but ungraded stakes, restrictions or specifications limiting eligibility to allowance races, or restrictions in claiming races having the same purse values, results charts tell the tale regarding numerous class changes of one kind or another. Handicapping author Steve Davidowitz years ago revealed a simple procedural method with charts that absolutely pinpoints the best races within any class.

The idea is to use a collection of charts to identify "key races." "Key" races are those so competitive that several horses in the field win next out. As Davidowitz says, either key races bring together the best fields, or fields of horses unusually fit and ready, and in either case several of them are likely to win next time, when presumably matched against a more ordinary lot. Once key races have been identified, handicappers can fairly expect big efforts from horses that raced well in them.

The procedural steps are simple. First, for the most recent race in the charts, check the date and race number of the winner's previous start, as indicated below. Caesar's Profile last raced October 22 at Santa Anita, the 9th race.

SEVENTH RACE 1 ⅛ MILES.(turf). (1.45⅘) ALLOWANCE. Purse $22,000. 3-year-olds and upward, which
Santa Anita have never won a race of $2,500 other than maiden, claiming or starter. Weights, 3-year-olds, 117 lbs.; older, 120 lbs. Non-winners of a race other than claiming at one mile or over allowed
NOVEMBER 4, 1981 3 lbs.

Value of race $22,000, value to winner $12,100, second $4,400, third $3,300, fourth $1,650, fifth $550. Mutuel pool $190,274. Exacta Pool $297,887.

Last Raced	Horse	Eqt.	A.	Wt	PP	St	¼	½	¾	Str	Fin	Jockey	Odds $1
22Oct81 ^{9}SA^{7}	Caesar's Profile		4	120	4	3	1^{hd}	$2^{1\frac{1}{2}}$	$2^{1\frac{1}{2}}$	1^{hd}	1^{nk}	Hawley S	6.70
[illegible]	Home Board	b	3	117	1	5	4^{2}	3^{1}	4^{6}	$3^{2\frac{1}{2}}$	2^{4}	Delahoussaye E	1.30
21Oct81 ^{2}SA^{8}	Desvelo		4	117	5	4	3^{hd}	4^{7}	3^{hd}	4^{3}	3^{nk}	Gallitano G	20.90
21Oct81 ^{5}SA^{3}	Prodigious	b	5	120	3	1	2^{1}	1^{hd}	1^{hd}	$2^{1\frac{1}{2}}$	4^{nk}	Olivares F	4.80
7Oct81 ^{7}SA^{7}	Summit Run		5	120	6	6	$5^{1\frac{1}{2}}$	5^{1}	5^{hd}	5^{2}	5^{4}	Pincay L Jr	7.30
22Oct81 ^{7}SA^{2}	Denali Ridge	b	3	114	2	2	6	6	6	6	6	McCarron C J	2.40

OFF AT 3:42 PST. Start good. Won driving. Time, :23⅘, :47, 1:10⅘, 1:35, 1:47⅗ Course firm.

$2 Mutuel Prices:	4-CAESAR'S PROFILE	15.40	4.40	3.40
	1-HOME BOUND		3.20	2.40
	5-DESVELO			5.40

$5 EXACTA 4-1 PAID $155.50

Dk. b. or br. c, by Roman Line—New Faces, by Swaps. Trainer Jones Gary. Bred by Carter Mrs M (Ky).

CAESAR'S PROFILE forced the pace outside PRODIGIOUS most of the trip, disposed of that one in the final sixteenth and drew off. HOME BOUND broke slowly, quickly moved up to a good position on the rail nearing the clubhouse turn, remained on the rail around the final turn, was trapped behind the leaders in the upper stretch, swung outside for racing room leaving the furlong pole, then closed strongly but was too late. DESVELO, reserved off the early pace, raced within easy striking distance of the early leaders but lacked the needed response rallying in the middle of the course through the stretch. PRODIGIOUS tired in the final furlong. SUMMIT RUN failed to menace. DENALI RIDGE showed a dull effort.

Owners— 1, Harrington L D; 2, Fluor Mr-Mrs J R; 3, Savoca & Winick; 4, Morrison A or Geri; 5, MacDonald B-K-M; 6, Triple Dot Dash Stable.

Scratched—L'Oiseleur (24Oct81 ^{1}SA^{4}).

Second, find the chart for the indicated race, and however the winner performed, **circle its name.** As seen below, Caesar's Profile finished 7th of eight October 22.

NINTH RACE
Santa Anita
OCTOBER 22, 1981

1 1/8 MILES. (1.45⅘) ALLOWANCE. Purse $22,000. 3-year-olds and upward which have never won a race or $2,500 other than maiden, claiming or starter. Weights, 3-year-olds, 117 lbs.; older, 121 lbs. Non-winners of a race other than claiming at one mile or over since April 22 allowed 3 lbs.

Value of race $22,000, value to winner $12,100, second $4,400, third $3,300, fourth $1,650, fifth $550. Mutuel pool $146,454. Exacta Pool $273,389.

Last Raced	Horse	Eqt.	A.	Wt	PP	St	1/4	1/2	3/4	Str	Fin	Jockey	Odds $1
11Oct81 ^{6}SA^{3}	Full Payment	b	4	121	1	1	1^{hd}	$2^{2\frac{1}{2}}$	2^{4}	2^{6}	$1^{2\frac{1}{2}}$	Hawley S	4.80
7Oct81 ^{7}SA^{9}	Princely Verdict	b	3	117	4	3	5^{3}	4^{1}	3^{hd}	$3^{1\frac{1}{2}}$	$2^{2\frac{1}{2}}$	Rivera M A	8.30
19Sep81 ^{8}Pom^{1}	Charly n' Harrigan	b	4	121	3	4	8	7^{1}	7^{6}	4^{hd}	3^{1}	Pedroza M C	50.30
3Oct81 ^{9}SA^{1}	Knight of Gold	b	4	118	2	2	2^{2}	1^{hd}	1^{hd}	1^{hd}	$4^{1\frac{1}{2}}$	Valenzuela P A	5.50
1Oct81 ^{7}SA^{2}	Midnite Copper	b	3	114	8	7	$6^{2\frac{1}{2}}$	6^{6}	$5^{2\frac{1}{2}}$	6^{3}	$5^{\frac{3}{4}}$	Lipham T	7.70
7Oct81 ^{7}SA^{8}	Charmande		4	118	6	5	4^{hd}	5^{hd}	6^{3}	$5^{\frac{1}{2}}$	$6^{4\frac{1}{2}}$	Castaneda M	5.40
11Oct81 ^{6}SA^{2}	Caesar's Profile		4	118	7	6	3^{hd}	$3^{\frac{1}{2}}$	$4^{\frac{1}{2}}$	7^{3}	$7^{\frac{1}{2}}$	McHargue D G	1.30
1Oct81 ^{7}SA^{4}	Port Velate		3	109	5	8	7^{hd}	8	8	8	8	Winland W M^{5}	36.90

OFF AT 5:35 PDT. Start good. Won ridden out. Time, :23⅘, :46⅘, 1:10⅘, 1:36⅕, 1:49⅘ Track fast.

$2 Mutuel Prices:	1-FULL PAYMENT	11.60	6.00	4.40
	4-PRINCELY VERDICT		9.00	5.40
	3-CHARLY N' HARRIGAN			11.20

$5 EXACTA 1-4 PAID $304.50

B. c, by Verbatim—Whitey III, by Sassafras. Trainer Rettele Loren. Bred by Elmendorf Farm (Ky).

FULL PAYMENT set or forced the pace from the outset, raced KNIGHT OF GOLD into defeat and drew clear in the final sixteenth. PRINCELY VERDICT, in good position while reserved off the early pace, rallied strongly in the final furlong but was too late. CHARLY N' HARRIGAN unhurried for six furlongs, rallied strongly between horses entering the stretch, almost ran up on the heels of the tiring KNIGHT OF GOLD in the final sixteenth and had to check sharply to the inside. The latter had little left after vying for the lead most of the trip. MIDNITE COPPER showed little. CHARMANDE had no excuse. CAESAR'S PROFILE gradually tired after six furlongs.

Owners— 1, Newman B; 2, Blum Maribel G; 3, Lerner P; 4, Schneider Berenice T; 5, Bannon & Haitsuka; 6, Keck H B Jr; 7, Tayhill Stable (Lessee); 8, Young Mrs M A.

The circle means Caesar's Profile won its next race.

Third, repeat the procedure for the winners of the previous six or seven days of racing, or 54 to 63 races, tracing the winners to their previous performances, and circling their names in those back charts. Valuable information will emerge, including the identity of highly competitive races, as indicated by several circles on the same chart. Any race having more than two circles represents a key race, a particularly well-run race within that class. Handicappers would look eagerly for

Steven Davidowitz, "Betting Thoroughbreds," *E. P. Dutton,* New York, 1977, Ch. 9, pp. 83-91.

other horses in the field in their next starts. The best performers in these races can often be followed indefinitely, as they win successively after shining in the key races.

Handicappers will occasionally light upon a key race such as the example below:

SIXTH RACE
Santa Anita
JANUARY 31, 1982

1 $\frac{1}{16}$ MILES. (1.40⅗) MAIDEN. Purse $18,000. Colts and geldings. 3-year-olds. Weight, 118 lbs. (Non-starters for a claiming price of $25,000 or less preferred.)

Value of race $18,000, value to winner $9,900, second $3,600, third $2,700, fourth $1,350, fifth $450. Mutuel pool $638,236.

Last Raced	Horse	Eqt.	A.	Wt	PP	St	¼	½	¾	Str	Fin	Jockey	Odds $1
17Jan82 $^{6}SA^{2}$	Lord Advocate	b	3	118	10	8	$7^{2\frac{1}{2}}$	$6^{\frac{1}{2}}$	$3^{2\frac{1}{2}}$	1^{hd}	1^{1}	Pincay L Jr	.80
17Jan82 $^{6}SA^{8}$	Berbereau		3	118	8	5	5^{2}	4^{1}	$2^{\frac{1}{2}}$	2^{5}	2^{5}	Delahoussaye E	7.20
17Jan82 $^{6}SA^{4}$	Charge Between	b	3	118	6	12	12	12	12	6^{hd}	3^{1}	Asmussen C B	14.00
7Jan82 $^{6}SA^{4}$	Rawlison	b	3	118	1	3	6^{1}	$7^{2\frac{1}{2}}$	7^{1}	$4^{\frac{1}{2}}$	4^{nk}	Hansen R D	55.10
20Jan82 $^{6}SA^{4}$	Funny Gum		3	118	9	4	4^{hd}	5^{2}	4^{1}	3^{3}	$5^{1\frac{1}{2}}$	Toro F	16.80
24Jan82 $^{3}SA^{5}$	Break and Try		3	113	7	7	10^{2}	$11^{\frac{1}{2}}$	10^{hd}	$5^{\frac{1}{2}}$	$6^{1\frac{1}{2}}$	Garcia J J^{5}	89.40
17Jan82 $^{6}SA^{5}$	Emerald Fox	b	3	118	11	11	11^{1}	$9^{\frac{1}{2}}$	8^{1}	7^{hd}	7^{2}	Harris W	38.10
14Jan82 $^{4}SA^{10}$	Kings Dawn		3	118	5	9	8^{2}	8^{1}	5^{hd}	8^{4}	8^{4}	Mena F	98.80
13Jan82 $^{3}SA^{4}$	King Darius		3	118	12	10	$9^{\frac{1}{2}}$	$10^{\frac{1}{2}}$	9^{hd}	9^{1}	$9^{1\frac{1}{2}}$	Lipham T	76.70
16Jan82 $^{6}SA^{9}$	Forebear		3	118	2	2	1^{hd}	3^{1}	6^{hd}	11^{2}	10^{2}	Shoemaker W	7.80
20Jan82 $^{6}SA^{2}$	Idaho	b	3	118	4	6	3^{3}	$1^{1\frac{1}{2}}$	1^{hd}	10^{2}	$11^{3\frac{1}{2}}$	Guerra W A	4.60
24Jan82 $^{3}SA^{6}$	Olden Age		3	118	3	1	2^{hd}	2^{hd}	11^{hd}	12	12	Valenzuela P A	43.70

OFF AT 3:26. Start good. Won driving. Time, :23, :46⅘, 1:12, 1:37⅘, 1:44 Track fast.

$2 Mutuel Prices:

10-LORD ADVOCATE	3.60	2.80	2.40
8-BERBEREAU		5.20	4.00
6-CHARGE BETWEEN			4.20

B. c, by Inverness Drive—Tort Lass, by Grey Eagle. Trainer Manzi Joseph. Bred by Manzi & Steiger Sherry (Ky).

LORD ADVOCATE, in hand after the start, remained unhurried until nearing the far turn, rallied wide at the far turn, collared BERBEREAU on the stretch turn, got the lead in the upper stretch and drew clear at the end. BERBEREAU, wide on the clubhouse turn, moved up to contention on the backstretch, got the lead on the final turn but could not outfinish the winner. CHARGE BETWEEN, outrun for six furlongs, offered a strong but belated rally in the middle of the track. RAWLISON saved ground into the stretch but could not menace the first two. FUNNY GUM saved ground most of the trip but lacked a strong finish. KINGS DAWN, checked in close quarters at the clubhouse turn. FOREBEAR was finished after six furlongs, as was IDAHO. OLDEN AGE tired quickly after five furlongs.

In his continuous research of the method, Davidowitz found the key race method particularly potent among maiden races. Since maidens lack class in any categorical sense, the key race procedure with charts regularly spots the most competitive of races for maidens. Other statistical evidence supports Davidowitz on the point, as it shows a good previous performance represents a strong predictor of success among maidens.

For the same reasons, Davidowitz recommends the approach for isolating competitive races among younger horses on turf, where few if any of the horses have much of a track record.

Handicappers can fairly extend the same logic to allowance races for nonwinners of one or two allowance races, and here a twist on the Davidowitz procedure is in order. The horses competing under preliminary nonwinners allowance conditions remain relatively unclassified. If the charts for these races reveal no circles, or a single circle for only the winner, mark the quality of the races down. The races reveal the horses do not boast much class at all.

Under any conditions, a pattern appreciated by many handicappers reveals a circle for the race winner and for the fourth or fifth finisher. Handicappers would watch like detectives for the next appearances of the second, third, and fourth horses. If they look solid, they very probably are.

Unmodified Speed Ratings and Class

Probability studies of past performance patterns have sought to determine whether *Daily Racing Form* speed ratings could be associated with class. The studies have succeeded, nobly. Handicappers armed only with the information in the past performance tables can identify classy horses by manipulating the *Form* speed ratings consistent with the following procedures and recommendations.

Proceeding from the elementary assumption that better horses run their races faster than do cheaper horses, Fred Davis rated horses in a field by averaging their two best speed ratings at today's distance. For sprints, six and/or seven furlong times were averaged. For routes, races at a mile or longer, and within 1/16 mile of today's distance, were averaged. Thus, a horse with an 87 at six furlongs and 82 at seven furlongs was rated at 84.5. Each lower average was then subtracted from the top average in the field, and horses were put into class categories as follows:

top average speed rating
below the top, by .5—2.0 points
below the top, by 2.5—4.0 points
below the top, by 4.5—7.5 points
below the top, by 8.5—14.5 points
below the top, by 15 points or more

A study including 3514 starters in sprints provides handicappers employing this technique with, as Davis put it, "a lot of clout." Of 395 horses having the top averaged speed ratings (11.2 per cent of all starters), 98 won (26.7 per cent of all starters). The study indicates horses having the highest averaged speed rating in sprints win 238 per cent their rightful share of the races.

Frederick S. Davis, "Thoroughbred Racing: Percentages and Probabilities," *Millwood Publications*, New York, 1974, pp. 14-15.

Moreover, horses below the top, but within 2 points of the top average, win 206 per cent their rightful share. Those are powerful probability statistics. If these sprint types measure up strongly on the remaining fundamentals of handicapping, and the odds allow, they represent solid investment opportunities.

To continue, horses in sprints below the top average by 2.5 to 4 points win about 134 per cent their fair share of the races, but horses with lower averages (below the top by 5 points or more) represent losing bets. By confining their action to horses on top or within four points of the top, handicappers would only need consider about one-third the sprint starters, but would be dealing with two-thirds the winners.

A study of 3295 starters in routes reflected the relative unreliability of speed ratings in distance racing, yet the top averaged rating performed unexpectedly well.

Of 454 horses having the top average, 117 won. Those horses represent only 13.8 of the starters, but 31 per cent of the winners. The probability of the top average speed rating making it home in routes is a powerful 225 per cent. If the top average router figures on comprehensive handicapping, it can be backed confidently—assuming its odds are realistic, of course.

All horses below the top figure horse in routes, even those a point or two below, are best distinguished on factors other than averaged speed ratings.

The powerful performance of unadjusted speed ratings as indices of class in probability studies reinforces the notion that as racing calendars expand to the end points and state-bred breeding programs materialize to fill nine races a day, month upon month, a serious decline in the quality of everyday competition plagues major racing, and speed of a common, everyday kind continues to seize its preeminent place as a determining factor in handicapping. It also reinforces the hallowed notion that the hallmark of thoroughbred class is speed.

These trends have continued unabated in the several years since the best of our probability studies have been completed, assuring handicappers the role of speed ratings has terrifically intensified.

Handicappers can do no less than keep in step with the changing scene.

The Principle of Maximum Confusion

A melancholy thought for many handicappers regards the collective wisdom of the betting public. No matter the genius of the individual handicapper, the crowd as a whole does it better. Imagine a select group of notable handicappers, to include perhaps Robert Dowst, Colonel Bradley, Howard Rowe, Ray Taulbot, Tom Ainslie, Andy Beyer, Steven Davidowitz, William Quirin, Huey Mahl, Henry Kuck, and the top two or three professionals on every local circuit. Could these experts not excel the crowd?

They could not.

Performing at their best, the small group of experts could be expected to lose approximately 15 per cent on investment. Public choices lose only 9 per cent. Actually, the experts 15 per cent loss would mean they estimated the real winning probabilities of horses exceedingly well, losing merely the house take. Yet the public, a crowd that includes those little old ladies from Pasadena, their intuition and hatpins and all the rest, estimates horses' actual chances so mysteriously well it loses less than 10 per cent and has outperformed every public selector in the history of the sport.

Thus, and not very surprisingly, it has come to pass that perhaps the surest mechanical betting approach ever devised departs from the scientifically-established performance of the betting public, yet the system gathers dust on bookshelves and is scarcely remarked in the literature. That is because the approach has been promoted in the strictest mathematical terms, together with theory, symbols, and formulae that might have guaranteed profits, but also disinvited mastery.

Regardless, the principle underpinning the system can be readily understood by anyone, however averse to mathematics. There is too a convenient alternative to grappling with the math. It substitutes intuition, of a practiced kind, and a normative measure of success.

In his eloquent and rigorous book *Horse Sense*, in which probability theory and mathematical methods are applied to betting propositions at the track, professor of ocean sciences Burton Fabricand befriends handicappers with a concise and lucid explanation of the Principle of Maximum Confusion. The Principle derives from the proposition that the betting public achieves its time-honored 9 per cent loss on favorites by over-betting some and underbetting others. Fabricand postulates the existence of races where the crowd underestimates the favorite's true probability of winning by more than 9 per cent, i.e., enough to turn loss into gain. The underestimated favorite presents handicappers with the only kind of favorable bet—a true overlay. Opposed to the underestimated kind is the overbet favorite, the kind that counterbalances the books into the 9 per cent loss. The handicapper's task is to distinguish profitable favorites from the others.

Enter the Principle of Maximum Confusion. This holds the public is most likely to underestimate the true winning probabilities of favorites in races where the past performance record of the favorite is highly similar to one or more other horses. The intuitive rationale for The Principle is the crowd's superior handicapping, i.e., there must be some reason or reasons not immediately obvious for the public to make one horse its choice, notwithstanding its similarity to other horses. Yet the public is sufficiently confused that it bets too much money on the similar horses. Thus, its favorite is underbet. The public's confusion is held to be maximal if enough other horses look enough like the favorite to make the favorite a good bet.

As to the converse of this circumstance, where one horse looks superior in every fundamental respect, it is certain the outstanding record will not be lost on the betting public. This kind is regularly favored by form players, public selectors, and experts, such that few would argue the horse does not deserve to be favored. But, as Fabricand notes, the question is not whether the horse should be favored, but whether it should be bet. His answer to that rhetorical question is a resounding "No." Why? Because the horse looks so obvious to all, it will

Burton Fabricand, "Horse Sense." *David McKay Company, Inc.*, New York, 1965. Ch. 5, pp 46-60.

almost certainly be overbet, or at least properly bet. No chance for profits long haul. Fat chance for losses of at least 9 per cent.

How might handicappers apply the Principle of Maximum Confusion, thus assuring themselves of continuous profits at upwards of 10 per cent? The trick is to recognize those races where the favorite is so similar to other contenders the public gets very confused. Fabricand supplies handicappers with seven rules comprising the definition of similarity, as well as the probability formulae for applying the betting methods. Here we present a simplified version of the definition rules, and an alternative to the math.

To wit, the favorite is similar to another horse if:

1. both show a race within the past 29 days, and

2. both have raced at today's track, or neither has, and

3. the favorite's last race was at a class level equal to or lower than the similar horse's, and

4. there is less than a 9-pound weight shift between the two horses off their latest races, and

5. both are male, or the favorite is female, and

6. both last-race finishes are the same, greatly similar, or the favorite's last out finish was slightly inferior to the other horse's, and

7. for sprints, the favorite is a sprinter (does not show a route in its pp's); for routes, the favorite is a router (last three races occurred in routes) or a sprinter that won its last race.

All seven rules of similarity must be satisfied (Fabricand).

All kinds of races are susceptible to The Principle, from the cheapest maidens to the highest class stakes. This is understandable, since the public is known to estimate the winning probabilities of favorites equally well regardless of the class of the race.

Handicappers that have isolated betting favorites that are similar to other horses in the field can fairly assume the public has been maximally confused. They can therefore presume the favorite will be underbet, and proceed to bet on it. To check the validity of the assumption, handicappers can employ a precious normative measure—their personal past performance with The Principle. Allow a distribution of 30 bets. The criterion of success is upwards of 10 per cent profit.

Of money management, the betting method should not be one sensitive to large mutuels. Favorites, even underestimated ones, do not yield these. Flat bets, of small amounts during the testing period, are appropriate. Bets might be enlarged in some proportion to the public's underestimation of its favorite's true chances, as handicappers intuit them, and this is surely preferable as the method becomes successfully familiar and habitual.

Reliance on norms (subjective standards) as substitutes for rigorous mathematical formulae is perfectly acceptable with complicated methods of handicapping and betting at racetracks, as the most meaningful index of performance at the track is one's personal performance. Once goals and criteria of success have been established, and notwithstanding the rigor or lack of same of one's applications, whatever the idea or method under experiment, satisfactory results can be readily determined, repeated, or even improved. Unsatisfactory results can be eliminated, merely by eliminating the activity contributing to the inadequate performance. If the Principle of Maximum Confusion does not work well enough as applied by individual handicappers, the normative approach will reveal that at small cost. These handicappers can abandon The Principle and return to the normal routine.

Even in the worst of scenarios, practice with The Principle might prove beneficial. Its application will reverse a greatly unfortunate tendency. Handicappers long have relished the overbet favorite. They anticipate the overlay elsewhere, if not so successfully. Much less enthusiasm is held towards underbet favorites. Many handicappers would benefit on both accounts by changing tactics. Rather than buck overwhelming favorites by plunging on reasonable horses at reasonable prices, as is far too often done, stimulating action, but not profits, handicappers can concentrate on underestimated favorites. When favorites are highly similar to nonfavorites, as Fabricand tells, the crowd will be uncharacteristically confused, and handicappers benefit by backing the nervous public choices. The Principle of Maximum Confusion will be on their side. It assures they will be betting a series of true overlays, and this without the customary demand for full-dress handicapping.

What could be less complicating than that?

Beyer Speed

In the mid-seventies speed handicapper Andy Beyer provoked a renaissance of his specialty and numerous successive investigations into same by describing an original and persuasive method of estimating the true speed of horses. Beyer's method concentrated on specifying final times that reflected the actual abilities of horses, and not just time differences due to differences in track surfaces. He flatly claimed his advanced technique for calculating daily variants as providing the best estimates available anywhere. He further assailed the concept of parallel time, replacing that with a concept of proportional time, and controversial techniques for calculating the proportions.

Now that the smoke has cleared, Beyer has been sustained. Not only that, he, along with selected others, can be justly credited for stimulating several scientific advances in speed handicapping that are genuinely useful and effective. So effective that all serious handicappers, regardless of religion, are fairly recommended to include among their weapons adjusted final times, calculated in the manner promoted by Beyer.

The advances in speed handicapping, theory and method, have proved so conclusively effective they have rendered obsolete for all times traditional practices associated with unadjusted final times (raw times), speed ratings as calculated by *Daily Racing Form*, or variants not sensitive to the influence of class. Before reviewing Beyer's method, it's instructive to consider those steps now fundamental to the effectiveness of any method of speed handicapping. To wit:

1. The construction of par time tables for class-distance categories at the local track.

2. The calculation of daily variants that reflect differences in class and the influences of track surfaces.

3. The conversion of raw final times into adjusted final times.

4. The conversion of adjusted final times into speed figures.

5. Modification of the basic figures.

6. Interpretation of the figures, in a context of full-dress handicapping that considers the fundamentals.

The last step should not be lost to speed handicappers whose figures do not seem to work well enough. If technique has been satisfactory, chances are the fault lies with the interpretation, not the numbers. On this point more broadly, speed handicappers have not yet done nearly enough to help its fanciers and detractors interpret and use speed figures intelligently. Until those guidelines are forthcoming, speed handicapping will remain a rarefied, subjective science in many quarters, but that's another story.

Practiced speed handicappers complete the steps listed, but proceed variously at each step. At step one, some handicappers construct local par time tables and many more purchase the pars constructed by others. When it comes to calculating daily variants, procedures, and the resulting variants, differ practically in exact proportion to the number of handicappers calculating them. Thus adjusted final times differ variously, and so too the ultimate speed figures, even before these have been variously adjusted for beaten lengths, distance changes, or track class.

Beyer speed reaches to the farthest frontier yet explored in speed handicapping. Beyer ignores par times, arguing the averages obscure class within a class, bringing together as they do time differences above and below average by several lengths. He replaces par times with projected times, estimates of how fast a small number of well-known horses should run. Thus projected times are expected standards against which actual running times can be more reliably compared.

The concept of projected times poses difficulties in practice, and Beyer's personal illustrations dramatize these. Beyer describes Horse A, with an adjusted time of 1:11, coming off a

---

Andrew Beyer, "Picking Winners," *Houghton Mifflin Company*, Boston, 1975, Chapters 7-9, pp. 119-151.

30-day layoff to beat by one length Horse B, with an adjusted time of 1:12. Beyer projects that A should beat B in 1:11 4/5, finishing four ticks slower than normally—a concession to form analysis. The alternative finds A winning in the customary 1:11, but meaning that B, only a length in arrears, would have improved four lengths. That projection is held not tenable. Convenient, but loose, and open to considerable if irreconcilable argument. Beyer's projections depend on (a) form (b) trainer intentions, (c) early pace, and, by extension, (d) any fundamentals of handicapping which might reasonably explain time differences.

If speed handicappers would rely on projected times of individual horses to calculate daily variants and determine speed figures, they might most advantageously depend on that small category of horses alluded to by Beyer. Those horses with highly reliable speed figures. Those final times are most stable and therefore most reliably projected. Where a half dozen of these can be spotted on a single card, the projected times represent best estimates of true speed. Variations from these times can lead handicappers to daily variants and speed figures well beyond the ken of the crowd, and of handicappers without figures. But handicappers need to be cautious about their everyday projections. Assumptions about the influences on final time of form, or trainer intentions, or early pace, are tricky at best. Handicappers best choose to be accurate rather than clever.

Of variants, Beyer cites a pair of classic problems. As illustrated in *Picking Winners*:

Race	Projected Time	Actual Time	Difference
1	1:13	1:13 3/5	slow by 3/5
2	1:12 1/5	1:13	slow by 4/5
3	1:12 4/5	1:13 4/4	slow by 5/5
4	1:12	1:10 2/5	fast by 8/5
5	1:12	1:12 4/5	slow by 4/5

Beyer notes the 4th race looks perplexing. He suggests the track appears dull, but this race is completed eight lengths faster than expected. Beyer first focuses on his projected time, in this case trying to find basis for a projection of 1:09 4/5, which would mesh with the others. Failing this, he concedes the point, asserts the race defies explanation—in terms of speed handicapping—and recommends the race be excluded from the variant's calculation. By extension, all extreme times, whether fast or slow, are best subjected to elision, if not to explanation. This is fair practice, by all means. In all statistical compilations, averages are oversensitive to extremes, a distortion wisely eliminated.

Here is another kind of problem:

Race	Projected Time	Actual Time	Difference
1	1:12	1:11 2/5	fast by 3/5
2	1:13	1:12 1/5	fast by 4/5
3	1:12 1/5	1:11 1/5	fast by 5/5
4	1:11	1:10 1/5	fast by 4/5
5	1:11 3/5	1:12 1/5	slow by 3/5
6	1:12	1:12 1/5	slow by 1/5
7	1:10 4/5	1:11 3/5	slow by 4/5
8	1:11	1:11 2/5	slow by 2/5
9	1:13	1:13 1/5	slow by 1/5

The track condition has changed abruptly during the card, perhaps for no apparent reason. Beyer's solution? Construct two variants. For races 1-4, fast by 4/5; for races 5-9, slow by 2/5.

The critical problem of comparing times earned by horses competing at different distances leads speed handicappers to the conversion of adjusted final times into speed figures, and introduces the notorious concept of parallel time. This logic suggests that horses that run such-and-such at six furlongs can be expected to run so-and-so at a mile and one eighth. Beyer cites Laurel, where his arbitrary speed figure of 80 equals six furlongs in 1:13 equals seven furlongs in 1:26 1/5 equals a mile and one-eighth in 1:54. In other words, an 80 is an 80 is an 80 is an 80, distance notwithstanding.

Is there basis in fact for the logic? Actually, studies of **sprint** final times indicate that time differences as between distances are equivalent at most tracks. But when sprint times are compared to route times at various tracks, the equivalence disappears. And the headaches begin.

Conceding that fast horses might be expected to change distances in time different from the time needed by slow horses, Beyer escorts handicappers closer to reality by promoting the concept of proportional time. Because one length or one-fifth of a second has greater value in faster races or at shorter distances, speed handicappers are urged to determine the percentage of a race one length (1/5 second) represents. Again using Laurel's pars, Beyer shows that in running 1:13 at six furlongs, a horse has covered the distance in 365/5, such that 1/5 represents .28 per cent of the entire race. At seven furlongs in 1:26 1/5, one fifth is 1/431 or .23 per cent of the race.

In that way 1/5 of a second is weighted for all distances at the local track. By moving the decimal point an integer to the right for convenience, handicappers can construct a speed figure table that reflects proportional time. If 1:13 is set at 80, 1:12 4/5 is really .28 per cent better, such that 1:12 4/5 is set at 82.8. Yet a change from 1:26 1/5 to 1:26 corresponds to a change from 80 to 82.3, reflecting the .23 per cent 1/5 represents at seven furlongs.

By this method, a portion of the Laurel speed chart at six and seven furlongs would look like so:

Six Furlongs		Seven Furlongs	
1:12	94.0	1:25 1/5	91.5
1:12 1/5	91.2	1:25 2/5	89.2
1:12 2/5	88.4	1:25 3/5	86.9
1:12 3/5	85.6	1:25 4/5	84.6
1:12 4/5	82.8	1:26	82.3
1:13	80.0	1:26 1/5	80.0
1:13 1/5	77.2	1:26 2/5	77.7
1:13 2/5	74.4	1:26 3/5	75.4

By removing the decimal points and rounding the numbers, handicappers can construct a speed figure table for every time at every distance at the local track. All that is needed are the basic equivalent times at each distance. Par times for a common class of horse at the regularly-run distances will do.

Beyer's chart does not pretend that every horse should cover an additional furlong in equivalent time, such as the 13 1/5 seconds difference between six furlongs at Laurel in 1:13

and seven furlongs there in 1:26 1/5. If a Laurel sprinter covers six furlongs in 1:10, the concept of proportional time would require its seven furlong time be something faster than 1:23 1/5. If a plodder goes six in 1:14 4/5, its seven furlong time must be something slower than 1:28. The faster horse would run the extra furlong proportionally faster than 13 1/5, the slower horse would run it proportionately slower than 13 1/5.

Referring to Aqueduct's basic time equivalents, Beyer's speed chart shows that a horse than runs six furlongs in 1:09 4/5 (a figure of 124) should cover seven furlongs in 1:22 2/5 (also a figure of 124), covering the extra furlong in :12 3/5 seconds. But a horse running six in 1:14 1/5 (a figure of 64) should go seven in 1:27 3/5 (also a 64), covering the last eighth in :13 2/5 seconds. In this way, proportional time replaces parallel time. Speed handicappers fly closer to reality by simulating Beyer. Figures in hand, they have a basis for comparing times at different distances, assuming the horses will be comfortable enough at the distance to approach their proportional times.

Beyer emphasizes the convenience of speed figures, once handicappers become familiar with them. Class-distance par times, for instance, can be converted to figures. When actual race times are converted to figures from simple reference to the speed chart, the actual figures can be compared to the par figures, in this way producing race variants, and ultimately the daily variant. Beyer supplies the following illustration from Aqueduct:

Class	Distance	Par	Time	Actual Figure	Difference
$10,000 Clm	1 mile	97	1:37 2/5	100	fast by 3
F-Maiden	6f	90	1:11 4/5	97	fast by 7
$15,000 Alw	7f	113	1:23 2/5	112	slow by 1
Stakes	1 1/8M	119	1:49 3/5	122	fast by 3
$17,000 Clm	6½f	102	1:17 3/5	105	fast by 3

Averaging the differences, Aqueduct's daily variant this day equalled −3. When a horse that competed this day runs again, speed handicappers merely subtract three points from its figure. Beyer also provides handicappers with a standardized chart for beaten-lengths adjustments. The numbers, which are reprinted at the end of this piece, are likewise subtracted from the winner's figure, after the variant has been added or subtracted.

Even as Beyer's method of speed handicapping was gaining recognition as something new and worthwhile, other forces were gathering throughout racing that would enhance the fundamental importance of speed. Racing days were increasing terrifically, lowering the quality of the general competition, thus assuring that more races than ever would go to the cheaper speed. State-bred breeding programs were materializing to fill racing cards, and these depended on speed as the trump. Probability studies began to demonstrate the importance of early speed, such that horses first, second, or third at first calls throughout the land were winning almost 60 per cent of the races. Racetrack surfaces were changing, favoring the speed. Suddenly the game had turned towards the speed horses. Beyer speed was fairly perceived as the surest route to the winner's circle.

Notwithstanding all the attention to speed and early speed, a significant point is that speed handicapping certified handicappers as consistent winners only after it had encompassed the relative influences of class. Par times and projected times are sensitive to class levels and real abilities. In a separate chapter of **Picking Winners,** on class, Beyer asserts his belief that class is relatively unimportant. Speed is the way and the truth. But Beyer's own method, paradoxically, belies his beliefs about class and reassures handicappers using figures that speed and class are interlocking, and had better not be conceptualized or treated separately.

Nowhere is evidence for the point more convincing than in Beyer's third chapter of his book's trilogy on speed handicapping, i.e., Speed Handicapping: III. In this chapter Beyer offers interpretive guidelines and illustrations of speed figures at work. He introduces the material by recalling the beatings he endured when in his earlier days he accepted the figures on faith, and with blind ambition attempted to beat the races with them and them alone. It didn't work for Beyer, and it won't work for handicappers who repeat the blind ambition. Beyer's method improved once he began winnowing out horses that did not measure up on other handicapping fundamentals. These include class, form, distance, pace, trainer, and footing criteria. Of speed figures, Beyer provides the following lessons:

—Discount figures a horse has earned with the assistance of a strong track bias.

—Discount figures a horse has earned on a muddy track, especially if the track is fast today.

—Discount figures a horse has earned by opening a big lead and maintaining it wire to wire.

—Distrust an outstanding figure resulting from a single exceptional performance.

—The latest figure is the most important, but consistently higher figures than those earned by the competition today represent the most unshakable bets of speed handicapping. (Beyer writes the three latest figures on the horses pp's, a particularly convenient procedure for comparison.)

—Speed figures can be trusted to explain whether horses moving up or down in claiming price can be expected to win.

Beyer speed may not tickle the fancy of handicappers everywhere, and its labor is demanding, yet aspects of the approach deserve experimentation, especially in the contemporary favorable climate towards speed. Computer-generated par time tables can be purchased, for instance, and daily variants calculated without much sweat. This produces adjusted final times sensitive to class.

Professional speed handicappers have taken Beyer's concept of projected times to heart, applying same to horses whose times they understand particularly well. Speed figures of that kind represent the most advanced stage of the art.

Beyer's beaten-lengths adjustment chart

(To use, look down the left column for the beaten-lengths. Move right across the row to the column for today's distance. Subtract the number from the winner's figure.)

BEATEN-LENGTHS ADJUSTMENT CHART

Margin	5 Fur.	6 Fur.	7 Fur.	Mile	1¹⁄₁₆	1⅛	1½
neck	1	1	1	0	0	0	0
½	1	1	1	1	1	1	1
¾	2	2	2	1	1	1	1
1	3	2	2	2	2	2	1
1¼	4	3	3	2	2	2	1
1½	4	4	3	3	3	2	2
1¾	5	4	4	3	3	3	2
2	6	5	4	4	3	3	2
2¼	7	6	5	4	4	4	3
2½	7	6	5	4	4	4	3
2¾	8	7	6	5	5	5	3
3	9	7	6	5	5	5	3
3¼	9	8	7	6	5	5	4
3½	10	9	7	6	6	6	4
3¾	11	9	8	7	6	6	4
4	12	10	8	7	7	6	5
4¼	12	10	9	8	7	7	5
4½	13	11	9	8	8	7	5
4¾	14	11	10	9	8	8	5
5	15	12	10	9	8	8	6
5½	16	13	11	10	9	9	6
6	18	15	12	11	10	9	7
6½	19	16	13	12	11	10	8
7	20	17	14	13	12	11	8
7½	22	18	15	13	13	12	9
8	23	20	17	14	13	13	10
8½	25	21	18	15	14	13	10
9	26	22	19	16	15	14	11
9½	28	23	19	17	16	16	11
10	29	24	20	18	17	17	12
11	32	27	23	20	18	18	13
12	35	29	25	21	20	20	14
13	38	32	27	23	22	22	15
14	41	34	29	25	23	23	16
15	44	37	31	27	25	25	17

To be sure, if the winner's figure for a mile race is 108, what figure is assigned to a horse beaten 6 lengths?

The answer is 97.

Pars

Among the most significant of all the scientific discoveries yet produced by probability studies of handicapping is the absolute correlation of speed and class. Not only do final times improve as class levels rise, the time differences tend to be standard from track to track. The practical consequences of this phenomenon have benefitted handicappers throughout the nation. They have been forever relieved of the research drudgery formerly required to construct accurate class-distance par time tables. As accurate pars (average final times recorded by a class of horses at a specified distance) precede the making of accurately adjusted final times and speed figures, handicappers without pars can receive little nourishment from their numbers.

Following Bill Quirin, par time tables for all classes and distances can be constructed for claiming races once the local pars for a particular class at the regularly-run distances have been determined. Quirin recommends $10,000 claiming horses represent the baseline. Of a single quiet afternoon, local handicappers need to consult their tracks latest results charts and record the final times for $10,000 older claiming horses at each distance. Only fast surfaces qualify. A sample of 15 races yields stable estimates. Throw out extreme times. Average the other final times.

The baseline erect, consult the table of standard claiming price adjustments abstracted here (below) from Quirin's studies and plug in the final times for each class at each distance.

To construct par time tables for nonclaiming horses, handicappers need baseline data for nonclaiming maidens at the various distances. These can be calculated during the same afternoon session. The maiden baseline data in hand, standard adjustments for class, sex, age, and time of season fall neatly into place. The standard adjustments follow:

Nonclaiming class adjustments

	Sprints	Routes
Maidens	0	0
NW 1	−2	−3
NW 2	−4	−5
NW 3	−5	−7
Classified Alw	−7	−10
Stakes	−9	−12

○ PAR TIMES FOR CLAIMING RACES ○

	3½F	4F	4½F	5F	5½F 6F 6½F	7F 7½F	1M 1⁴⁰M	1⁷⁰M 1₁₆M	1⅛M
$50,000	−3	−4	−5	−5	−6	−7	−9	−9	−10
$40,000	−3	−4	−5	−5	−6	−6	−8	−8	−9
$35,000	−3	−4	−5	−5	−5	−5	−7	−7	−8
$30,000	−3	−4	−5	−5	−5	−5	−6	−6	−7
$25,000	−2	−3	−4	−4	−4	−4	−5	−5	−6
$20,000	−2	−2	−3	−3	−3	−3	−4	−4	−4
$18,000	−2	−2	−2	−2	−2	−2	−3	−3	−3
$15,000	−1	−1	−2	−2	−2	−2	−2	−2	−2
$13,000	−1	−1	−1	−1	−1	−1	−1	−1	−1
$10,000	0	0	0	0	0	0	0	0	0
$8,500	+1	+1	+1	+1	+1	+1	+1	+1	+1
$7,500	+1	+1	+1	+2	+2	+2	+2	+2	+2
$6,500	+1	+1	+1	+2	+3	+3	+3	+3	+3
$5,000	+2	+2	+2	+3	+4	+4	+4	+4	+4
$4,000	+3	+3	+3	+4	+5	+5	+5	+5	+5
$3,500	+3	+3	+3	+4	+5	+5	+5	+6	+6
$3,200	+4	+4	+4	+5	+6	+6	+6	+7	+7
$3,000	+4	+4	+4	+5	+6	+6	+7	+8	+8
$2,500	+5	+5	+5	+6	+7	+7	+8	+9	+9
$2,000	+5	+5	+6	+7	+8	+8	+9	+10	+11
$1,750	+6	+6	+7	+8	+9	+9	+10	+11	+12
$1,500	+6	+6	+7	+8	+9	+10	+11	+12	+13
$1,250	+6	+7	+8	+9	+10	+11	+12	+13	+14
$1,000	+6	+7	+8	+9	+10	+11	+13	+14	+15

So $5,000 claimers normally run six furlong 4/5 of a second slower than $10,000 claimers do, at any track. And $20,000 claimers normally cover 1-1/8 miles 4/5 of a second faster than $10,000 claimers do. Anywhere.

William Quirin, "Winning at the Races: Computer Discoveries in Thoroughbred Handicapping," *William Morrow and Company, Inc.*, Ch. 16, pp. 154-159.

Standard par time adjustments, various:

Fillies and Mares (all classes). Sprints +2, Routes +3

Maiden claimers (same age, sex, & class). Sprints +5, Routes +7.

Seasonal adjustments for nonclaiming maidens and nonwinners allowances.

Jan-Feb	−2
Mar-Apr-May	−1
June-July-Aug	0
Sept-Oct	+1
Nov-Dec	+2

For races restricted to 3-year-olds at various times of year.

	6F	6½F	7F	$1M-1^{40}M$	$1^{70}M-1\frac{1}{16}M$	$1\frac{1}{4}M$		
+9							Jan. 1	+9
+8							Feb. 1	+8
+7						Jan. 1	Mar. 15	+7
+6					Feb. 15		May 1	+6
+5				Jan. 1	Apr. 15		June 1	+5
+4		Jan. 1	Jan. 1	Apr. 15	June 1		July 1	+4
+3	Jan. 1	Feb. 1	Mar. 15	June 1	July 1		Aug. 1	+3
+2	Apr. 15	June 1	June 15	July 15	Aug. 15		Sept. 15	+2
+1	July 1	Aug. 1	Aug. 15	Sept. 15	Oct. 15		Dec. 1	+1
0	Nov. 1	Dec. 1	Dec. 15	—	—		—	0

For example, in comparison to races open to older horses, races for 3-year-olds at six furlongs are completed 3/5 of a second slower on Jan. 1, 1/5 slower on July 1, with no difference by Nov. 1.

If handicappers determine the local par for $10,000 older claiming males at six furlongs is 1:11, they can readily answer the following by consulting the adjustment charts.

What is the par for older $4000 males at six furlongs?

What is the six furlong par for $20,000 older mares?

What is the six furlong par $12,500 older males?

What is the six furlong par $8000 3-year-olds during May?

What is the six furlong par for $40,000 maiden 3-year-old fillies, entered to be claimed on August 29?

The first four pars are 1:12, 1:10 4/5, 1:10 4/5, and 1:11 3/5.

The fifth question par requires the following adjustments:

$40,000 level	−6
Maidens	+5
Fillies	+2
August 29 3-year-olds	+1

Par is 1:11 plus 2, or 1:11 2/5.

In like manner, handicappers can determine the following pars, if they know older nonclaiming maidens at the mile average a final time of 1:38, at 1-1/16M average 1:44 3/5, and at 1-1/8M 1:51 2/5.

What is par for NW 3 males traveling a mile and one-sixteenth on July 4?

What is par for NW 1 older fillies and mares at one and one-eighth miles February 15?

What is par for stakes fillies, 3-years-old, going one mile October 20?

What is par for classified 3-year-old fillies traveling a mile and one-eighth August 15?

The first three pars would be 1:43 1/5, 1:51, and 1:36 2/5.

The fourth question's par requires these adjustments:

Classified	−10
Fillies	+3
Three-year-olds, Aug 15, at 1-1/8M	+3

Par is 1:51 2/5, minus 4, or 1:50 3/5.

The most constructive use of pars for handicappers, regardless of persuasion, is the calculation of daily track variants sensitive to class differences. Handicappers who compare actual times to par times and average the differences for a nine-race card have calculated a variant sensitive to both class levels and track surfaces. When the variant is added or subtracted to the raw final times, the resulting times are adjusted final times that represent better estimates of true speed.

Properly adjusted final times help handicappers understand class within a class, and they have reliable application to the calendar's largest category of races, claiming races open to older horses. Adjusted final times also reflect the relative quality of maiden races, providing indicators as to which of these winners might proceed successfully to preliminary non-winners allowance competition. Variants calculated by reference to par time tables can be obtained within minutes. Many professionals recommend calculation of both a sprint and route variant, by averaging the day's time differences (pars plus or minus raw times) in each category. Handicappers can honor the dramatically-improved role of speed in handicapping by spending the time and effort to obtain pars and daily variants. Those who do will prosper with a set of adjusted final times that shed light on numerous handicapping mysteries.

CRUDE OIL IN ALLOWANCE FIELDS

On publishing a surprisingly effective detector of class in allowance races, Fred Davis fretted that handicappers would judge the technique crude. On the other hand, he asserted, the statistics stand firm. The only way to adjust them is statistically, with better studies.

The source of Fred's anxiety was his finding that in allowance races horses that have been entered in stakes races, of any commodity, anywhere, have a much better-than-expected chance to win. It does not matter what happened to the horses in the stakes competition. They might have been beaten to a frazzle. If returned now to allowance conditions, the horses enjoy a statistical advantage, and not a narrow one at that. Fred Davis wondered about that, and worried. Handicapping texts had consistently held that mere presence in a stakes race did not amount to stakes quality. What mattered was the quality of performance in the stakes. Fred was about to go public with new evidence, of the kind he had trouble accepting himself.

Davis in fact has helped thousands of handicappers without result charts by studying whether the **types of races** a horse has entered might indicate its relative class in allowance races. He shuffled starters in allowance races into three categories: (a) has appeared only in allowance and maiden races (maiden special weights in the East) (b) has entered one or more stakes races, and (c) has entered one or more claiming races. Whereas the **a** group was defined as moving neither up nor down in class, the **b** group was assigned to a higher class and the **c** group to a lower one. Where horses had entered both stakes and claiming races, the more recent stakes or claiming start was accepted.

Here are the results that perplexed the researcher, and many handicappers besides:

	STARTERS		WINNERS		
Category	How many	Percent	How many	Percent	I.V.
Stakes	596	28	118	47.5	1.70
Alw-Mdn	893	42	92	36.5	.82
Claiming	638	30	40	16.0	.53
	2126		250		

As fascinating as the probability statistic indicating stakes starters in allowance races win 170 per cent the fair share of the races are the stats persuading handicappers how poorly the other two categories perform. Neither group holds its own in allowance competition, and horses previously entered to be claimed win merely half their rightful share of allowance starts.

Handicappers without charts now have at easy disposal a technique for spotting classier entrants in allowance races. They merely spot the horses that have already entered stakes races, those results notwithstanding. Where two or more stakes starters appear, as happens frequently, handicappers need sharper criteria, such as actual performance in stakes competition, average purse earnings, conditions of eligibility completed successfully, or the kinds of horses challenged and defeated, and charts contain this kind of information. In another approach to relative class in allowance races, Davis found horses that have competed successfully for purses 30 to 60 per cent higher than today's hold a significant edge (I.V.'s of 1.86 to 2.16).

The stakes starters often appear under nonwinners allowance conditions, for nonwinners of three or more allowance races. With developing horses in particular (three-year-olds and sparsely-raced four-year-olds), trainers typically follow a second allowance win with entry in a stakes. If the stakes start ends with a shellacking, the horses might lose competitive form for a time. In a few weeks they again gather their forces together, and now they face allowance competition. Entry in a stakes suggests the trainer felt the horse had enough quality to handle itself, or perhaps win. The Davis

Frederick S. Davis, "Thoroughbred Racing: percentages and probabilities," *Millwood Publications*, Millwood, New York, 1974, pp 12-13.

statistics apply strongly to this kind. When a similar horse remains eligible for nonwinners twice other than maiden or claiming—now challenging horses that have not yet won two allowance races or better—its stakes experience suggests it outclasses the conditions. The better the stakes performance, the better.

If handicappers can appreciate how stables progress with nicely-bred, lightly-raced, nicely-developing younger horses, they need not be tentative about backing stakes starters that fared miserably when these prospects return to allowance ranks. Stables might be abjectly wrong about the stakes potential of a fine young thoroughbred, but that horse is very likely a good thing against ordinary allowance fare.

THE RACE WAS WRITTEN FOR HIM

A thirst among handicappers for knowledge about eligibility conditions accounted for the instant success of the most comprehensive treatment of that topic yet published. In *The Handicapper's Condition Book* horses well-suited to race conditions were elaborately described, and contrasted to horses not so well-suited to conditions. Where more than one kind of horse fit the conditions nicely, these were profiled in descending order of preference, though handicappers were cautioned to consider the suitable profiles as interchangeable, depending on factors other than class. The book defined the role of race conditions as essentially prescribing or limiting the class of the horses eligible to compete. Many handicappers regarded the work as an advanced treatment of the class factor. They were largely correct.

From time to time at every major track the racing secretary writes a race specifically for one horse, almost invariably the star of the division, if not the local, regional, or national champ. The star's trainer may complain he needs an overnite race to prepare for the upcoming stakes. Or a preliminary stakes may be wiped out by rain, hindering the bigshot's conditioning, and necessitating an overnite substitute race before the next big stakes on the agenda. Once upon a recent Saturday, the fourth race at Santa Anita early in January was carded specifically for the Eastern stakes invader **Five Star Flight**, there to contest that track's Strub series, three closely-matched graded stakes uniquely limited to new four-year-olds. The first leg of the Strub series had been covered with mud a week before, and **Five Star Flight** had scratched out. Thus an overnite race was written for him, to insure his continued conditioning. The conditions of eligibility for the special race looked like this:

FOURTH RACE

Santa Anita

JANUARY 9, 1982

7 FURLONGS. (1.20) CLASSIFIED ALLOWANCE. Purse $40,000. 4-year-olds and upward. Non-winners of $19,500 since December 25, which are non-winners of two such races since July 28. Weights, 4-year-olds, 121 lbs.; older, 122 lbs. Non-winners of two such races since April 20 allowed 3 lbs.; of such a race since September 29 or a race of $22,500 in 1981, 5 lbs.; of a race of $19,500 since July 28, 8 lbs. (Claiming races not considered).

Value of race $40,000, value to winner $22,000, second $8,000, third $6,000, fourth $3,000, fifth $1,000. Mutuel pool $281,471. Exacta Pool $407,330.

By barring winners of big money since only December 25, the racing secretary kept the Eastern horse clear of extra-sharp stakes winners at the young meeting, notably the winner of the Malibu stakes, the previously-remarked first leg.

On the rare occasions when this occurs handicappers gaze upon the miserly odds on the bigshot under overnite conditions, and scream that the race was written for him. True enough, but upsets are common enough under these special circumstances. **Five Star Flight** finished fourth of five on his special day. After all, the stars come into the race short on a fundamental factor of handicapping, current form. So they sometimes lose.

The screaming handicappers can benefit in this regard from recognition of a much greater truth about eligibility conditions. If not for a particular horse, in fact every race on the card is written with a particular **kind** of horse in mind. That's the racing secretary's main purpose, to provide winning opportunities for every horse in the barns. Handicappers who learn to recognize in the past performances the kinds of horses **most likely** to win each kind of race have leaped ahead of the crowd by miles.

From the handicapper's condition book, here are the conditions of eligibility in major racing and the kind of horses best suited to each. If it sets up as the only horse of its kind in the field, the race was written for him.

Maidens, 3-and-up, or 4-and-up, any distance.

The horse that finished second last time out.

Maiden claiming, all ages, any distance.

The horse moving from a maiden or maiden special weight race, provided form is intact, it has a front-running or pace-pressing running style, and its speed figures for either of its previous two races are among the top two in the field.

Allowance, nonwinners of two races, or nonwinners of a race other than maiden or claiming.

Lightly-raced younger maiden winners that have raced close once or twice with above-average clockings under similar conditions.

Allowance, nonwinners two times other than maiden or claiming.

Lightly-raced impressive younger horses, especially nicely-bred improving three-year-olds, that recently have won an allowance race easily or impressively in better-than-average (par) time.

Allowance, nonwinners three times other than maiden or claiming.

Impressive winners of two recent allowance races that performed evenly or better in a stakes or handicap.

Allowance, nonwinners four times other than maiden or claiming.

Previous stakes winners, preferably of open stakes.

Conditioned stakes, bars previous stakes winners or winners of a specified amount since a specified date.

Horses that recently have finished in-the-money or have run close in an open stakes of relatively high purse value, provided form remains intact or continues in the improvement cycle.

Stakes, Grade 1.

Previous Grade 1 stakes winners.

Stakes, Grade 2.

Previous Grade 1 or Grade 2 stakes winners, preferably a well-meant Gr. 1 horse.

Stakes, Grade 3, or ungraded but open.

In the absence of well-meant Gr. 1 or Gr. 2 winners, a recent persuasive winner of an open stakes, preferably of a purse comparable to or greater than today's.

Classified allowances, relatively unrestricted.

Any horse whose basic class, as indicated by purse values won, restrictions of prior classified conditions, or the quality of horses engaged in its recent best efforts, is superior to today's conditions, especially open stakes winners, provided form is acceptable, and the distance, footing, and probable pace are comfortable.

Classified allowances, relatively restricted.

Currently **sharp** horses that have been competing for purses of comparable or better value, and are particularly well-suited to today's distance, footing, and probable pace.

Claiming races, all ages, all prices.

Any horse dropping in claiming price by 30 per cent or more, provided form is acceptable, improving, or peaking, and the horse has high to satisfactory early speed.

Starter races, all ages, all prices.

Horses that have won or run close previously at the highest open claiming price, especially a horse that has won a prior race in the starter series, or one which became eligible by a drop in claiming class last time out.

Regarding classified allowance conditions, relatively unrestricted conditions are not very restricted at all. They are open to all but the classiest horses on the grounds. Thus, class rules. Relatively restricted conditions bar all horses that have accomplished anything of late, and therefore provide ordinary and inferior horses a better chance to win. Thus, class bows to form.

Of claiming conditions, the ideal bet in any claiming race is the horse that combines (a) high early speed (b) peaking form, and (c) a drop in class. The 30 percent or greater drop in claiming class is handicapping's most powerful probability statistic. It wins 375 percent its rightful share of the claiming races.

PADDOCK INSPECTIONS REVISITED

Until Bonnie Ledbetter broke into print with descriptions of equine body language, handicappers assigned most if not all horses with copious kidney sweat to the no-bet category. None could be fairly regarded as betting stickouts. All worlds change. Sweating horses are sometimes the sharpest horses in the field. The sweat is part of a keyed-up profile of the **sharp**, impatient horse clamoring for competition. Handicappers can now not only recognize the **sharp** horse that might be sweating, they can distinguish it unmistakenly from the **frightened** horse that is sweating as well. Ms. Ledbetter has spelled out the differences.

Ms. Ledbetter has also revealed that the most critical object of the handicapper's paddock and post parade inspections is a part of the horse barely touched by previous literature—the ears. More on that momentarily.

In a collaboration altogether helpful and rewarding to handicappers everywhere, when Tom Ainslie combined the body language of horses, as supplied by Ms. Ledbetter, to formal principles of handicapping, the resulting inspection guidelines serve to extend the knowledge base in this esoteric area tremendously, and to alter several preexisting notions that no longer apply.

Even the foundations of the paddock visit have been shaken. The purpose heretofore was to look for negative signs. If horses that figured on paper failed the paddock inspection, races were passed, or at times second choices upgraded. Handicappers now are advised that horses inseparable on paper can sometimes be distinguished in the paddock and post parade. This represents a fundamental departure in procedure. If contenders are separated at the paddock, previous unplayable races turn playable, action increases, and handicappers had better understand what they are about.

Ainslie reminds that 90 per cent of all races are won by horses described as **sharp, ready,** or **dull.** The remaining 10 per cent are taken by **frightened, angry,** and **hurting** horses, which handicappers presumably avoid. Sweat and kidney lather can be characteristic of both the **sharp** and **frightened** horses, which represent by far the most interesting dichotomy of body language. Handicappers can support **sharp** horses on those grounds alone, avoid **frightened** horses for like reasons. They should set out to become expert about the two profiles. Ledbetter-Ainslie are greatly reassuring on the point, asserting the body language of each kind is unmistakable.

Of the **sharp** horses, these may not only sweat, but dance and wheel almost fractiously, affecting apprehension or nervousness, but otherwise are the embodiment of health and vigor. The coat luxuriates with a shine or dapple. Mane and tail gleam. Neither fat nor bony, its rear muscles haunch and perhaps ripple. The animal prances on its toes, a picture of eagerness, often with neck arched, head tucked downward towards the chest, the ears pricked forward, tail up to signal readiness. The horse is alert to the crowd and surrounding commotion. It is not quiet in the saddling stall, but rather full of itself, almost showing off, head in the air, dancing confidently, and this language intensifies during the parade to the post. Lead riders may have to take a short hold of it in the parade, lifting its nose in the air, lest the **sharp** horse throttle the lead pony. When warm-ups begin, the **sharp** horse strides out strongly off the hind haunches in the first couple strides, tail up, muscles tensing. Sometimes the horse's head will almost touch its chest, neck arched, ears pricked fully forward. The horse almost lunges into the gate and once inside stands firm, back feet planted, fronts at times shuffling and restless. It springs out of there like jet propulsion. There might not be many of these sharpsters, but they are well worth the hunt. They are, in the banker's lexicon, bettable.

The **sharp** horse's opposite number, the **frightened** horse, begs the player's automatic elimination. Its sweat and fractiousness are not symbols of excitement, but of fear. Reluctant and resistant, en route to the paddock ceremonies, there, and

Tom Ainslie and Bonnie Ledbetter, "The Body Language of Horses," *William Morrow and Company, Inc.* 1980, Ch. 7, pp. 164-173.

in the walking ring its head is held high and in continuous motion, eyes rolling so that the whites become visible, ears flicking rapidly in all directions, unsynchronized. Leg action in front is high and uncoordinated, tail swishes from side to side or up and down. The handler might control the horse with a stud chain over the nose, under the lip or across the mouth. The horse fights the chain, perhaps moving in a semicircle in front of the lead horse, pulling and yanking to get away from it all.

During saddling, walking, and mounting the horse washes out and moves about kicking and stomping in unorganized maneuvers. Eyes roll, ears flick, nostrils flare. It resists its handlers, who in turn fight back. In the walking ring the **frightened** horse may wheel and circle away as the jockey attempts to mount. During the post parade the jockey has a tight hold, even as the horse clings to the lead pony as much as possible, perhaps extending its head and neck across the pony. If the lead rider prevents that with the chain, the horse's head is high, eyes and ears moving wildly, the front legs stepping high and sideways. The lead horse proceeds straight down the course, but the **frightened** horse moves in short, spastic jumps at an angle to the pony.

Before the starting gate arrives, all energy and hope has been lost. These kind also throw tantrums in the gate, casting themselves or hanging over the partitions. Coincidence determines what happens when the gate opens. Often **frightened** horses burst out first, as if fleeing, but they exhaust themselves in a panicky run long before the homestretch. If they break tardily, they typically show keen bursts of speed that catch the others but deplete the horses of late speed, such that they are absolutely exhausted just as the stretch run begins.

Handicappers already may be familiar with the **ready, dull,** and **hurting** horses, but not so with the **angry** horse, characterized by Ledbetter as the sour kind easily provoked during the pre-race ceremonies. Ill-tempered, **angry** horses range from mildly irritated to wildly furious, and all but the mildly irritated should be expected to lose. Angry body language differs from the language of fright, but the result is the same. **Angry** horses rarely sweat. The telltale sign of its annoyance is flattened ears, or in furious moments, ears pinned directly onto the head. Handicappers should not fail to consult Ledbetter for the **angry** profile and are well-advised to renew acquaintances with the **ready, dull,** and **hurting** kind.

Handicappers are also alerted that **sharp** horses can turn **angry** during any phase of the prerace ceremonies, if distracted or upset by handlers or circumstances. If horses behave fractiously when parading before the stands, dancing sideways, rearing or bucking, head tossing up and down, and tail swishing, handicappers who have not visited the paddock and many who have will have difficulty recognizing whether the horses remain **sharp** or are seriously fractious. What differentiates the two conditions at this crucial point is the position of the ears. The ears of the **sharp** horse remain alert and in the forward position, or perhaps turned backwards to the chirping rider, but straight. But if the ears flatten or become pinned or assume the airplane position, even as the tail swishes and pops irritably, the horses are now out of sorts. Handicappers should continue to watch the horses, paying attention to the ears. If they remain flattened or pinned, avoid the horses.

Ainslie relates the body language of horses to the fundamental factors of handicapping in numerous important ways. A few:

Closely-matched contenders can sometimes be separated at the paddock. If one looks particularly **sharp,** and the odds beckon, the bet makes sense. These horses not only are overlays and figure well enough on fundamentals, they look like winners in the flesh. In this special context, handicappers prosper by inspecting horses for positive signs of fitness and readiness.

Dramatically-improved form together with dramatically-improved appearance equals a potentially sweet bet.

Of horses that appear **dull** or **hurting** only those that have won previously when in comparable condition can be considered a potential play.

The most debilitating and negative experience for a young horse is the stumble or actual fall. As Ms. Ledbetter tells, for a horse loss of balance is perceived as a threat to survival.

If a horse's behavior deteriorates as soon as the jockey climbs aboard, and the jockey has lost with the horse while others have won, handicappers can fairly assume incompatibility between horse and rider. They should not expect a triumphal return.

More than ever before, handicappers can prepare themselves to benefit from the body language of horses. The language is not learned quickly. Familiarity and practice make the difference. The study of horses' body language moves from Ledbetter-Ainslie to the paddock, walking ring, and post parade, and back again, numerous times a season.

UNIT WAGERS AT THE ODDS

The records of professional handicappers have taught them how to make seasonal profits. These result from betting to win, but not so often at odds below 3-1. To be sure, horses at 8-5 might represent outstanding overlays (true chances better than public odds) and these can be bet confidently. An overlay at any price is part of a mathematical pattern that must end in success. Yet the record shows handicappers earn their profits from bets on better-priced horses. The dividing line is reported at 3-1. Above that, handicappers' win percentages may drop, but not enough to alter the profit picture. Students of win-loss ratios above and below odds of approximately 3-1 report that handicappers win frequently enough at the higher odds to concentrate the higher bets there.

The implications of this for unit wagering ($2 or $5 or $20 or $200 or whatever) are clear, if difficult to apply. The size of the bets should increase as the odds increase.

Fred Davis has recommended the following escalation:

At 3-1 or below, one unit.

At 7-2 or 4-1, two units.

At 9-2 or 5-1, three units.

At 6-1, four units.

At 7-1 or above, five units.

All studies agree handicappers win enough at the higher odds to justify the higher wagers. At the same time, unit wagering at 3-1 or below amounts to little more than spinning wheels. Neither the profits nor losses become significant. If unit bets correlate with size of the odds, a $20 bettor will bet $100 when his selection goes at 7-1 or greater. If he is the kind of handicapper that wins 40 percent at 2-1 or 30 percent at 3-1, earning 20 percent on the dollar, raising the bets as odds grow will improve the rate of return.

Tom Ainslie, who long has advocated fixed percentage wagering, advises that unit wagering in ratio to the odds should not be tried with 5 percent of capital as the basic unit. Otherwise, handicappers bet 25 percent of capital when the 10-1 horses arrive. Theoretically, this works, but few of us have the temperament for the bets. Ainslie recommends 1 percent at the base, thus 5 percent on the longshots.

To sustain profits that are not seasonal, perhaps weekly or monthly, unit wagering in this manner can include place bets. The pros tolerate place bets when (a) horses stand out at 7-2 or greater, and (b) the favorite figures to lose. If both conditions prevail, handicappers can bet one unit to win and two units to place when their selection is:

7-2 or better in a field of seven starters or more,

3-1 in a six-horse field, and

5-2 in a field fewer than six.

To repeat, the race favorite must smell like a loser.

Perhaps the most simplified of all the acceptable longterm wagering methods, the main problem experienced with unit bets that increase as odds increase is the psychology of the approach. Having been conditioned forever to bet more on shorter-priced horses, handicappers have difficulty extinguishing that baseless approach and learning to bet more when the risk goes up. Regardless, as the books assert, there can be little doubt many handicappers can tolerate the new approach and profit extensively from it.

Tom Ainslie, "Ainslie's Encyclopedia of Thoroughbred Handicapping," **William Morrow and Company, Inc.,** 1978, pp. 150-151.

SPOT PLAYS AT MINOR TRACKS

In major league racing the purse quickens the pulse. Stables, trainers, and jockeys concentrate their strategies and energies there, however much they might appreciate a few points in the odds. Handicappers need know little more about owner-trainer-jockey practices than which ones succeed most often at the expense of the others. At minor tracks purses are small. Stables cannot survive and trainers cannot prosper without cashing a bet or two. Handicappers need as much information about the ways and means of these individuals as researchers and their computers can generate. The most advantageous information is the kind that has not been captured in the past performances or results charts.

On this remote front the most useful and instructive body of knowledge has been accumulated by James Selvidge and his associates at Jacada Publications, as presented quarterly in that outfit's hardcore handicapping periodical, *Hold Your Horses* (HYH), which has much that is valuable to say to handicappers at the majors as well. Selvidge regularly provides handicappers at Longacres in Seattle and other tracks with an array of spot plays that have thrown seasonal profits, as well as the wagering experiments that cost-effectively reveal whether the spot plays continue to win. The work is laboriously empirical. It involves collecting every piece of information about every owner, trainer, jockey, and horse on the grounds, and microscopically examining the data in all its combinations. Computers are necessary handmaidens. The idea is to produce patterns of performance that show seasonal profits that are otherwise invisible to handicappers.

To illustrate the possibilities this sort of data bank can arouse, Selvidge in 1979 astonished the handicapping fraternity by reporting that the use of an obscure piece of equipment by a select group of Longacres trainers was tossing out fantastic profits. HYH referred to it as the "Tongue-Tie phenomenon." Certain horses that wore tongue-ties constituted the most powerful spot play at the track. To quote HYH:

> "Backing tongue-tie starts above 3-1 by the 22 trainers spotted in 1979 created a profit of $5,451.90 by midseason. . .It also had a period of waffling, but then kicked on the after-burners and generated another $2500 late-season profit."

The phenomenon repeated itself so in 1980 with an enlarged group of 34 "power" trainers that Selvidge demonstrated how a seasonal flow of his base-bet-plus-square-root-of-profits money management method would have resulted in profits of $30,000 and a rate of return on investment of 1000 percent.

Tongue-tie freaks at Longacres and other minor tracks to which this epidemic might have spread are dependent on HYH or its counterpart for generating the trainer information, and for other system modifiers, such as the cutoff at 3-1 odds or greater. Moreover, the logistics of implementing the system can approach the machinations of a relay team, involving as they do inspection of the horses from the trip to the paddock until they are deposited into the starting gate, a routine not easily characterized as handicapping. Yet the researcher's retort is not easily dismissed. The data shows a trend that works.

Of more conventional performance patterns, Selvidge each year identifies profit flows involving trainer/jockey relationships, owner/trainer relationships, trainer performance specialties (2-year-old racing, distance racing, sprint to route, route to sprint, alw to stks, exactas, et. al.), repeat winners at designated times of the season, pedigree performance in juvenile racing, and shippers. To enhance the reliability of the data, three-year baseline periods must pass muster before the performance pattern is designated as profitable enough to warrant play. Even then, investment is protected by employing a money management technique that allocates risk capital

James Selvidge, "Hold Your Horses Quarterly," Vol. 1, No. 5, Fall 1980, *Jacada Publications*, Seattle, Washington, p. 15.

enough only to support 15 consecutive losing bets. If that kind of loss is sustained, Selvidge advises abandoning the performance pattern, previous statistics notwithstanding. Because the profitable performance patterns are best regarded as angles, as opposed to selections resulting from a fundamental kind of handicapping, they are continuously subject to experiment and reevaluation. Angles eventually stop working. Even when working at full steam, the angles often win at a rate of 20 percent or so, but the average payoffs just as often are high enough to sustain them. Spot plays of the kind HYH discovers by looking behind the scenes at minor tracks can be of tremendous value to handicappers with access to the information, so long as they do not run amuck with it. Continuous study is critical. Blind ambition with handicapping angles that work for a time, but not for all time, leads ultimately to the poorhouse.

Another handicapper-author who has assisted handicappers at minor tracks by studying the racing routines there is the peripetetic Steve Davidowitz. He warns handicappers who seldom see a top-drawer horse at their tracks not to forget to incorporate notions about class in their methods. In this regard Davidowitz has elaborated a classification code that pinpoints the relative class of claiming races having the same selling prices at minor plants. To use the scheme, handicappers need a full set of results charts for the current and previous seasons.

Davidowitz' classification code fastens on the eligibility conditions of claiming races. After studying the charts of Charles Town in West Virginia, Davidowitz reported that 90 percent of the claiming races had restrictive clauses in the conditions. The restrictions produced a class hierarchy within a specified claiming level referred to by Davidowitz as "class within a class." He cited a series of $1500 claiming races during 1976. The first $1500 race was limited to horses that had not won a race in 1976. The second was for nonwinners of three races in 1976; the third for nonwinners of two races lifetime; and the fourth for nonwinners of a race during 1975 or 1976, perhaps the lowest $1500 races ever written. Another series of $1500 claiming races restricted eligibility to nonwinners since a number of specified dates.

Davidowitz found that not only were the class differences within the $1500 level measurable in terms of final times, those differences were in fact greater than the differences between the average $1500 race and the average $2000 race. As Davidowitz noted, it was more difficult at Charles Town to move up within the $1500 class than it was to step up from $1500 to $2000. When horses win $1500 races at Charles Town they normally lose eligibility at a more restricted level, and next must compete against horses with more recent victories, thus they face stiffer competition. For this reason horses at minor tracks have greater difficulty winning back to back, and the slower horses at each class level remain trapped for months. They cannot move ahead until all the horses at their class level, as all the $1500 horses that are better, have advanced to the next level of competition. Handicappers can imagine the plight of slow horses at these gradations.

Below is Davidowitz' classification code for $1500 and $2000 claiming races at Charles Town. With minor variation the code is highly transportable to minor tracks elsewhere. It reveals how steep a class ladder these rock-bottom horses are forced to climb.

Charles Town Classification Code for $1500 and $2000 Claiming Races

O—open race, unrestricted eligibility (top class)

A—nonwinners of 2 races in the past two months or 3 races in the past three months

B—nonwinners of 2 races in three to five months

C—nonwinners of 2 races in six to nine months or 3 races in nine to twelve months

D—nonwinners of 2 races in nine to twenty-four months

E—nonwinners of a race in nine to twenty-four months

M—nonwinners lifetime (Maidens)

Davidowitz offers precious guidelines for working with the code and the class factor at minor tracks.

1. The easiest class jump is from M to E. This being so, E-class horses are the most chronically trapped. Most of these have little ability, and consistently face recent maiden win-

ners. Thus recent M graduates are among the best bets at minor tracks, when they move ahead the small step to E.

2. If a horse is entered at A or B when still eligible for C or D, handicappers can throw it out. Such horses are either out for exercise or their trainers are darkening form.

3. Horses showing recent signs of life at A or B make excellent prospects when dropped to D or E, for which they remain eligible.

Handicappers at minor tracks might be enthused to know Davidowitz has called the hidden class maneuver immediately above (from A or B to D or E) the most powerful dropdown angle in all of racing.

Handicappers at Charles Town, Thistledown, River Downs, Waterford Park, Lincoln Downs, Green Mountain Park, Penn National, Finger Lakes, Commodore Downs, Longacres, and Fonner Park, plus a dozen others like them, are well-advised as a first resort to develop a classification code for their place. Davidowitz stresses it will be the most important homework they complete for this or any season. He predicts genuinely astounding results, as when at Green Mountain Park he spotted a 14-1 shot in a $2000 D-race that had recently flashed high early speed in a $1500 A-race. As Davidowitz tells, despite the apparent rise in claiming price, the longshot was dropping down big in class. It won by nine lengths.

COMPREHENSIVE HANDICAPPING

Promoted by Tom Ainslie variously in his seven books and private method, Comprehensive Handicapping as method recognizes that **all** the factors of handicapping play **a part** in the outcomes of races. Arguing that all the factors of handicapping are intertwined, Ainslie makes systematic the player's handling of each, underscoring their interrelations, and establishing their priorities under various conditions of racing. Because the method features the interactions among several factors, it is essentially analytical and evaluative in approach, asking handicappers to break a race down into component parts, put those pieces together again in a new coherent whole, and make final decisions with a judgment formed by extensive knowledge and experience. Not easily susceptible to quantification, the method relies on qualitative analyses. Because the method derives only from fundamental and comprehensive knowledge about the sport of racing and skill of handicapping, it not only achieved a breakthrough of its own, equipping thousands of racegoers with considerable knowledge and systematic procedure encompassing the entire range of the handicapping art, but also advanced the frontiers of knowledge about the sport itself.

And because it depends on fundamental knowledge, the method begs revision whenever the knowledge base of handicapping gets extended through research or changes in the sport itself. First set forth in *The Compleat Horseplayer* (1966), and following successive revisions from 1968 through 1979, the latest version incorporates well the new evidence regarding the importance of early speed and the need to liberalize standards of form.

Taking distance and form as the starting points, and proceeding to jockeys, weight, class, age, sex, and consistency, Ainslie first presents elimination guidelines, standards of performance against which horses' records must pass muster, or the horses themselves are eliminated from further consideration. The survivors are the contenders. These are next differentiated on pace. The separation process continues by comparing horses' records on a list of plus factors, these designed to reflect the subtleties of handicapping. Next comes the paddock and post parade inspections, where horses that figure best on paper must look acceptable in the flesh. If selections survive all of this, handicappers finally can check the odds and decide whether they have found a good bet.

In systematic but not mechanical manner, handicappers proceed to apply a series of negative guidelines that identify contenders to the application of a series of positive guidelines that separate the contenders. Noting that handicappers might start with any factor that suits their personal tastes, as comprehensive handicapping eventually must touch all the factors, Ainslie recommends distance and form considerations to begin, as these two factors reliably eliminate the largest number of noncontenders.

Of class, Ainslie reminds that the handicapping process sometimes ends abruptly here, if one horse outclasses its rivals notably. Handicappers already know the horse is suited to the distance and in acceptable form. If a final check indicates the horse's class edge should not be nullified or seriously blunted by today's probable pace, it figures, and the handicapping for all practical purposes has been completed.

To separate contenders, Ainslie emphasizes that pace analysis supersedes pace ratings, and in the latest edition of the method he stresses that pace analysis should begin by estimating the influences and probable effects of the early speed. Where early speed looks inconclusive, pace analysis concerns the relationship between fractional times and final times. Ainslie sets out to find the horse that either will set and maintain the fastest fractions, or will track and overcome the early fractions. The Plus Factors cover the full range of the handicapping process but many of them reflect the critical interplay as between class and form.

If no horse qualifies, or too many do, comprehensive han-

Tom Ainslie, "Ainslie's Complete Guide To Thoroughbred Racing," *Simon and Schuster*, New York, 1979 (Revised Ed.), Chapters 7-17.

dicapping has found the race unplayable, and therefore unbeatable. The method is designed to determine whether one horse has an unusually good chance to win, and not to provide action on unreliable horses or overly competitive races.

Full-dress comprehensive handicapping is more intricate than the above capsulization suggests. Once unfit, outclassed, and horses ill-suited to the distance are eliminated by applying the negative guidelines, what counts is how handicappers relate performance on each factor to all others. Weight and post position normally have incidental effects on race outcomes, for example, but those influences will have more or less effect depending on the horses' comfort with the distance, degrees of class, or relative fitness. To attempt a condensation of comprehensive handicapping as method almost necessarily violates the basic tenet of the method, which, after all, honors **comprehensiveness**. Handicappers wishing to examine the method or to review it again are best advised to consult Ainslie's latest version (1979). For now, it will be instructive to review some of the basic elimination guidelines for the fundamental factors of distance, form, and class. These eliminate systematic errors of the grossest sort. Handicappers who continually support horses whose records violate one or more of the following precepts are prone to mistaken judgments of the most fundamental character.

The following guidelines apply to horses aged three or older.

Of distance, a horse qualifies at today's distance if

(a) it has won a race of this exact distance, or

(b) it has finished close (within three lengths) to the winner at today's distance in respectable time and the race occurred this season, or

(c) it finished fourth and within two lengths of the winner at the distance this season.

The concept of "respectable time" is defined in terms of speed ratings. The cutoffs are:

90—Sprints of handicap and stakes quality

88—High grade allowance sprints

85—Handicaps and stakes run around two turns

80—High grade allowance routes, lesser allowance sprints, and sprints for claiming horses valued above $7,500

78—Cheap claiming sprints

73—Route races for better claimers

69—Route races for claimers valued at $4000 or less

Excepting the occasional sprinter that might take the early lead and control the pace, horses 4-and-older competing at new distances are best eliminated.

Of form, when analyzing claiming races

(a) horses at seven furlongs or less must have raced within the past calendar month at today's track, a sister track, or a track of superior class

(b) a horse at longer than seven furlongs must show a race within the past month plus two workouts in the meantime. If it has raced within two weeks and shows one workout, it is acceptable. If it has raced within the past week, no workouts are necessary.

(c) a horse entered at seven furlongs or less can be regarded as a potential contender even if it has been unraced for 45 days, providing it hs been working out at intervals of four or five days and has previously won after absences of such length.

When considering allowance, handicap, and stakes horses, these need not have raced so often to maintain sharpness, but they are seldom acceptable unless they have worked out frequently, recently, and with respectable times (12 seconds a furlong).

Regarding basic fitness and soundness standards

(a) throw out any horse that bled, ran sore, or finished lame in its last race

(b) throw out any horse that lugged in or bore out in its last race

(c) throw out any horse that is stepping up in class after a race it won while losing ground in a driving stretch run

(d) throw out any cheaper four-year-old or older horse that engaged in driving finishes in each of its last two races.

(e) throw out any horse aged five or older whose best effort at today's distance occurred in its last race, unless the horse is a male that demonstrated reserve speed in that race.

(f) throw out any claimer whose last race was a "big win" more than two weeks ago.

Of class, eliminations remain consistent with these guidelines.

(a) no horse aged four or older is acceptable in a handicap or stakes unless it usually runs in such company and either has won or finished in-the-money when so entered.

(b) no three-year-old is a good candidate in a handicap or stakes race against older horses unless it has already beaten such a field, or has been running with exceptional power against its own age, suggesting a clear edge in intrinsic class and condition.

(c) to be acceptable as a contender in an allowance race, a horse whose last start was in a claimer should have won an allowance race on this circuit or one of equal class, or should be facing other nonwinners of such allowance races, and should not be asked to defeat another contender that has run in the money in a handicap or stakes within the last three months.

(d) in claiming races no horse can step up as much as 50 percent when comparing the top price today with the claiming price at which the horse was entered last time.

(e) in maiden races and races for nonwinners of two races, three-year-olds are almost invariably better prospects than the older, chronic losers they meet in such fields.

Finally, no horse can be conceded an advantage in class because it has raced against higher-class horses than it will meet today unless the horse beat at least half the field or showed high early speed in the higher-class race.

Because the method is at once basic and intricate, comprehensive handicapping is simultaneously appropriate for beginners and intermediate-advanced handicappers. Because it is comprehensive, the method has something for practically everyone, regardless of persuasion.

BRED FOR GRASS

Pedigree studies having largely revealed that breeding for performance represents the sport's richest crap shoot, breeding as a factor in handicapping has merited only limited application. William Quirin's probability studies changed that forevermore. They demonstrated irrefutably that talent on turf is strongly related to pedigree. Moreover, horses whose breeding promises good performance on turf regularly win at boxcar prices when first tried over grass. If the dirt performances have ranged from ordinary to awful, the public will shy from the horses, but handicappers in the know can back them enthusiastically when they switch to the grass. Quirin has identified a prepotent sire line and all the contemporary sires and broodmare sires whose get go best on the lawn. Handicappers are rightly urged to commit the names to memory.

The sire line of Prince Rose is the prepotent family. His most potent grass sons for four generations appear on the pedigree flow accompanying this piece. Handicappers can appreciate the important influence of Princequillo, whose grandson Stage Door Johnny is the most influential turf sire of today. As the chart indicates, two sons of Princequillo, Prince John and Round Table, have exerted the most influence on successful grass racing. Another son, Prince Chevalier, has engendered a less well-known but important line.

Probability studies have identified the sires and broodmare sires that afford handicappers not only a significantly better-than-expected chance of winning, but also of netting profits on a series of $2 wagers. Here in descending order of their profit potential are the most potent sires on the turf.

William Quirin, "Winning At The Races: Computer Discoveries In Thoroughbred Handicapping," *William Morrow and Company, Inc.,* 1979, Ch. 22, pp. 227-240.

Sires (10 performers)	Winning Probability	Net on a $2 Bet
Verbatim	429%	$9.68
One For All	264	5.80
Stage Door Johnny	347	4.64
Hoist The Flag	378%	$4.18
Prince John	140	4.10
Round Table	212	4.00
Le Fabuleux	305%	$3.81
Grey Dawn II	143	3.50
Chieftain	147	3.42
Vent du Nord	198%	$3.34
Exclusive Native	187	3.30
Intentionally	147	3.11

The entire Princequillo line wins 160 percent their expected share of turf races and returns handicappers a $3.25 net per $2 bet while doing so. The following sires win more than their share while yielding profits on a series of $2 bets:

T. V. Commercial   Herbager
Dr. Fager   Nijinsky II
Mongo   Prince Rose Line
Sea-Bird

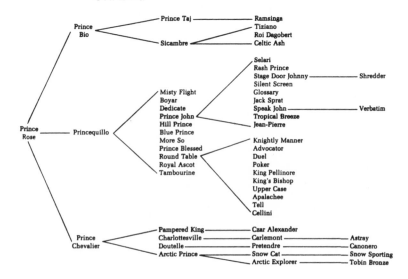

As broodmare sires, the entire lines of Prince Rose and Princequillo win much more than expected with $2 profits ranging from $3.49 to $3.61, powerful performance statistics.

The leading individual broodmare sire is Round Table, whose daughters' produce win twice their share of turf races and return a dollar profit of 137 percent while winning. Other leading broodmare sires for win percentage and profits include Prince John, Ribot, Intentionally, John's Joy, Amerigo, and Sir Gaylord.

Quirin combined the data on these sires along with selected others in numerous ways to discover the most propitious ways handicappers might proceed towards profits in turf racing. These findings can be accepted as maxims:

1. Horses with potent turf breeding should be bet when attempting their first-or-second starts on grass. The horses are generally underbet, in opposition to horses that have raced on turf without winning, and therefore represent overlays that yield seasonal profits.

2. Most profits await handicappers who play turf breeding on horses that go postward at odds of 10-1 or greater. This might represent the richest source of longshots handicappers have ever discovered scientifically!

3. If both sire and broodmare sire are influential turf parents, results can be expected to be all the better.

4. The first start on grass of appropriately bred horses can be either sprints or routes.

5. Good form on dirt is not a prerequisite for backing horses with turf breeding when they switch to grass. Dirt form helps, but is not necessary. Poor dirt form horses win less frequently, but return larger profits.

6. The most rewarding 2nd start on turf is one that immediately follows the 1st start. If the horse returns to dirt before a 2nd start on grass, its attraction diminishes greatly—no play.

7. Horses that win the 1st turf start do very well when bet right back, but horses that lost their first start "with honor," finishing within a length of the winner, do even better. These win 313 percent their appropriate share of their next races, return a 30 percent dollar profit.

8. Appropriately-bred horses do best when their first turf start occurs in maiden races or in nonwinners allowance races.

Quirin's updates of his original tabulations appear annually. The researcher has found horses carrying the blood of stallions on the original list do especially well themselves. Handicappers can expect these younger sires to carry the cause:

Secretariat	Majestic Light
Tentam	King Pellinore
Big Spruce	Fifth Marine
Shredder	Little Current

Horses that were turf champions themselves, although not bred for grass, should be expected to pass turf ability along. Look for the get of Cougar II, Snow Knight, Youth, Caro, Lyphard, and Roberto.

Handicappers also benefit by avoiding horses that, despite gathering a reputation for getting turf runners across the seasons, did not measure up well enough in the statistical studies. Horses by Sir Gaylord, Graustark, Tom Rolfe, and T.V. Lark win more than their fair share on grass, but do not pay enough to matter. Of these sires, selected overlays maybe, but not consistent action. Finally, here's a list of suspected turf sires whose horses do not win enough or pay enough.

Sir Ivor	Arts and Letters	Assagai
Drone	In Reality	Vaguely Noble
Ribot	Hawaii	John's Joy

AN APPROACH TO NONCLAIMING 3-YEAR-OLDS

In *The Handicapper's Condition Book* this writer argued that nonclaiming three-year-olds present handicapping problems peculiar to them. In contrast to older, well-established horses their class levels remain uncertain, form cycles uneven, and distance-footing-pace preferences elusive. Not much about them is reliably known or understood for a time, not even to their owners and trainers. This regularly contributes to upsets of one kind or another, as either horses do not repeat big wins or others in apparently dull form snap suddenly to life, and win waltzing.

What to do?

The proper solution treats nonclaiming three-year-olds as the developing horses they are. It requires of handicappers that they analyze three-year-olds' past performance tables using methods particularly suited to younger, still-developing horses. Such methods must diverge from absolute commitment to class-consistency handicapping, or speed handicapping, or even comprehensive handicapping, as these rely one and all on recent races and best efforts to provide telltale indicators of what should happen today. For older horses, recent races and best efforts normally supply accurate and stable indicators of true performance. But the past performances of nonclaiming three-year-olds may provide neither.

An alternative to common practice was termed "total performance handicapping," and demanded study of the entire three-year-old record. Only in that way, handicappers were advised, could they appreciate a young racer's pattern of development. All three-year-olds were held to proceed to true levels of performance by one or an admixture of four patterns of development that were characterized as stereotypical. Further, by recognizing the attributes of class young horses demonstrate in their races and relating these to the typical class demands of today's race, handicappers best understand whether horses fit conditions. The stereotypical patterns of development are reproduced here. The class demands of races progress from the moderate speed and basic competitiveness of maiden races to the increasingly necessary combinations of speed, endurance, and competitiveness required to win allowance, classified, and stakes races. Handicappers equipped to identify performance patterns and to match attributes of class to the class demands of races not only eliminate errors of the grossest kind, but also zero in on nonclaiming three-year-olds that outclass eligibility conditions or fit those conditions especially well.

In practice, total performance handicapping systematically examines three component parts of a three-year-old's record. **Present** performance refers to the last out or two, and indicates whether current form can be regarded as weak or strong under today's conditions. The **Power** component begins the critical assessment of class and potential class. Handicappers find the horse's best performance under the most difficult conditions it has faced. What qualities of class were exhibited there? How well did the horse do? What evidence about class and potential class does the race provide? Next handicappers examine the race following the power performance, to determine whether expected improvement or performance actually occurred. Is the power performance and its aftermath consistent or contradictory? If inconsistent, contradictory, or inexplicable, how to reconcile?

Finally, handicappers supplement indices of current form and class potential with information about the **entire pattern of development**. They go back to the first three-year-old race, and proceed upwards through the past performances to the present. This procedure illuminates overall achievement and potential, yields best indications of distance-footing-pace preferences, often explains apparent inconsistencies and contradictions in the recent record, and determines whether the horses fit today's conditions well, outclass them altogether, or merely figure to lose.

Here's an instructive example of how total performance

James Quinn, "The Handicapper's Condition Book," *GBC Press*, Las Vegas, Nevada, 1981, Chapters 8-9, pp. 143-198.

handicapping can expose attractive nonclaiming three-year-olds that really do not fit the race as potential winners should. It's October, 1980, at Santa Anita. Read the conditions, and apply the proposed method to **Back'n Time's** entire three-year-old record.

7th Santa Anita

1 MILE. (1.33⅗) ALLOWANCE. Purse $40,000. 3-year-olds and upward, which have not won two races of $13,750 at one mile or over since April 7. Weights, 3-year-olds, 116 lbs.; older, 120 lbs. Non-winners of $13,750 since July 21 allowed 2 lbs.; since June 1, 4 lbs.; since April 7, 6 lbs. (Races when entered for $40,000 or less not considered.)

Back'n Time

Dk. b. or br. c. 3, by First Back—Exigency, by Prize Host
Br.—Post Time Stables (Cal)

Own.—Post Time Stables **110** Tr.—McAnally Ronald

| | | | | | | | | 1980 | 5 | 3 | 0 | 1 | $24,825 |
| | | | | | | | | 1979 | 0 | M | 0 | 0 | |

21Sep80-10OMF	6f :21² :43⁴ 1:07⁴ft	*1-2 113	1hd 1⁴ 1⁷ 1⁸	Valenzuela P A¹	Alw 98	Bck'nTime,VoomVoom,AmnBrothr 9
6Sep80-7Dmr	6f :21² :44 1:08²ft	*1-2 118	1½ 11½ 1⁴ 14½	Pincay L Jr⁴	Alw 96	Back'nTime,StatelyNtive,BronzeStr 7
22Aug80-6Dmr	6f :22 :44¹ 1:08¹ft	*9-5 117	11½ 16 16 11⁶	Pincay L Jr³	⑤Mdn 97	Back'n Time,TrammelLuck,Donald 11
10May80-2Hol	6f :21⁴ :44⁴ 1:10¹ft	5½ 118	42½ 31½ 32½ 32½	McHargueDG⁵	M50000 84	Olympd'sSon,WtrfrdBlly,Bck'nTm 11
5Jan80-3SA	6f :21³ :45 1:10³ft	13 118	52½ 63½ 83½ 59½	McHargueDG⁹	⑤Mdn 76	WoodindLd,SgcosStory,FortClqry 12

Oct 20 SA 1ft 1:43⁴h   ●Oct 15 SA 7f ft 1:25¹h   Oct 8 SA 6f ft 1:14²b   Oct 1 SA 4f ft :59⁴b

As *The Handicapper's Condition Book* explained:

"This classified mile admitting three-year-olds during Oak Tree at Santa Anita 1980 provides an instructive note on which to end this discussion.

"To recall, classified conditions of fall can often favor late-developing three-year-olds, which have projected a higher class under nonwinners conditions. The colt Back'n Time certainly fits that description. Moreover, six months of the core season have elapsed since April 7, the specified date of the classified restrictions. Any horse that has won two or more routes of classified or stakes quality has effectively been barred from the competition, the usual layups excepted. The conditions are thus relatively restrictive. So much more in favor of developing three-year-olds.

"Does Back'n Time figure to win in a breeze? Not according to total performance handicapping procedures, which are enlightening in this instance, as is so often the case.

"Having won a maiden race and two allowance races, Back'n Time can be credited with having proceeded to advanced nonwinners allowances. Its power performance Sept. 21 at Del Mar surely indicates Back'n Time will be a monster sprinting under NW3 conditions if not pressed hard on the front. What that victory says about future races under classified or stakes conditions at longer distances or on turf is far more speculative, much more risky.

"The total record is similarly of concern. After a hapless performance Jan. 5, the colt was not favored in a maiden claiming sprint four months later, which it lost. No one wanted the claim. Next came the rejuvenating workouts and the devastating maiden and preliminary nonwinners races at Del Mar. Back'n Time might have an exceptional future, after all.

"But the time to bet on it was not the Oak Tree classified mile. Not only was the fast colt attempting a distance of two turns for the first time, but also it was jumping greatly in class. Do the Del Mar races support the combined moves? They do not. Anyone who watched the Del Mar romps saw a fast but free-running colt, and ability to get middle distances had to be of concern. With classier horses running at it, that concern should have mounted. At low odds, handicappers prefer to pass, rather than risk good money.

"Back'n Time weakened in the final sixteenth of the Oak Tree mile and lost the decision to a middling classified miler of no previous distinction. Had better horses been eligible, Back'n Time would have lost more persuasively, notwithstanding its strong betting favoritism. As events proceeded, a nondescript animal proved good enough to handle this developing three-year-old. But the race was written for just that kind of nondescript classified maverick. I hope handicappers who begin paying stricter attention to racing conditions will stop betting on young colts that are not favored by the conditions, and therefore do not figure to win."

Three-year-olds' patterns of development:

The races entered by nonclaiming three-year-olds often reveal them as horses of a kind. Developing horses proceed to the core of competition in one of four stereotypical patterns, depending on abilities exhibited in their earliest races. They can be referred to as Class A-B-C-D. Here are the four patterns handicappers can identify.

Class A

Maiden, nonclaiming
Allowance, nonwinners other than maiden or claiming

Allowance, nonwinners twice other than maiden or claiming

Allowance, nonwinners three times other than maiden or claiming, or Conditioned Stakes

Allowance, nonwinners four times other than maiden or claiming, or Open Stakes, nongraded or lower grade

Grade 2 stakes

Grade 1 stakes

Grade B

Maidens, nonclaiming

Allowance, nonwinners other than maiden or claiming

Allowance, nonwinners twice other than maiden or claiming

Allowance, nonwinners three times other than maiden or claiming, or Conditioned Stakes

Claiming races, at relatively high price brackets, or Allowance, nonwinners three times other than maiden or claiming

Claiming races, at high to moderate price brackets, or classified allowances, or minor stakes or conditioned stakes

Class C

Maiden, nonclaiming

Allowance, nonwinners other than maiden or claiming

Allowance, nonwinners twice other than maiden or claiming, or Claiming, at relatively high price brackets

Claiming races, at high to moderate price brackets, or Allowance, nonwinners once or twice (if eligible)

Claiming races, at moderate to low price brackets

Class D

Maiden claiming

Claiming races, at moderate to high price brackets, or Allowance, nonwinners other than maiden or claiming

Claiming races, at moderate to low price brackets

Claiming races, at relatively low price brackets

The classifications overlap, the sequences vary. Class A three-year-olds of April, competing then in nonwinners three times allowances or conditioned stakes, may be struggling against Class C claiming horses by September.

Handicappers often get a direct line on three-year-olds by examining the sequence of good performances, however embedded in the total record.

ROBERT SAUNDERS DOWST FOR THE 80's

Beyond publishing the books and magazine articles that established him as the high priest of handicapping in the thirties and forties, Robert Saunders Dowst went public in 1936 with perhaps the only fundamentally sound system capable of continual seasonal profits. Dowst's system had been born a year earlier, 1935, when a St. Louis betting commissioner, no less, a gentleman sporting the handle of "Liberal Tom" Kearney, burst into print with the unerring observation that the only way to beat the races was to play winners. Other than indicating that the horse **Adobe Post** in 1934 had won 20 of 50 starts and a bet on each would have netted profits, the commissioner provided his followers with no directions as to how to select the winners in advance of the races.

But Dowst did.

In *Profits on Horses,* the Dowst Consistency System came to life. In its simplicity and scope it was indeed a system for all times. Dowst postulated two verifiable assumptions, from which he derived one principle of selection and eleven rules of exclusion. Following "Liberal Tom's" magnificent insight, the Dowst system was based on the precept that good horses can beat bad horses. Good horses, said Dowst, were those that beat members of a specific class consistently. Thus, Dowst put forth his two premises: (a) all Thoroughbreds are divisible into fixed classes and (b) when a horse wins a race or runs close he normally does so by virtue of his own speed, gameness, and quality, and not by the advantage of jockey, post position, or a clever trainer.

The chief difficulty was establishing the operational definition of consistency. After tinkering with diverse formulae, which did not work, Dowst hit on the one that did. To wit, the Dowst principle of selection:

Play to be limited to horses which had won at least a third of their starts while finishing in the money at least half of the time, provided any qualifying horse is the only one of its kind in the race.

A horse with 10 starts this year can be rated on this season's record alone. If starts number fewer than 10, rate the horse on this year's and last year's records cumulatively, regardless of total races.

When the system appeared in book form and in *Esquire*, the national stampede began. As Dowst had predicted, the system rung up munificent profits during the whole of 1936. It repeated the feat in 1937, by which time Dowst had prepared a list of the horses that qualified as a play.

For a time the sweet smell of success permeated the air. The secret of beating the races was out, and it worked. But it came to pass that Dowst was wrong on one important point. Dowst himself had argued the system would remain fail-proof unless so many of the public bet on consistent horses that their prices bottomed out under the weight of the money. Knowing the contrariness of the horseplayer, Dowst dismissed that dismal possibility. On that he erred. The public bet Dowst's consistent horses off the board, and the Dowst Consistency System stopped working.

Five decades later, in the context of contemporary handicapping literature, what is the legacy of Robert Saunders Dowst? Does the Dowst Consistency System deserve a revival?

Dowst on racing and handicapping is not so out of date, as the leading authority of the century's first half has left a rich and pungent body of work. He has left to handicappers as a first contribution a theoretical definition of class not yet improved. Good horses still beat bad horses, and a horse's class is arguably best assessed by identifying the specific class of horses it can beat consistently. The Dowst system worked, not because he eventually discovered a working definition of consistency, but because he had precisely comprehended the true nature of Thoroughbred class. Dowst repeatedly contended

Robert Saunders Dowst, "Profits on Horses," *Morrow and Company*, New York, 1937.

class held the key. Indeed The Dowst Consistency System would have been better named The Dowst Class-Consistency System, as the essential ingredient was **demonstrated ability against a specific class of horse**. Dowst's exclusion rules (reprinted below) honored his high regard for class repeatedly, and Rule 8 prevented play on system horses when "definitely stepped up. . .". Others forbade playing fillies against colts, horses aged seven or older, chronic quitters, and claiming horses valued at $1500 or less.

Where the Dowst system falls flat today is on the center point of consistency. The probability studies of William Quirin concluded that consistency was overrated. Horses that have won three or four of their past 10 starts do win more than their share of the races, but (a) the public overbets that kind and (b) inconsistent horses win enough. Quirin showed that horses that won just one of their 10 previous starts won almost a fair share of their starts. Fred Davis' probability studies supported Quirin on the matter of inconsistency, concluding this was insufficient reason to regard horses as noncontenders, particularly in claiming races.

Yet the Davis data did suggest a modern variation of Dowst. Davis found that recent consistency outperformed consistency. Recent consistency was defined as winning two of the latest six starts. Moreover, recent consistency proved more important among better horses, and in studies of allowance races recently consistent horses performed significantly better than inconsistent ones (won one or none of their latest six). Davis did not report whether recently consistent horses in allowance races returned profits.

A modified application of The Dowst Consistency System is tenable, at small investment until profit margins are determined. The principle of selection now holds:

> Play to be limited to horses in allowance races which have won at least two of their latest six starts, provided any qualifying horse is the only one of its kind in the race.

Before presenting the rules of exclusion, which apply without exception, it's instructive to consider why Dowst's carefully-calculated operational definition of consistency no longer applies. To be sure, it's a matter of modern Thorough-bred form—the methods trainers use to regulate form, the demands on form of the modern racing calendars, and the resulting variations in horses' form cycles. Dowst did not take the form factor seriously. Excepting downright unsoundness, his system ignored it. In Dowst's time approximately 8000 horses were in training to compete on a limited calendar. Relatively sound and able to begin with, when racing began the 8000 were relatively fit and ready to race. Trainers did not have enough time to race horses into top condition and fewer horses became severely overworked during the shorter season. On these points times have changed. During 1981, no less than 72,205 horses competed on 7,661 racing days. Untalented, un-fit, and overworked horses do not easily become consistent horses. Nowadays handicappers best find the class of the field, not so much by identifying the kinds of horses a horse has whipped consistently, but by closely evaluating form cycles, to determine whether one horse is ready to run at its authentic best today.

Dowst's rules of exclusion:

1. No plays on tracks slow, heavy, muddy, or otherwise off; a track must be fast or good to permit a system-wager.

2. No fillies or mares are to be played against colts, horses, or geldings from April 1 to September 1 of each year.

3. No plays on two-year-olds.

4. No plays on aged horses (animals over six).

5. No chronic quitters are to be played.

6. No horse known to have any physical infirmity, to be un-sound in any way, is to be played.

7. No horse entered in a claiming race at a valuation under $1500 is to be played in any event (the modern equivalent of this rule remains unknown, but might hover at $5000).

8. No horse is to be accepted as a play under this system when definitely stepped up, in comparison with earlier races, in point of the class of opposition he is entered against.

9. No horse otherwise qualifying as a play can be accepted if he is conspicuously overweighted.

10. No sprinters are to be played in route races.

11. No route-type horses are to be played in sprints.

As Dowst insisted, the rules are easy to apply. Only the eighth and ninth, of class and weight, require knowledge and skill in handicapping.

Postscript. Handicappers interested in pursuing Dowst can consult the following bibliography.

1934 *Playing the Races* (with Jay Craig), Dodd, Mead and Company, New York.

1935 *Winners and How to Select Them*, Cosmic Press, New York.

1937 *Profits on Horses*, William Morrow and Company, New York.

1938 *Horses to Bet*, William Morrow and Company, New York.

1945 *Straight, Place, and Show*, M. S. Mill Company, Inc., New York.

1947 *Winners at Prices*, M. S. Mill Company, Inc., New York.

1954 *In the Stretch*, Dodd, Mead and Company, New York.

1959 *The Odds, the Player, the Horses*, Dodd, Mead and Company, New York.

TRACK BIASES

If there is one pervasive influence on the handicapping experience, wrote Steve Davidowitz in *Betting Thoroughbreds*, track bias comes very close to filling the bill. Davidowitz went on to argue that handicappers who did not weigh the significance of the track surface could not expect to make profits. However much they catered to track bias before Davidowitz anointed that factor to cardinal status, handicappers everywhere paid even more devotion to their ovals afterwards. Davidowitz, whose writings more than those of others reflect a studied synthesis of widely diverse experiences, excepted no racetracks. He insisted biases operate everywhere, only more or less so.

Some specific examples are worth repeating. At **Pimlico** in Maryland the tendency for inside posts at 1-1/16 miles to dominate when the first turn is a short ways from the gate is sharply exaggerated, biased toward posts one, two, and three, and away from posts nine, ten, eleven, and twelve. Many racetracks share that bias to various degrees. Davidowtiz names **Fair Grounds** and **Churchill Downs**, where conventional wisdom unwisely believes stretch runs of 1300-plus feet eliminate post position biases. But the two turns are acutely sharp, and favor speed horses that can accelerate around them.

At **Keystone, Garden State**, and other tracks where winter racing endures, Davidowitz says the extra top soil mixed with antifreeze agents affects track surfaces notably. The effectiveness of the antifreezing varies significantly. In consequence, the rail may be a paved highway, or it may be a swampy trap.

Racetracks also change surfaces. Storied **Saratoga** changed in 1974 from a graveyard for frontrunners to a freeway where they might threaten time records. Speed on the rail can be a tremendous positive bias.

When horses switch courses on the same circuit, handicappers aware of the biases at each track can make the quickest adaptations, as horses cannot. **Calder**-to-**Gulfstream** is cited as from endurance to lickety-split speed. Yet speed horses at **Calder** today cannot be tossed aside as formerly, when that track was new.

Of weather, a sudden rainstorm on an otherwise normal surface usually places a premium on early speed. But if the rain continues for a few days, handicappers experience the bane of all abnormalities, unpredictable results. The same sorry situation results from a sudden frost or extreme heat.

Davidowitz reassures handicappers they can readily spot significant track biases when at the track. Observation skills make the difference. Here are the guidelines:

1. Watch the turns. Are horses gobbling up ground on the outside, or is the rail the only place to be?

2. Watch the break from the gate. Are particular post positions sluggish during the early going, even when occupied by early speed horses?

3. In route races around two turns, watch the run to the clubhouse turn. Do horses exiting the outside posts settle into position comfortably, or are they laboring noticeably?

4. Watch the top jockeys. Do the best boys continually direct their mounts to one part of the track? Handicappers are advised that most jockeys remain insensitive to biases themselves, but that every track's colony contains one or two who know where to be after two or three turns of the course. Davidowitz salutes Sandy Hawley, Jorge Valasquez, Angel Cordero, Willie Passmore, Mike Venezia, and Vince Bracciale, Jr. at his East coast haunts.

For infrequent track visitors or handicappers arriving from out of town, Davidowitz urges consultation with recent results charts. Look for running patterns that reflect biases. Underline phrases and clauses that betray strong biases. Here are four illustrations from Saratoga 1976.

Steven Davidowitz, "Betting Thoroughbreds," *E. P. Dutton*, New York, 1977, Ch. 4, pp. 27-43.

FIRST RACE
Sar
August 21, 1976

6 FURLONGS. (1:08). MAIDENS. CLAIMING. Purse $7,500. Fillies. 2-year-olds. Weight, 119 lbs. Claiming price, $20,000; 2 lbs. allowed for each $1,000 to $18,000.
Value to winner $4,500; second, $1,650; third, $900; fourth, $450. Mutuel Pool, $93,684.
Off-track betting, $82,077.

Last Raced	Horse	EqtAWt	PP	St	¼	½	Str	Fin	Jockeys	Owners	Odds to $1
13 Aug76	1Sar³	By by Chicken	b2 115	8	1	1½	2³	1h	1h	JVelasquez	Harbor View Farm	1.70
13 Aug76	1Sar⁹	Sun Bank	b2 119	5	2	2h	1h	2²	2²½	MVenezia	B Rose	b-4.30
13 Aug76	1Sar⁸	Mean Katrine	b2 115	1	3	5²	5½	4²	3½	ASantiago	Robdarich Stable	7.50
		Peach Flambeau	2 117	4	5	4h	4½	3½	4½	DMcHargue	J W LaCroix	a-7.60
		I Gogo	b2 112	6	9	6h	6½	6¹	5²½	KWhitley⁷	Brookfield Farm	18.50
13 Aug76	9Sar⁶	Good Party	2 115	3	4	3²	3½	5½	6no	EMaple	N A Martini	12.50
25 Jly 76	2Del⁵	Tootwright	b2 119	2	10	7½	7³	74	7⁵	PDay†	D Sturgill	3.80
		North Ribot	2 115	7	8	8²	8¹	8½	8h	MPerrotta	Betty Rose	b-4.30
27 Jun76	9Bel⁸	Hot Dogger	b2 117	9	6	9¹	9½	9¹½	9½	TWallis	Judith McClung	21.30
13 Aug76	9Sar⁴	Behavingaise	b2 117	10	7	10	10	10	10	RTurcotte	J W LaCroix	a-7.60

†Seven pounds apprentice allowance waived.
b-Coupled, Sun Bank and North Ribot; a-Peach Flambeau and Behavingaise.
OFF AT 1:30 EDT. Start good. Won driving. Time, :22⅖, :46⅗, 1:12⅗. Track fast.
Official Program Numbers ↘

$2 Mutuel Prices:

7-BY BY CHICKEN		5.40	3.40	2.80
2-SUN BANK (b-Entry)			4.60	3.40
3-MEAN KATRINE				3.60

B. f, by The Pruner—Chicken Little, by Olympia. Trainer, Lazaro S. Barrera. Bred by Carl L. Broughton (Fla.).

BY BY CHICKEN saved ground while vying for the lead with SUN BANK and prevailed in a stiff drive. The latter raced outside BY BY CHICKEN while dueling for command and narrowly missed. MEAN KATRINE finished evenly while saving ground. PEACH FLAMBEAU rallied approaching midstretch but hung. I GOGO failed to seriously menace while racing wide. GOOD PARTY tired from her early efforts. TOOTWRIGHT off slowly, failed to be a serious factor. NORTH RIBOT was always outrun. BEHAVINGAISE showed nothing.
Claiming Prices (in order finish)—$18000, 20000, 18000, 19000, 20000, 18000, 20000, 18000, 19000, 19000.
Scratched—Lots of Flair.

SECOND RACE
Sar
August 21, 1976

1⅛ MILES. (1:47). CLAIMING. Purse $8,500. 3-year-olds and upward. 3-year-olds, 117 lbs.; older, 122 lbs. Non-winners of a race at a mile and a furlong or over since Aug. 1 allowed 3 lbs.; of such a race since July 15, 5 lbs. Claiming price, $12,500; 2 lbs. allowed for each $1,000 to $10,500. (Races when entered to be claimed for $8,500 or less not considered.)
Value to winner $5,100; second, $1,870; third, $1,020; fourth, $510. Mutuel Pool, $131,988.
Off-track betting, $95,870.

Last Raced	Horse	EqtAWt	PP	St	¼	½	¾	Str	Fin	Jockeys	Owners	Odds to $1
7 Aug76	1Sar⁶	Tingle King	b4 114	1	3	2½	3⁴	11½	15	16	RTurcotte	Vendome Stable	5.00
7 Aug76	1Sar⁴	O'Rei	7 113	4	5	4h	4h	44	33	24	TWallis	Mrs L I Miller	1.00
13 Aug76	3Sar¹	Mycerinus	b5 122	8	7	7	7	6²	47	3no	MVenezia	Audley Farm Stable	1.00
7 Aug76	2Sar⁷	Good and Bold	5 117	5	2	3⁴	2½	2³	2½	49½	EMaple	S Sommer	4.80
18 Aug76	7Sar⁸	Slaw	3 107	7	4	6²	6½	7	5½	58	RD'g'diceJr⁵	Betty Anne King	28.60
7 Aug76	1Sar⁹	Gene's Legacy	b4 106	6	6	5¹	5⁴	5¹	6¹	64½	KWhitley⁷	Beau-G Stable	10.40
13 Aug76	3Sar²	Mister Breezy	4 113	3	1	1½	1½	3¹	7	7	JCruguett	M M Garren	2.30

†Two pounds apprentice allowance waived.   ‡Five pounds apprentice allowance waived.
OFF AT 2:05 EDT. Start good. Won handily. Time, :23⅖, :47, 1:11¾, 1:36⅘, 1:50¾. Track fast.

$2 Mutuel Prices:

2-TINGLE KING		12.80	5.80	4.20
3-O'REI II.			5.20	4.00
7-MYCERINUS				3.40

B. c, by Bold Legend—Miss Tingle, by Avant Garde. Trainer, Flint S. Schulhofer. Bred by D. Shaer (Md.).
TINGLE KING raced forwardly into the backstretch, took over while saving ground into the far turn, drew away while being mildly encouraged. O'REI II., never far back, finished well to be second best while menacing the winner. MYCERINUS, void of early foot, passed tired horses. GOOD AND BOLD, a factor to the stretch, tired. MISTER BREEZY stopped badly after showing speed to the far turn.
Overweight—Tingle King, 1.
Claiming Prices (in order of finish)—$10500, 10500, 12500, 12500, 12500, 10500, 10500.
Scratched—Campaigner.

THIRD RACE
Sar
August 21, 1976

6 FURLONGS. (1:08). CLAIMING. Purse $9,000. 3-year-olds and upward. 3-year-olds, 117 lbs.; older, 122 lbs. Non-winners of two races since Aug. 1 allowed 3 lbs.; of a race since then, 5 lbs. Claiming price, $20,000; 2 lbs. allowed for each $1,000 to $18,000. (Races when entered to be claimed for $16,000 or less not considered.)
Value to winner $5,400; second, $1,980; third, $1,080; fourth, $540.
Mutuel Pool, $157,960. Off-track betting, $94,849. Exacta Pool, $158,817. Off-track betting Exacta Pool, $231,460.

Last Raced	Horse	EqtAWt	PP	St	¼	½	Str	Fin	Jockeys	Owners	Odds to $1
16 Apr76	6Aqu⁸	Gabilan	4 117	7	2	1h	12	15	13	EMaple	S Sommer	6.20
7 Aug76	2Sar²	Rare Joel	b4 117	1	7	7¹½	7½	6½	2h	JVelasquez	Elysa M Alibrandi	5.40
25 Jly 76	3Aqu⁵	Snappy Chatter	b4 117	5	5	5h	4¹	2½	3½	JAmy	May-Don Stable	8.80
7 Aug76	2Sar¹	Commercial Pilot	b4 113	2	4	4½	5²	3h	4¹	DMcHargue	Lovir Stable	6.50
10 Jly 76	2Aqu⁴	Odds and Evens	5 108	8	8	8	6h	7¹½	53	RDelg'riceJr⁵	Colvie Stable	17.10
7 Aug76	4Sar²	Native Blend	b6 108	4	3	3³	2¹	4¹	63	KWhitley⁷	Hobeau Farm	1.60
23 Jun76	7Bel⁹	Chaulky Long	b4 118	3	6	6⁵	8	8	7²½	BBaeza	A Rosoff	4.40
7 Aug76	4Sar⁴	What A Lucky Star	b4 117	6	1	2½	3²	5¹	8	PDay	J W LaCroix	14.90

• 114 •

OFF AT 2:45 EDT. Start good for all but ODDS AND EVENS. Won ridden out.
Time, :21⅘, :44⅗, 1:09⅘. Track fast.

$2 Mutuel Prices:			
7-GABILAN	14.40	6.20	4.20
1-RARE JOEL		6.00	4.40
5-SNAPPY CHATTER			5.20

$2 EXACTA (7-1) PAID $89.60.

Dk. b. or br. c, by Penowa Rullah—Little Buzzy, by Royal Coinage. Trainer, Frank Martin. Bred by L. P. Sasso (Md.).

GABILAN sprinted clear approaching the stretch and, after opening a good lead, was ridden out to hold sway. RARE JOEL, void of early foot, finished full of run. SNAPPY CHATTER rallied from the outside entering the stretch, lugged in near the final furlong and continued on with good energy. COMMERCIAL PILOT split horses nearing midstretch but lacked the needed late response. ODDS AND EVENS broke in the air. NATIVE BLEND, a factor to the stretch, gave way. CHAULKY LONG was always outrun. WHAT A LUCKY STAR stopped badly after entering the stretch.

Overweight—Chaulky Long, 1.

Claiming Prices (in order of finish)—$20000, 20000, 20000, 18000, 18000, 19000, 20000, 20000.

FOURTH RACE Sar August 21, 1976 — 6 FURLONGS. (1:08). MAIDENS. SPECIAL WEIGHTS. Purse $9,000. Fillies and mares. 3-year-olds and upward. 3-year-olds, 117 lbs.; older, 122 lbs. Value to winner $5,400; second, $1,980; third, $1,080; fourth, $540. Mutuel Pool, $223,335.

Last Raced	Horse	EqtAWt	PP	St	¼	½	Str	Fin	Jockeys	Owners	Odds to $1
	Love for Love	3 117	2	4	[illegible]	2½	$2^{2\frac{1}{2}}$	1^{2}	PDay	Rokeby Stable	1.10
13Aug76 ^{5}Sar^{7}	Solo Dance	3 117	1	3	[illegible]	$7^{1\frac{1}{2}}$	5½	2no	JVelasquez	Elmendorf	5.60
13Aug76 ^{5}Sar^{8}	Ready Again	b3 117	5	1	[illegible]	1^{1}	1^{h}	$3^{1\frac{1}{2}}$	MVenezia	Dogwood Stable	21.10
13Aug76 ^{5}Sar^{3}	Cornish Pet	3 117	6	6	[illegible]	3½	3½	4^{h}	JCruguet	Verulam Farm	5.00
	Skater's Waltz	3 117	4	5	[illegible]	4^{1}	6^{1}	5^{h}	RCSmith	A G Vanderbilt	16.60
13Aug76 ^{5}Sar^{2}	Like for Like	3 117	3	2	[illegible]	$5^{1\frac{1}{2}}$	4½	6no	JARodriguez	Waldemar Farm	6.10
	Naivasha	3 110	8	8	[illegible]	8	$7^{1\frac{1}{2}}$	$7^{6\frac{1}{2}}$	KWhitley^{7}	King Ranch	28.50
13Aug76 ^{5}Sar^{4}	Artful Levee	3 117	7	7	[illegible]	6½	8	8	RLTurcotte	Whitney Stone	5.90

OFF AT 3:21½ EDT. Start good. Won handily. Time, :22⅗, :46⅗, 1:12⅕. Track fast.

$2 Mutuel Prices:			
2-LOVE FOR LOVE	4.20	3.20	3.40
1-SOLO DANCE		4.80	4.40
5-READY AGAIN			6.40

Dk. b. or br. f, by Cornish Prince—Rare Exchange, by Swaps. Tr., Elliott Burch. Bred by Mellon Paul (Va.).

LOVE FOR LOVE prompted the pace into the stretch, took over from READY AGAIN just inside the final furlong and proved clearly best under confident handling. SOLO DANCE, eased back along the inside early, finished well to gain the place. READY AGAIN saved ground while making the pace and weakened under pressure. CORNISH PET made a bid from the outside leaving the turn but hung. SKATER'S WALTZ, between horses much of the way, lacked a late response. LIKE FOR LIKE rallied along the inside leaving the turn but failed to sustain her bid. ARTFUL LEVEE failed to be a serious factor.

Handicappers are urged to remember too that biases equal excuses. A speed horse on a dead rail is almost certain to perish. An off-pace horse might survive, if it has a definite class edge. When the outside plays like The Bermuda Triangle, horses disappearing this week might return to win next. Handicappers with keen observation skill and well-marked charts do not often get caught in the switches.

ABILITY TIMES

Social science researchers refer to operationally-defined variables that exist solely in testable hypotheses as constructs. These are usually single measures of two or more factors whose true relationships are otherwise difficult to define. The measures are admittedly artificial and sometimes arbitrary, obtaining validity only to the extent they can be shown to work admirably well for given purposes in the real world.

Who would've believed it? The study of the great game of handicaping has by 1982 become so scientific a pursuit that handicappers have now had delivered to them the game's first demonstrably-effective construct. It has been called **ability times**. In *Investing at the Racetrack* author William L. Scott carefully defines **ability time** as "an artificially constructed time element out of a portion of a race, **designed to represent both speed and class.**"

Having determined through extensive preliminary research of his own that speed and class were two of the three factors that distinguished thoroughbreds the best, Scott next set out to determine whether he might establish a figure that accurately represents horses' abilities in terms of their combined speed and class. He succeeded, notably, as a companion piece in this anthology documents (see Fully-Insured Investments in Completely-Systematized Handicapping), with the discovery of ability times, an invention Scott ultimately converts to standard figures, to be modified in turn by considerations of Form and Early Speed.

It is all curiously compelling, particularly the logic that not only sustains Scott's fundamental ideas, but also supports his numerous adjustments to the basic times and figures, as well as his rules for constructing "ability" figures and for applying them. What makes Scott's logic still more compelling is his repeated assertion, so true, that however much other handicappers beg to differ with it, this is precisely what works. That is to say, Scott's arguments have been handed down after the fact. They evolve only after months of laborious empirical research have finally revealed the winning formulae.

Although Scott's pursuit of a speed-class figure that reflects horses' basic abilities was only part of a more ambitious campaign to prove a fail-safe system of handicapping for profit, the ability time construct will undoubtedly be lifted out of that grand context. On the thought that speed handicappers and class handicappers everywhere might wish to incorporate into their methods an adjusted time that represents both factors satisfactorily, Scott's methods for constructing ability times can be usefully generalized here.

Scott's measure of racing ability in sprints is the final-quarter time of the race, called lead time, modified by two adjustments, for lengths gained and for energy expended. The calculation is quite easy.

Consider the latest race of the New York claiming sprinter **Self Pressured.**

Self Pressured — Dk. b. or br. h. 5, by The Pruner—Self Made, by Gun Bow

Own.—Schwartz B K — **113** — Br.—Peters L J (Fla) — Tr.—Trovato Joseph A — $45,000

1982	8	0	2	3	$12,160
1981	17	4	2	4	$60,940
Turf	4	0	0	0	$1,020

Lifetime 55 6 10 9 $119,180

16Apr82-1Aqu	6f	$:22^2$	$:45^3$	$1:10^3$ft	2¼	113	6^{13}	6^{12}	6^8	3^7	Velasquez J^4	45000	81	HappyCannibal,Cphl,SelfPressured	6
26Mar82-5Aqu	6f	:23	$:46^4$	$1:11^4$ft	4¼	113	$8^{8¼}$	$8^{7¾}$	$6^{6¼}$	4^3	Velasquez J^4	45000	79	‡Priority, Piece of Ice,SilverScreen	8
26Mar82—Placed third through disqualification															
17Mar82-3Aqu	7f	$:23^1$	$:46^3$	$1:24^1$gd	4	117	9^{11}	$7^{6¾}$	6^5	$5^{4¾}$	Martens G^2	50000	75	Raise A Buck, Mr.Wilford,JefferyC.	9
28Feb82-5Aqu	6f	⊡:23	$:46^2$	$1:10^4$ft	5	117	8^9	$7^{6¼}$	$6^{2¼}$	$3^{3¼}$	Martens G^3	50000	87	RingofTruth,RiseABuck,SlfPrssurd	9
18Feb82-5Aqu	6f	⊡:23	$:46^3$	$1:11^1$ft	9½	117	9^{10}	9^{10}	5^3	2^{nk}	Martens G^2	40000	88	InfiniteSg,SelfPressurd,RisABuck	11
10Feb82-5Aqu	6f	⊡:23	$:46^1$	1:11 ft	21	113	$9^{5½}$	$5^{3½}$	$6^{4¾}$	$6^{5¼}$♦	Graell A^6	45000	84	Happy Cannibal, Waj.Jr.,RainPrince	9
♦10Feb82—Dead heat															
30Jan82-6Aqu	6f	⊡:23	:46	$1:11^2$ft	7½	117	$9^{8½}$	$8^{8½}$	$8^{8½}$	$6^{6¾}$	Hernandez R^2	50000	80	Hotspur, Bold Ruddy, Propaganda	9
15Jan82-5Aqu	6f	⊡$:22^4$	$:46^1$	$1:11^2$ft	12	117	14^{11}	$11^{6½}$	$3^{1½}$	2^{nk}	Hernandez R^9	35000	87	HppyCnnbl,SlfPrssurd,It'sAChllng	14

Apr 30 Aqu 6f ft $1:13^4$ h ●Apr 23 Aqu 5f ft $:59^1$ hg Apr 11 Aqu 3f ft :37 b

Here are the procedures that apply:

1. The lead time from the quarter pole to the finish, or second call to final call, is :25 seconds.

2. Between the two calls, **Self Pressured** is credited with gaining only 1 length.

The horse actually gained five lengths, as indicated in the past performance table, but Scott found that the lengths-gained calculation should not be made from a 2nd call beaten lengths number greater than 8 lengths. Thus **Self Pressured** advanced from "8" lengths behind at the second call to 7 lengths behind at the final call, a gain of 1 length.

In Scott's formula for lengths gained (shown at end of article), which translates lengths gained to fifths of seconds, and is based on the finding that five lengths gained equates to four-fifths seconds, a gain of 1 length equals one-fifth of a second gained.

The lengths-gained time equivalent is subtracted from the lead time for the race. Thus Self Pressured's ability time, adjusted for lengths gained (1), is :24 4/5.

3. The energy adjustment concerns the expenditure of early speed, and depends on a horse's ability to reach the second call in less than 47 seconds (46 seconds in California). If the horse does, no adjustment is made. If a horse runs to the second call in 47 seconds or slower, an adjustment is required according to the following formula:

:47 to :47 4/5	add one-fifth
:48 to :48 4/5	add two-fifths
:49 to :49 4/5	add three-fifths
:50 to :50 4/5	add four-fifths

Twelve lengths behind a :45 3/5 lead time at the second call, **Self Pressured** is estimated to have run to the quarter pole in a tardy :48 seconds, a 2/5 penalty.

By adding 2/5 to :24 4/5, handicappers arrive at **Self Pressured's** ability time. It is :25 1/5.

Regarding these calculation rules, and numerous others in the original work, the researcher's chant applies. To wit, these are the rules that work the best. In technical language, they are empirically valid.

Scott recommends handicappers calculate several ability times in a horse's past performance table, and use the two best. At sprint distances other than six furlongs, as with **Self Pressured** on March 17, final times must first be equated to six furlong final times and Scott provides a formula for the conversion.

Interestingly, Scott's use in sprints of final-quarter times as indicators of speed-class dynamics traces to his discovery that **differences in final-quarter times** for horses racing over fast and slow track surfaces respectively, i.e., California strips and Eastern strips, were smaller than comparable **differences in final times**. Where final time differences were of a full second or greater, final-quarter times often differed by as little as two-fifths or one-fifth. Scott replicated that finding when studying fast and slow surfaces in Florida. Thus he reasoned the final-quarter times represent a truer index of basic ability across horse populations than final times, **track speed notwithstanding**.

In route racing the distances from the second call to the finish varied so they render those time comparisons impractical. Scott found that for those regularly-run routes where the first and second calls represent four and six furlongs, the most accurate estimates of basic ability relied on the time differences between first and second calls. Lead times are calculated, and the lengths gained and energy adjustments are applied, as for sprints. Where the first two calls do not represent four and six furlongs, Scott has treated each distance independently. Handicappers wanting to calculate ability times for horses in the various route races should consult Scott in his provocative book.

There handicappers will find too the means for converting ability times to speed-class figures, as well as the rules for further refining those figures, based on fundamental considerations of form and early speed. They will discover much else besides, all of it adding up to a veritable model of empirical research at the racetrack. Few handicappers might choose to apply Scott full-scale. On the other hand, few can afford to ignore this large, meticulous field study, and the significant contributions it contains. For example, the formula just below:

Scott on Lengths Gained, To Wit:

"Therefore, we now adopt a 5-for-4 formula for lengths gained as converted to fifths of seconds. We shall equate five lengths with four fifths of a second. We can also deal with fractional lengths with more flexibility, and these fractional lengths will embrace slight shadings of error and leave us with a more realistic rating all around. Here is a simple chart showing how we will treat lengths behind in terms of fifths of a second where a gain is involved.

Gain in Lengths	Gain in Fifths of Seconds
Less Than One	None
1 to 1 3/4	One
2 to 2 3/4	Two
3 to 3 3/4	Three
4 to 4 3/4	Three
5 to 5 3/4	Four
6 to 6 1/4	Four
6 1/2 to 7 1/4	Five
7 1/2 to 8	Six
8 and More	Six

"This is one of the most important tools to be applied in rating horses. You must learn this formula, accept it, apply it. It is relatively easy to learn, even though it may look difficult. As soon as you use it a few times, it will become much easier. Surrounding five for four, it flows up and down in proper sequence."

Handicappers can fairly substitute Scott for their own beaten-lengths calculations, and anticipate better results.

HORSE AND JOCKEY SWITCHES

Probability studies demonstrate generally that changes of jockey, weight, and post position have incidental effects on race outcomes, except when combined with changes that are more fundamental. Handicapper-writer-lecturer Mark Cramer has combined the fundamental and the incidental to elaborate a demonstrably effective system of play at major tracks that over successive monthly time frames has provided handicappers with unusually complementary rewards, high action and high profits. The profits regularly soar. A May 1981 workout at Hollywood Park returned 98 percent on investment. A December workout returned 91 percent, after Cramer lopped off two longshot winners as not representative. Cramer's data indicates handicappers can expect approximately 33 percent winners on 60-65 plays a month, with average winning mutuels near $11.00. The longest losing skein has been seven.

The system is pleasing to the handicapping taste as well, and readily digested. If two events occur simultaneously, Cramer hypothesized, (a) a class drop and (b) a favorable jockey change, the trainer has a live horse and is taking out insurance. The rationale for the system emphasizes trainer intentions. As all know, when the horse is primed to win, its chances improve against easier competition and with superior jockeys. Regardless of whether the race is actually easier or the jockey better, trainers perceive these differences, and believe the switches favor their horses.

Systematizing the rationale involves two simple rules:

1. The horse must be taking a drop in class.

2. The trainer must be switching jockeys from either a lower to a higher category of winner, or from within the same winning category, unless the jockey switch is to a rider that

handled the horse in its latest victory, or to a rider that is perceived as a specialist under today's conditions.

The class drops are defined as (a) stakes to allowance, (b) allowance to claiming, and (c) higher claiming to lower claiming. Magnitude of the drop is irrelevant.

Jockeys are categorized by win percentages. Jockey standings for the past season and the current meet produce a normal curve that identifies "leading," "excellent," and "good" categories. To illustrate, Cramer notes the final 1980 standings in Southern California showed that Lafitt Pincay and Chris McCarron won at above 20 percent, with the next best jockeys clustered near 15 percent. Pincay and McCarron were defined as "leading." The next cluster, "excellent," included Eddie Delahoussaye, Sandy Hawley, Bill Shoemaker, and Darrel McHargue. At "good" were jockeys Patrick Valenzuela, Fernando Toro, and Terry Lipham. The curve is regenerated after each meeting. Jockeys are systematically added, dropped, or reclassified. By year-end 1981 in Southern California, for example, jockey Marco Castenada had emerged from the obscure ranks to "excellent," his agent and resulting business having changed dramatically. Jockey Lipham had to be dropped. In categorizing jockeys, handicappers are best guided by two indices: current win percent, and trainer perceptions. Is the jockey winning consistently? Is the jockey "hot," and perceived to be "hot"? Remember the jockey changes can be from any lower to higher category, or from within a given category that is favorable.

To break ties (more than a single horse qualifies), a horse must have any one of the following attractions:

1. Switching to a rider who has **won before** with the horse.

2. Switching to a "leading" jockey.

3. Dropping from allowance to $40,000 claiming or less.

4. Switching to a rider with a well-known talent for the type of race, i.e., in Southern California jockey Fernando Toro is widely perceived as a talented specialist in turf racing.

If ties are unbroken and two horses qualify, play both.

Mark Cramer, "Jockey Angle: Dropping To Win," American Turf Monthly, *Amerpub*, New York, Dec. 1981, pp. 6-7.

If three or more horses qualify as an unbroken tie, discard the race.

Successive workouts with the system indicate a normal distribution of winners, similar to results achieved by fundamental handicapping selections, with profits unbiased by unrepresentative longshots. Implementing the system requires neither results charts nor arithmetic, just the past performance tables. All qualifying horses must be played, irrespective of odds.

The results of two monthly workouts, six months apart, are highly similar, as indeed the workout distributions themselves:

Results of System Workouts

	May 1981	December 1981
Playable races	65	62
Amount invested ($2 base)	$130	$124
Profit	$127.60	$104
Percent of winners	35	33
Return on investment (dollar)	.98	.91
Average mutuel	$ 11.20	$ 11
Most successive losses	5	5

The continuity and internal consistency of Cramer's system at Southern California tracks suggests that when dropdowns are mounted by more favorable jockeys handicappers have come within arms-length of systematic profits. To the extent the findings generalize to other major tracks, handicappers everywhere can enjoy the same sweet fruits of Cramer's research.

SMART AND SILLY MONIES IN EXOTICS

In a longitudinal study of money management wholly without external validity (not generalizeable to other populations of events) and troubled in its most provocative findings by sampling bias that might have been easily avoided (selecting nonrandom samples of races and small testing periods that are positively skewed), the controversial and sometimes enigmatic Gordon Jones formulated a principle of exotic wagering that throttled the major racing meetings in Southern California during 1975 and may generalize to major racing elsewhere. Given seasonal handicapping selections at odds that show a profit when bet to win, Jones found that, in opposition to straight betting,

".....exacta and daily double wagering can maximize profit on profitable key horse selections and minimize loss on unprofitable key horse selections. They (exotic wagers) can even turn slightly losing key horse selections into a profit if the key horses are bet scientifically through the daily double and exacta."

If fundamentally-sound handicapping selections that are profitable return even greater profits by exotic wagering, those same profits can be maximized exponentially if play is limited to profitable selections at odds between 5-1 and 20-1. Depending on how key selections are combined with other horses in exactas, for example, Jones found that his own selections returned profit margins ranging from 41 percent to 106 percent. Win and place profits on the same horses were 37 percent and 16 percent. Jones' studies have much to say about exotic betting procedures that maximize profits. More on this shortly.

The rationale for greater profits through exotic wagering is silly money. The betting public is held to behave foolishly at the exacta and double windows. They bet jockey combos, trainer combos. They bet number sequences. They bet birthdays, anniversaries, addresses, ages, and phone numbers. Saturated with bets based on whim, whisper, sentiment, and hope, exotic pools do not resemble the normal distributions of money characteristic of straight pools. Moreover, the public's tendency to oberbet its favorite and lower-priced contenders is intensified in exotic wagering. Favorites are almost instinctively included in exotic combinations, and in a hopeful bet the favorite is often hooked to the longest shots in the field. Thus, the real longshots are overbet in exotics, even as are favorites and short-priced contenders. The cutting points, as Jones tells, are 5-1 and 20-1. Horses inbetween tend to be underbet or properly bet. The smart money concentrates its action on these odds, and reaps the greatest possible return across the season.

In his 1975 study of key selections (5 to 1 or greater) at Hollywood Park and Santa Anita, Jones found that exotic wheels do not yield the highest returns, either in the exactas or doubles. Better that handicappers combine their key selections with one, two, or three other contenders in multiple denominations. Betting on horses that have little real chance is largely a waste of money, and of profit potential from the top contenders.

Here is Jones' exacta betting chart indicating rates of return on several kinds of combinations (Key horses combined top and bottom):

Exacta Betting Chart

Combination	Rate of Profit
Key Horse to Top Contender	106 percent
Key Horse to Top 2 Contenders	84 percent
Key Horse to Top 3 Contenders	49 percent
Box Top Three Selections	47 percent
Key Horse Top Wheel	41 percent
Key Horse to Win	37 percent
Key Horse to Place	16 percent

Gordon Jones, "Smart Money," *Karman Communications*, Huntington Beach, CA., 1977, Chapters 4-5, pp. 42-74.

Jones reminds handicappers that to the extent the key selections show a profit to win or come close to showing a profit, the better the dynamics of exotic wagering.

Interestingly, the key horse at odds of 9-2 or less showed an exotic profit when combined top and bottom **with the second choice only.** If key horses at those odds were combined with two or three contenders, profit dropped to 5 percent. If three horses were boxed, profit disappeared. Wheeling the key horse works at 5 to 1 or better, but reduces longterm profits. Wheeling the race favorite on top costs 10 to 20 percent. But a back-wheel of the favorite returns anywhere from 20 percent profit to 10 percent loss. If favorites must be wheeled in exactas, this is the way to do it—the favorite on bottom.

On the latter procedure, a back wheel, Jones asked whether wheels, top and bottom, did better than straight betting when key horses were 5-1 or better. It depends. Here are the 1975 results:

Win bet on key horse at 5-1 and up	30 percent profit
Top wheel on key horse at 5-1 and up	40 percent profit
Bottom wheel on key horse at 5-1 and up	40 percent profit

A back wheel is clearly preferable to any place bet on key selections at 5-1 and up, as place bets return about 10 percent. Of top wheels, the greater the odds above 5-1 the more likely the win bet will approach or excel top wheel profits. This is particularly so where second or third choices are overbet but solid. It is decidedly so where straight odds are 20-1 or better, as the public overbets these longshots in exotic pools.

A two-year, five-meeting study of key horse selections in daily doubles shows persuasively that (a) exotic wagering beats straight wagering, and (b) the most profitable procedure links the top choice in the key race to the top three selections in the other half. Here is Jones' betting chart for the double:

Daily Double Betting Chart

Combination	Profits
Key Horse to Top 3	69 percent
Key Horse to Top 2	46 percent

Key Horse Wheel	29 percent
Key Horse to Top 4	25 percent
Key Horse to Top 1	19 percent
Key Horse to Win	2 percent loss

Perhaps there is more silly money in double pools than in exacta pools. Jones emphasizes that restricting play to key horses that go postward at 5-1 or better increased profit margins to 100 percent or more on investment.

Jones' daily double studies provided other basic investment guidelines.

1. A key horse wheel is best when the other half is mysteriously unpredictable, in the usual cases because either too many first starters will race or too many horses are returning from lengthy layoffs, or because the track is extremely muddy, heavy, or slow.

2. Race favorites are notorious underlays in the double.

3. Selections by public selectors are underlays in the double.

4. The same program numbers and the same jockeys in the double pay less than straight win parlays.

How much should handicappers bet on exotic wagers? Jones found that 4 percent of capital (or less) avoids the bankruptcy extended losing streaks in exotic play can accelerate, if money is not managed smartly. The standard applies equally to exactas and daily doubles.

The Jones research suggests the smart money can take advantage of the silly money in exotic wagering, and do better than it can in straight wagering. The brightest prospects, for handicappers with the temperament for the style, are horses that figure to win and set at odds between 5-1 and 20-1. Even greater overlays in the exotic pools, these maximize profits when manipulated properly in exotic combinations. As Jones cautions, playing smart money in exotic wagering situations does not substitute for ineffective handicapping. As is ultimately true about all money management principles and practices, better selections yield better profits.

TREND ANALYSIS

Whether totalizator action signifies inside money or not is less important to handicappers than whether the action represents a betting trend that wins frequently enough to matter. A field study of pari-mutuel price fluctuations lasting an amazing 18 years has identified only two winning betting trends. At the same time it reveals a losing trend that often fools handicappers into expressing false confidence with real money. In presenting his research, engineer Milt Gaines muddied the issues with extravagant claims of financial success traceable solely to biased samples of exotic wagering, and weakened his case with sloppy illustration, yet some of the substantial evidence not only survives, it may be persuasively useful to handicappers who prefer their key selections get inside support on the board. Gaines is not a handicapper, rather a tote watcher and trend taker. Thus his method is trend analysis. When Gaines spots a winning betting trend, he bets. As he carefully points out, the best of all worlds unites a winning betting trend with a solid handicapping selection.

The two betting trends that frequently signify inside action ("insiders" are held to have more information or knowledge than the average customers), and win, are characterized by odds lines moving in opposing directions. In one the odds first fall below the morning line, shift quickly upwards, and finally fall again. In the second the odds first change to a line higher than the morning line, eventually but not immediately fall significantly lower, and may rise again near the end of the betting. Gaines presents two variations of each pattern, detailing each trend in terms of the kinds of odds changes handicappers should expect as the minutes before posttime trickle by. Here we illustrate the two positive trends, and describe the variations. Of much concern too is a variation of the most frequently successful trend that is an abject loser. That trend too is illustrated below.

The most frequently successful betting trend Gaines refers to as an H1 trend (H honors the late Lou Holloway who studied price fluctuations and trend analysis and delivered in 1957 the most important work on the topic, "The Talking Tote,"). It looks like this:

Morn Line	Open Line	10 Min Line	5 Min Line	2 Min Line	Bet Line	Close Line
4/1	8/5	9/5 2/1 5/2	3/1 3/1	3/1 5/2	8/5 8/5	8/5

or like this:

10/1	2/1	5/2 3/1 4/1	6/1 8/1	8/1 6/1	5/1 9/2	9/2

An H1 trend satisfies these rules:

1. The first odds change (Open Line) shows a line lower than the morning line by at least half.

2. The odds move upwards until post time nears (2 Min Line).

3. The odds drop once or twice near the end of betting.

Gaines refers to Step 2 as absorption, meaning the public interprets the early inside betting as dropping the horse below its true odds, and therefore not worth a bet, thus the odds steadily rise. Step 3 Gaines calls confirmation, whereby the inside money that did not bet early now reacts to the public's misinformed generosity. Late betting is essential to an H1 trend. If it does not occur, no play.

In a positive variation of H1 (H6), the initial change is lower than the morning line odds, but not by half. The subsequent trends remain firm.

In a more important variation of H1 called H2, the well-backed horse can be fully expected to lose. In the opening flash, the odds indeed fall below the morning line by at least half. But they stay low. In fact, they never again exceed the first flash (Open Line). Gaines provides this example of H2:

Milt Gaines, "The Tote Board Is Alive and Well," *GBC Press*, Las Vegas, Nevada, 1981, Chapter 3, pp. 28-39.

Morn Line	Open Line	10 Min Line	5 Min Line	2 Min Line	Bet Line	Close Line
2/1	1/1	1/2 1/2 1/2	4/5 3/5	4/5	4/5 3/5	1/2

H2 horses are getting strictly public money. These likely look solid in the past performances and were probably selected by several public experts. The inside money steers clear of this kind, and Gaines advises handicappers to do the same. The horses are underlays. As such, a series of bets on them guarantees loss. Gaines' data supports the point. If handicappers believe the horses won't lose, Gaines urges they pass the races.

More common than the H1 trend, but not as successful, is H8. It goes like so:

Morn Line	Open Line	10 Min Line	5 Min Line	2 Min Line	Bet Line	Close Line
5/1	12/1 16/1	14/1	12/1 8/1 6/1	7/1 8/1	9/1	10/1

To qualify as an H8 trend:

1. Open odds (Open Line) must be at least twice the morning line.

2. Several successive drops must occur prior to the 2Min Line. Importantly, the drops must each be more than a single point.

3. Near the end of betting, the odds rise again.

In this trend the inside money bets **between** the end points of the public action. The horses figure better than the public realizes, and the insiders know it. Since inside money tends to be big money, odds can be expected to drop by more than a single point. At lower odds, the drop simply might skip the next logical level, i.e., the 4-1 horse drops to 3-1, skipping the conventional 7-2 level.

H8 horses being common, these often find their way into races that also contain H1 horses. If the two trends conflict, and just one H1 trend has begun, handicappers should back the H1 horses relentlessly. Gaines' data show the H1 horses win 70 percent of the races where this type of conflict arises. But if two or more H1 horses have been entered against a single H8 horse, the H8 horse figures to upset. Handicappers' money belongs on H8.

Trend analysis is held applicable at both major and minor tracks. Here are selected guidelines supported by Gaines' data.

1. Do not consider trends until a meeting has been active for at least two weeks. **Insiders are less likely to bet until form over the track begins to emerge.**

2. Do not bet trends where one or more horses in the race are first starters. Maiden and juvenile races are susceptible to trend analysis, but not until all starters have started previously

3. Do not bet on a trend until the final two minutes. The later the better, especially when considering the H1 trend.

4. Be skeptical of early action on the strongest of public selectors' horses. Winning trends on horses **not** selected by public selectors represent much better bets.

5. Demand the bettable horses be outstanding illustrations of the winning trends. If trends look vague or ambiguous, pass. Best bets equal outstanding trends combined with outstanding handicapping selections.

6. Beware of races having two H1 trends, especially at smaller tracks. The insiders are playing games.

THE HANDICAPPER'S MORNING LINE

When—if ever—the literature of handicapping can produce a morning line that reflects the actual probability of each horse's winning, it will have settled a knowledge frontier still faraway, and the practice of appraising past performance tables will have moved from art to science. As well, tutored handicappers will have moved within an arm's reach of the absolute overlays that guarantee profits. Until that time, overlay identification remains a finely artistic endeavor, challenging even to the most talented, accomplished, and sophisticated of the pastime's practitioners. Progress towards the scientific pole has begun in the past decade, and this reviews the current state of the art.

First, as most appreciate, morning lines published by racetracks bear only coincidental resemblance to horses' actual chances. Recognizing their limitations in this practice, the tracks intend only that morning lines predict how the customers will rate the horses, but even so the predictions are as a rule despairingly poor. The reason is obvious. Almost none derive from fundamental handicapping. They result instead from the intuition and guesswork of racetrack employees who are not handicappers. This is an amenable disservice to the paying public, but that's another matter.

As handicappers understand, to bet on no horses but those that are overlays is the surest route to long-haul profits. If an actual 3-1 shot looks best to the crowd, it likely will go postward at less than true odds, perhaps at odds nearer to 8-5. Handicappers abstain. If another horse attracts the crowd's favor, the actual 3-1 horse might slide to 4-1. That's an overlay, and handicappers might decide to bet. In situations where the crowd's favorite is overbet but figures to lose, many handicappers will bet two or three other horses that are contenders running at higher odds than real chances warrant.

Studies demonstrate handicappers make profits on horses sent postward at relatively high odds, from 3-1 to 8-1 or such, but they make little or nothing on short-priced horses. The explanation is that higher-priced horses more frequently represent overlays. These win more often than expected, and pay better than they should. In this way, and this way alone, talented handicapers prosper. The handicapper's best bet arrives any time his top-rated horse is underestimated by the crowd. The greater the underestimation, the better the bet.

Identifying overlays, in practice, remains a kind of artistic pursuit, dependent on knowledge and experience. The most talented, most prosperous handicappers can be fairly presumed to do it best. Of the genuinely scientific attempts to elaborate a morning line based on actual probabilities, the most advanced appeared in *Probability Computation*, by Fred Davis. In a companion work Davis had determined the probability values associated with the winning percentages of numerous past performance characteristics. Probabilities were called impact values, such that a value greater than 1 held an impact on race outcomes stronger than expected. Through multiplication Davis simply combined several impact values for each horse, such that each horse obtained a total impact value which reflected its status on the fundamentals of handicapping. When individual horses' total impact values were added and that sum divided back into each horse's individual rating, the resulting percentage for each horse reflected its share of the handicapping values held to have an impact on the outcome. Finally, each horse's percentage was converted to an odds line (using the odds-percentage table included here). The odds were held to reflect the actual probabilities of each horse's winning, or, more precisely, best estimates of same. If public odds exceeded the handicapping odds that reflected horses' true chances, handicappers had come face to face at last with a true overlay.

The method was correct, but complaints about the independence of the combined impact values were lodged. That is to say, each impact value should represent something uni-

Fred Davis, "Thoroughbred Handicapping: Probability Computation," *Millwood Publications*, New York, 1974.
Tom Ainslie, "Ainslie's Encyclopedia of Thoroughbred Handicapping," *William Morrow and Company, Inc.*, New York, 1978, pp. 167-168.

que in terms of handicapping value, but this was argumentative. Statistical objections were raised, and held valid. More practically, the procedure required the multiplication of many impact values for each horse, plus still further multipliers that reflected values associated with local tracks, such that it was suitable to computer generation, but not to individual handicapping routine. When handicappers gain access to morning lines tailored by the Davis probabilities and math, computers will do the dirty work and spit out the final odds, available for a price.

The most logical facsimile to Davis yet to appear for public consumption was developed by Tom Ainslie and presented in his 1978 encyclopedia of handicapping. Characterized as a simplification of Davis, the Ainslie formula is strictly arithmetical, adding and subtracting points from a base of 10, as determined by handicapping values contained in horses' past performance tables. As such formula absolutely must be, the Ainslie formula is very carefully-calculated, such that differences among numerical values reflect actual differences among handicapping values, as best as these have been empirically and statistically determined. For example, the Ainslie formula quantifies form by valuing a horse's finish in its latest race. But form is passed altogether if a horse has not raced in more than 30 days, as research has determined that factor loses impact at that point. Ainslie's morning line reflects horses' relative standing on five factors: Class, Form, Consistency, Early Speed, and Weight. I present the formula **verbatim**. As noted, each horse begins with 10 points.

Class. When handicapping a CLAIMING RACE, add 4 points if the horse has ever finished first or second when entered at today's top claiming price or higher. Subtract 3 points if the horse has not done that. If today's is an ALLOWANCE RACE, add 7 points if the horse has started in a STAKES race and has not raced in a claimer since then. If the horse has raced only in allowances and non-claiming maiden races, neither add nor subtract. If the horse has raced in a claimer and has not raced in a stakes since then, subtract 4. When handicapping a stakes race, add 6 if the horse has already won a stakes and subtract 4 if it has never raced in a stakes. Otherwise add or subtract nothing.

Finish in Last Race. If the horse has not raced in more than 30 days, skip this altogether. Otherwise use its latest race:

Won	+5
Second	+7
Third	+2
Fourth	0
Fifth	−1
Sixth	−2
Worse	−4

Consistency. Check each horse's six most recent races—fewer if it has raced less than six times. Credit it with 2 points for each win in a non-maiden race at a track of today's quality or higher, and 1 point for a win in a non-maiden race at a minor track (or a track of considerably less quality than your own minor track). Credit it with 1 point for a second-place finish in a non-maiden race at a track of today's quality or higher. Now add these consistency points and modify the horse's previous rating as follows:

Six consistency points or more	+8
Five points	+6
Four	+4
Three	+3
Two	+1
One	−2
None	−4

Early Speed. Find each horse's two best running positions at the first call in past races at today's distance or shorter. Total the numbers. Example: If the horse was first at the first call once and second at the first call on another occasion, 2+1=3. Find the three horses with the lowest totals. In case of ties, four or more horses may be involved here. Whether three or more are found, give each 3 points. Deduct 2 points from all others.

Weights. After adding to the horses' posted weights whatever APPRENTICE weight allowances have been subtracted, give 4 points to the three horses with the highest weights (four or more horses if ties necessitate). Subtract 3 points from all the other starters.

Computing the Odds. Add all the final ratings. Divide each final rating by the total of all of them. Convert each resultant percentage into its equivalent morning-line odds by using the odds-percentage table that accompanies this essay.

Ainslie's formula applies only to races on the main track. With practice its application becomes facile. Nonwinners allowance contests, for example, can be difficult races on which to get an accurate fix. Let's see how the formula sorts out just that kind of allowance mile, carded during January, 1982, at Santa Anita.

6th Santa Anita

1 MILE — SANTA ANITA — START • FINISH

1 MILE. (1.33⅗) ALLOWANCE. Purse $25,000. 3-year-olds which have never won three races. Weight, 122 lbs. Non-winners of a race of $20,000 at one mile or over allowed 3 lbs.; of such a race of $10,000, 5 lbs.; of a race of $15,000 any distance, 8 lbs. (Claiming races not considered.)

Coupled—Prince Khalid and Bargain Balcony.

Algardi — Ch. c. 3, by Avatar—Abergwaun, by Bounteous
Br.—Blue Bear Stud (Ky) — 1981 6 2 1 1 $16,784
Own.—Mandysland Farm 114 Tr.—Doyle A T — Turf 4 2 1 1 $16,784
14Nov81-8Hol 7f :211 :432 1:22 ft 18 119 612 613 612 68½ ShoemkrW2 Hol Prvu 78 Sepulveda,GatoDelSol,DesertEnvoy 6
30ct81-8SA 7f :221 :454 1:231ft 7½ 119 66 56 66¾ 69 DihossyE4 Sny Slope 75 Dena Jo, Ring Proud, SpeedBroker 8
23Jun81♦3Pontefract(Eng) 6f 1:15 fm*1-2 132 Ⓣ 25 Piggott L Castlecare My Dad Tom, Algardi, Pinxton 6
4Jun81♦4Epsom(Eng) 6f 1:14 gd *1 123 Ⓣ 12½ PiggottL Staff Ingham Algardi, Little Robert, Pauls Ivory 7
16May81♦5N'wmarket(Eng) 5f 1:024gd*2-3 130 Ⓣ 32¾ Baxter G Felix Leach Chris's Lad, Chulia Street, Algardi 4
1May81♦5N'wmarket(Eng) 5f 1:032gd*3-2 123 Ⓣ 11½ Piggott L Chevington Algardi, House Pitch, HelloCuddles 7
Jan 23 SA 6f sl 1:15 h Jan 16 SA 1 ft 1:382 h Jan 10 SA 6f ft 1:13 h Jan 5 SA tr.t 4f sy :491 h

Maggie's Best — Ch. c. 3, by Maggie's Pet—Zamora, by Hill Prince
Br.—Sabinske R J (Cal) — 1982 1 0 0 0
Own.—Sabinske R J 119 Tr.—Mayer V James — 1981 7 2 0 2 $27,050
Turf 1 1 0 0 $12,100
10Jan82-8SA 7f :213 :44 1:22 ft 18 117 117½117¾ 87½ 812 Sibille R9 Ⓢ Cal Brdrs 78 PrncSpllbond,Glc'sSport,CrystlStr 11
13Dec81-7Hol 1 Ⓣ:4721:1141:362fm 13 115 63½ 42½ 1hd 12½ Sibille R2 Alw 87 Mggie'sBest,King'sFindr,RdCurrnt 10
29Nov81-8Hol 1 1/16 :481 1:141 1:474sl 76 121 65¾ 87¾ 814 815 Toro F11 Hol Fut 41 Stalwart, Cassaleria, Header Card 12
22Nov81-6Hol 1 1/16 :48 1:132 1:444ft 6½ 117 1hd 1hd 1hd 12½ Sibille R1 Mdn 71 Mggie'sBest,ChrgeBetween,BluJstr 8
7Nov81-3SA 6½f :221 :452 1:163ft 18 118 85¾ 811 1015 512 Sibille R9 Mdn 75 Bunnell,ProspectiveStar,WterBnk 11
2Aug81-6Dmr 1 :462 1:113 1:39 ft 5½ 116 2hd 3½ 53½ 76¼ Baltazar C4 Mdn 67 ThreeDocs,OkieCityLad,ShdyCreer 10
18Jly81-4Hol 6f :213 :45 1:112ft 7¾ 116 610 59½ 45½ 35¼ Olivares F6 Ⓢ Mdn 75 Songhay, Tular, Maggie's Best 10
10Jly81-6Hol 6f :22 :452 1:111ft 22 116 55½ 57 56 35¼ Baltazar C8 Mdn 75 Muttering,LuckyLegnd,Mggi'sBst 12
Jan 24 SA 5f ft :593 h Jan 4 SA tr.t 6f sl 1:154 h Dec 27 SA 4f ft :471 h Dec 20 SA 5f ft 1:01 h

Prince Khalid — Dk. b. or br. c. 3, by Bold Hitter—Nancy's Fancy, by Glanwin
Br.—Royal Oaks Farm (Cal) — 1982 1 0 0 0 $7,500
Own.—Greene–Marino–Sheridan etal 114 Tr.—Hirsch Arthur — 1981 6 2 3 0 $23,815
10Jan82-8SA 7f :213 :44 1:22 ft 6½e117 96½ 95¼ 53¼ 44¾ GrrWA10 Ⓢ Cal Brdrs 85 PrncSpllbond,Glc'sSport,CrystlStr 11
20ct81-8BM 6f :222 :452 1:093ft *9-5 117 54 22 22 25 LamnceC3 Sr Fr Drke 87 Tohottocri,PrinceKhlid,MdboutJoe 7
16Sep81-11Bmf 6f :221 :451 1:111ft 4½ 122 69 68½ 56 2hd LamanceC3 Md Pnsla 84 Songhay,PrinceKhalid,MadboutJoe 7
4Sep81-11Sac 1 :45 1:10 1:36 ft 8-5 113 55½ 31½ 13 110 LmncC7 St Fr Champ 96 PrinceKhalid,Stuntman,GallantFool 8
27Jly81-4SR 6f :23 :461 1:104ft *2 118 1hd 12 14 18 Lamance C1 Mdn 90 Prince Khalid,CountElite,Stuntman 9
17Jly81-7Sol 5½f :221 :45 1:04 ft 3 118 56 32 22 23 Lamance C9 Mdn 90 LittleTis,PrinceKhlid,NtivRflction 10
3Jly81-3Pln 5½f :22 :443 1:033ft 6½ 118 57½ 513 49 47 Lamance C8 Mdn 87 DancingFriend,FlyDancer,Stuntman 8
Jan 23 SA 6f sl 1:162 h Jan 8 SA 4f sl :484 h ●Dec 18 Hol 6f ft 1:142 h Dec 8 Hol 5f ft :584 h

Native Stepper — B. c. 3, by Dewan—Native Sue, by Raise a Native
Br.—McLean & Miller (Ky) — 1981 9 2 2 1 $34,575
Own.—Greene Mr–Mrs H 119 Tr.—Lukas D Wayne
23Dec81-8Hol 1 1/16 :471 1:113 1:431ft 31 116 52½ 52½ 54½ 66¼ Toro F3 Ald Lng Syn 73 Muttering, King's Finder,Cassaleria 9
6Dec81-5Hol 1 :472 1:122 1:381ft *3-2 115 2hd 1hd 2hd 1nk Toro F5 Alw 75 NativeStepper,AlmoStrnger,AHero 7
310ct81-8SA 1 1/16 :461 1:103 1:421ft 56 118 1½ 2hd 31½ 69¼ Toro F8 Norfolk 81 Stalwart, Racing Is Fun,GatoDelSol 9
240ct81-7SA 1 :461 1:104 1:361ft 8½ 115 41½ 31½ 3½ 34¾ Valenzuela P A1 Alw 83 Stalwart, BoldForli,NativeStepper 10
100ct81-7SA 6½f :221 :452 1:17 ft 10 118 1½ 1½ 2½ 21¼ Valenzuela P A6 Alw 84 LuckyLegend,NtivStppr,Glic'sSport 8
12Aug81-8Dmr 6f :22 :45 1:11 ft 18 116 44 46½ 45 45 Lipham T2 De Anza 78 King'sFinder,Heln'sBu,RmmbrJohn 5

31Jly81-8Dmr 6f :223 :46 1:112ft *1 120 33 21½ 32 21 McHargue D G1 Alw 80 GalaArray,NativeStepper,Subdivide 7
20Jly81-4Hol 6f :221 :453 1:111ft 3½ 116 1hd 2hd 1hd 11½ McHargue D G4 Mdn 81 NtivStppr,ExplosivTwist,SpnishJoy 6
21Jun81-6Hol 5½f :222 :46 1:05 ft 8½ 116 89½ 912 1011 99½ Hawley S3 Mdn 76 AdvnceMn,SpnishDnD.,LuckyLgnd 12
● Jan 23 SA 4f sl :47 h   Jan 14 SA 4f ft :484 h   Jan 8 SA 5f sl 1:022 h   Dec 18 SA 5f ft 1:02 h

Bison Bay
B. c. 3, by Queen City Lad—Cosmic Time, by Jig Time
Br.—Fink L (Ky)   1981 10 2 1 3 $37,050
Own.—Spreen R H   119   Tr.—Lukas D Wayne   Turf 1 0 0 0
23Dec81-8Hol 1 1/16 :471 1:113 1:431ft 23 116 2hd 3nk 712 714 SibilleR6 Ald Lng Syn 65 Muttering, King's Finder,Cassaleria 9
13Dec81-7Hol 1 Ⓣ:4721:1141:362fm *2½ 117 73¾ 84 74¼ 75½ McCarron C J1 Alw 82 Mggie'sBest,King'sFindr,RdCurrnt 10
8Nov81-6SA 1 :454 1:102 1:362ft 2½ 116 31½ 43 1½ 11 McCarron C J2 Alw 87 BisonBay,RoyalCaptive,Prosperous 7
31Oct81-10LA 7f :22 :453 1:241ft 9½ 117 41½ 32½ 21½ 22½ WinlndWM5 Juaneno 86 Tropic Ruler, BisonBay,SafeAtFirst 8
25Oct81-3SA 1 :454 1:111 1:38 ft 5 116 33 2hd 1½ 11 Valenzuela P A5 Mdn 79 Bison Bay, Berbereau, Crystal Star 8
18Oct81-2SA 1 1/16 :464 1:114 1:424ft 3½ 118 2hd 2hd 23 311 Pincay L Jr5 Mdn 76 Cassaleria,ChargeBetween,BisonBy 7
2Sep81-6Dmr 1 :454 1:11 1:37 ft 2½ 117 11 2hd 22 64½ Pincay L Jr1 Mdn 78 StandupComedian,Durable,Partags 7
16Aug81-6Dmr 6f :223 :453 1:112ft 3½ 118 84¾ 67½ 55¾ 35 Winland W M2 Mdn 76 Mill Stream, Jato Unit, Bison Bay 12
24Jun81-8Hol 5f :22 :454 :583ft 17e 115 2hd 51¾ 77 86¾ Lipham T4 First Act 79 Helen'sBeu,HeyRob,B.RichGeorge 12
13Jun81-4Hol 5f :221 :454 :583ft 12 116 84¾ 67¾ 53¾ 31¼ Valenzuela P A4 Mdn 85 Helen's Beau, Zanyo, Bison Bay 10
● Jan 15 SLR tr.t 5f gd 1:003 h   Dec 9 SA 5f ft 1:032 h   Dec 3 SA 5f ft 1:004 h

Bargain Balcony
B. g. 3, by Bargain Day—Balcony Doll, by First Balcony
Br.—Barnes Dr G & Darlene (Cal)   1982 1 0 0 0
Own.—Greene H F   119   Tr.—Headley Bruce   1981 9 3 1 0 $49,080
10Jan82-8SA 7f :213 :44 1:22 ft 6¾e 117 61½ 63½ 98¾ 914 ShmkrW8 Ⓢ Cal Brdrs 76 PrncSpllbond,Glc'sSport,CrystlStr 11
27Dec81-4SA 1 :471 1:12 1:362ft 3½ 114 11½ 11 12½ 15 Shoemaker W3 Alw 87 BargainBlcony,Botrell,AlmoStrnger 8
8Nov81-6SA 1 :454 1:102 1:362ft 4½ 115 1hd 33 46½ 46 McHargue D G4 Alw 81 BisonBay,RoyalCaptive,Prosperous 7
14Oct81-8SA 1 1/16 :462 1:113 1:433ft 36 117 75¼ 77 812 820 MrquezC2 El Rio Rey 63 PrincSpllbound,Muttrng,SpdBrokr 10
30Sep81-6SA 6f :214 :444 1:10 ft 2½ 115 52¾ 57 69½ 614 McCarron C J1 Alw 74 PrincSpllbound,LuckyLgnd,Wcklow 7
9Sep81-8Dmr 1 :453 1:111 1:372ft 37 115 41¾ 62¾ 4¾ 42¾ Marquez C4 Dmr Fut 78 GatoDelSol,TheCaptain,RingProud 10
26Aug81-5Dmr 6f :221 :452 1:104ft 8-5 117 4¾ 32½ 31 1hd Pincay L Jr1 50000 84 BrginBlcony,KingKlku,RoylMemory 6
10Aug81-1Dmr 6f :222 :452 1:113ft 6½ 120 42 36 34½ 21 Pincay L Jr1 40000 79 Spiritino,BrginBlcony,AntiqueRuler 7
27Jly81-2Dmr 6f :23 :464 1:131ft *1 118 33 44 22 1nk ChpnTM4 Ⓢ Mc32000 72 BrginBlcony,Crrie'sTen,KingDrius 12
3Jly81-11Pln 5½f :214 :444 1:042ft 2½ 114 32½ 32½ 43½ 42½ ChpTM8 Ⓢ Almda Fut 88 Demarday, Royal Memory, FleetBid 9
Jan 23 SA 5f sl :594 h   Jan 18 SA 5f ft 1:04 h   Dec 21 SA 1 gd 1:444 h   Dec 15 SA 7f ft 1:253 h

Formula application: (allot each horse 10 points to begin).

Horse	Class	Last Finish	Consistency	Early Speed	Weight Rating	Total
Algardi	7	0	1	−2	−3	13
Maggie's Best	7	−4	4	−2	4	19
Prince Khalid (E)	7	0	2	−2	4	21
Native Stepper	7	0	3	3	4	27
Bison Bay	7	0	4	3	4	28
Bargain Balcony (E)	7	−4	1	3	4	21
Bunnell	7	5	5	−2	4	29
Gala Array	7	−4	4	3	−3	17

Total rating points = 175

Odds computation: (individual ratings divided by 144[1]).

Horse	Point Percentages	Handicapper's Morning Line
Algardi	9.0	10-1
Maggie's Best	13.0	7-1
Prince Khalid (E)	14.0	6-1
Native Stepper	18.0	9-2

Bison Bay	19.0	9-2
Bargain Balcony (E)	14.0	6-1
Bunnell	20.0	4-1
Gala Array	11.0	8-1
Total	118.0	

(See the Odds-Percentage table that accompanies article.)

A version of fundamental handicapping reveals nothing close to a probable winner or strong favorite, practically assuring handicappers the public choice will race as an underlay. So probably will second and third choices. Below are the track's morning line odds and the betting public's odds, as taken from the track program and *Form* result chart.

Horse	Track Morning Line	Public Line
Algardi	6-1	9-1
Maggie's Best	5-1	11-1
Prince Khalid (E)	3-1	3-1
Native Stepper	6-1	7-1
Bison Bay	10-1	14-1
Bargain Balcony (E)	3-1	3-1
Bunnell	7-5	4-5
Gala Array	15-1	15-1

[1]Reduction for pari-mutuel take of 18 percent.

When the handicapper's morning line is compared to the track's morning line, the horse Bunnell shapes up as an illegitimately short price. The entry Prince Khalid-Bargain Balcony deserves attention, for although individually each horse is overestimated, together the two account for 25 percent of the percentage table for the race, and thus will be properly bet at 3-1. Of the others, only Gala Array represents a potentially lucrative overlay, but the colt looks seriously short of winning form, having benefitted not at all from the sloppy sprint it did not like January 20.

When the handicapper's morning line is compared to the public's betting line, Bunnell becomes a dreadful proposition. Anyone seriously interested in this kind of horse at this kind of price belongs instead in deep consultation with another game.

Handicappers might have benefitted from the financial avalanche falling on Bunnell, but the entry has been properly bet, and nothing else looks tempting enough on handicapping fundamentals. Bison Bay represents an overlay when odds alone are considered, but fundamental handicapping cannot regard the colt a logical contender. Nothing doing in this everyday allowance mile.

Here is the result chart.

SIXTH RACE
Santa Anita
JANUARY 27, 1982

1 MILE. (1.33$\frac{4}{5}$) ALLOWANCE. Purse $25,000. 3-year-olds which have never won three races. Weight, 122 lbs. Non-winners of a race of $20,000 at one mile or over allowed 3 lbs.; of such a race of $10,000, 5 lbs.; of a race of $15,000 any distance, 8 lbs. (Claiming races not considered.)

Value of race $25,000, value to winner $13,750, second $5,000, third $3,750, fourth $1,875, fifth $625. Mutuel pool $422,895.

Last Raced	Horse	Eqt.	A.	Wt	PP	St	¼	½	¾	Str	Fin	Jockey	Odds $1
10Jan82 ^{8}SA^9	Bargain Balcony	b	3	119	6	3	$2^{1\frac{1}{2}}$	$2^{2\frac{1}{2}}$	1^{hd}	1^1	$1^{\frac{3}{4}}$	McHargue D G	a-3.20
14Nov81 ^{8}Hol^6	Algardi		3	116	1	8	8	8	$6^{2\frac{1}{2}}$	3^{hd}	2^1	Delahoussaye E	9.20
10Jan82 ^{8}SA^8	Maggie's Best	b	3	119	2	1	$5^{\frac{1}{2}}$	7^4	4^1	5^3	$3^{\frac{3}{4}}$	Shoemaker W	11.60
20Jan82 ^{8}SA^7	Gala Array	b	3	117	8	2	1^{hd}	1^{hd}	2^2	$2^{\frac{1}{2}}$	4^2	Hansen R D	15.30
23Dec81 ^{8}Hol^6	Native Stepper		3	119	4	4	$4^{1\frac{1}{2}}$	5^{hd}	3^{hd}	$4^{\frac{1}{2}}$	$5^{\frac{1}{2}}$	Pincay L Jr	7.30
10Jan82 ^{8}SA^4	Prince Khalid		3	114	3	6	6^{hd}	4^{hd}	$5^{\frac{1}{2}}$	6^2	$6^{2\frac{1}{2}}$	Guerra W A	a-3.20
9Jan82 ^{7}SA^1	Bunnell		3	119	7	7	7^3	$6^{\frac{1}{2}}$	8	8	$7^{2\frac{1}{2}}$	Asmussen C B	.90
23Dec81 ^{8}Hol^7	Bison Bay		3	119	5	5	$3^{\frac{1}{2}}$	$3^{\frac{1}{2}}$	7^1	7^1	8	Valenzuela P A	14.50

a–Coupled: Bargain Balcony and Prince Khalid.

OFF AT 3:18. Start good. Won driving. Time, :22$\frac{4}{5}$, :45$\frac{4}{5}$, 1:10, 1:35$\frac{3}{5}$ Track fast.

$2 Mutuel Prices:

1–BARGAIN BALCONY (a–entry)	8.40	4.00	2.80
2–ALGARDI		8.00	4.60
3–MAGGIE'S BEST			5.40

B. g, by Bargain Day—Balcony Doll, by First Balcony. Trainer Headley Bruce. Bred by Barnes Dr G & Darlene (Cal).

BARGAIN BALCONY engaged for the lead inside of GALA ARRAY soon after the start, took the lead when roused on the stretch turn and held his rivals safe through the drive. ALGARDI, unhurried until the final turn rallied between horses entering the stretch, responded gamely in the drive but could not overtake the winner. MAGGIE'S BEST, never far back, swung out wide to rally in the drive and finished strongly. GALA ARRAY set or forced the pace to the upper stretch and weakened. NATIVE STEPPER, always within easy striking distance, lacked the needed closing response. PRINCE KHALID rallied between horses in the drive but hung near the end. BUNNEL was wide and failed to respond when called upon. BISON BAY was finished after six furlongs.

Owners— 1, Greene H F; 2, Mandysland Farm; 3, Sabinske R J; 4, Fairmeade Farm; 5, Greene Mr-Mrs H; 6, Greene-Marino-Sheridan et al; 7, Hooper F W; 8, Spreen R H.

Overweight: Algardi 2 pounds.

To conclude the exercise, when setting odds lines from handicapping probabilities, Ainslie and others have recommended as important operational guidelines:

1. Handicappers' profits usually trace to horses at good odds, with returns on short-priced horses amounting to little or nothing.
2. Best bets are top-rated horses at overlaid odds.
3. Opportunities arise when logical contenders remain inseparable by handicapping, but one becomes a strongly overestimated favorite. Bets on the underestimated others should result in lucrative seasonal profits.
4. Price bets alone do not succeed. Attractively-priced horses must also be contenders according to the fundamentals of handicapping.

Odds-Percentage Table

(If actual odds line does not appear, use the nearest odds.)

Odds	Percentage	Odds	Percentage
1-9	90	9-2	18
1-5	83	5-1	17
2-5	71	6-1	14
1-2	67	7-1	12
3-5	62	8-1	11
4-5	56	9-1	10
1-1	50	10-1	9
6-5	45	11-1	8
7-5	42	12-1	8
3-2	40	13-1	7
8-5	38	14-1	7
9-5	36	15-1	6
2-1	33	18-1	5
5-2	29	25-1	4
3-1	25	30-1	3
7-2	22	40-1	2
4-1	20	70-1	1

PACE ANALYSIS BEATS PACE RATINGS

Pace as a fundamental factor in handicapping can be mishandled as readily as any other, perhaps more so. Among the most serious malfunctions has been the tendency to treat a horse's performance during a single race segment, or combinations of segments, as the critical index of its pace ability. It's a variation on the strictly rhetorical question: which is the most important factor in handicapping? Pace fanciers seek to know: which is the most important segment of the race? The answer to both questions is the same: None.

The early Ray Taulbot, for example, promoted pace to the half mile in sprints, and to the three-quarters in routes, as the critical indicators. His contemporary Hugh Matheson argued the opposite, that the third quarter mile of sprints, the third and fourth quarter times of routes, were most important. Huey Mahl proposed a hybrid approach, whereby the first quarter combined with the final quarter told the tale. Colonel E.R. Bradley remains celebrated for his lasting remark that any horse which last time out had completed the final quarter-mile of a race in 24 seconds or less was worth a bet next out.

None of these assertions squares with the classic definition of pace, i.e., pace refers to the **relationships between** fractional times and final times. Thus it should not be surprising that the most comprehensive study of pace yet conducted has revealed that segments of the race are not as important as the race taken in its entirety. Even as no single factor is most important in handicapping, no single segment of a race's pace should be considered most important, at least not in the absolute sense many handicappers set sails to discover.

John Meyer, "The T.I.S. Pace Report," **The National Railbird Review,** Vol II, Nos. 8 and 9, San Clemente, CA, 1981.

John Meyer, publisher of the prestigious National Railbird Review, selected thousands of races nationwide to study the relative importance of eight pace segments. Defining pace as a rate of speed, measured by dividing distance by time (feet divided by seconds equals feet per second), Meyer asked what percentage of winners in four types of races also had run at the fastest pace during each of the segments.

Here is a summary of the findings:

Percentages of Winners by Pace Segments During Which They Ran at the Fastest Rate of Speed

Types of Races	Start to 1st Call	1st Call to 2nd Call	2nd Call to Finish	Averaged Pace, 1st 3 Calls
Dirt sprints	.25	.19	.09	.31
Dirt miles	.21	.16	.26	.16
Dirt routes	.43	.09	.09	.35
Grass routes	.20	.17	.23	.27

	Start to 2nd Call	Start to Finish	1st and Last Call Combined	3rd and 4th Calls Combined
Dirt sprints	.22	.41	.19	.03
Dirt miles	.16	.32	.26	.26
Dirt routes	.43	.39	.17	.09
Grass routes	.23	.30	.17	.27

The relatively high percentages in the "start to finish" column indicate that generally the greatest number of winners can be found by determining which horses can maintain the highest rate of speed throughout the race, and not just for particular segments of races.

As Meyer's study of pace did not report the percentage of starters having the highest rate of speed for each race segment, the observed winning percentages cannot be compared to expected winning percentages, yielding probability values, but a number of the observed relationships beckon for comment.

As 43 percent of Meyer's winners in dirt routes (1 1/16M to 1 1/2M) also had shown the highest rate of speed to the first call, and to the second call, a much higher winning percent than that of sprints, Meyer suggests handicappers pay greater attention than traditionally supposed to early pace leaders in routes.

In both dirt sprints and dirt routes, speed to the first call is associated with many more winners than speed demonstrated between the first two calls, or between the second call and the finish. In the same kinds of races, however, speed from the start to the first call and speed from the start to the second call are associated with comparable percentages of winners. Apparently handicappers can fairly interchange first or second call fractional times in their calculations of pace ratings.

Handicappers who concentrate their pace calculations on the combined final segments (3rd and 4th calls) of races are working with less than five percent of the winners in sprints and less than 10 percent of the winners in routes. Such handicappers will be making many dismal forecasts. Only slightly more advantaged are handicappers who combine the first and last calls in their pace ratings, as Mahl has recommended.

Meyer concluded handicappers will be keeping company with the greatest number of winners if they base pace calculations on entire races or at least on the averaged rate of speed for the first three race segments. Thus his findings support the definition of pace as the relationships between fractional times and final times.

The Meyer study supports too a conclusion about pace far more fundamental. Pace analysis supersedes pace ratings. Instead of rushing to ratings, by focusing on the rate of speed dished out during one favored race segment or another, handicappers benefit if first they consider how races might be run today, which horses might contest or press the lead at the various points of call, and what might be the likely effects of the pace confrontations at each point. This kind of pace analysis will be most effectively completed in a broader context that simultaneously considers Class and Form. To put it simply, pace analysis extends a fundamental kind of race analysis.

And so it goes, if a horse that figures to contest the early pace also figures to be outclassed by early rivals, it does not figure to win, its previously high pace ratings notwithstanding. Likewise, the prospects of horses suited to the class demands of early pace duels, but short of form, or dulling in form today, are dim prospects. Such horses might lose even if they carry the race to the second or third calls, and even if they wield the highest pace ratings. The high ratings presumably were earned when the horses raced in tip-top shape.

After analyzing which horses should do what, in relation to the probable pace to each point of call, and deciding what the likely effects at each call will be, handicappers have identified those horses that figure to survive a comprehensive pace analysis.

Now handicappers can pace rate the identified horses, relying on key races within recent times, and applying methods whose resulting numbers reflect horses' abilities at both fractional points and final points.

As Meyer's study reminds, when handicappers set out to discover with arithmetic whether one horse is likely to set and maintain the fastest pace, or to track and overcome that pace, they best limit the calculations to horses that already have distinguished themselves as genuine contenders on pace, as revealed by pace analysis.

When at last pace ratings are employed to separate contenders, Meyer recommends handicappers calculate horses' rates of speed in feet-per-second. The method describes a ratio between distance travelled and time recorded, and eliminates the common practices whereby one length is equated to one-fifth of a second. The one-to-one equation is not sufficiently accurate.

By Meyer's method, a horse that ran a furlong (660 feet) in 12 seconds would be credited with a rate of speed at 55 feet-per-second. The horse that does a furlong in 11 3/5 seconds goes 56.9 feet-per-second. When a final time is considered, the beaten-lengths adjustment used by Meyer is 11 feet per length. The small differences in feet-per-second that normally result from these pace calculations need not be so upsetting to handicappers. As Meyer shows, even tiny differences in feet-per-second translate to significant differences in ground covered during the race. To illustrate the point, Meyer shows how a .05 feet-per-second difference represents approximately a yard of ground in a six furlong sprint completed in 1:11 seconds.

Or enough to explain the difference between victory and defeat.

AN OPERATIONAL DEFINITION
OF RECENT FORM

As horses vary so in their individual form cycles and training patterns, not to mention changes of physical condition related to soundness or maturation, handicappers have generally conceded the form factor remains the most elusive and perplexing of their art. Not merely a few professionals practically ignore the complexities of form, preferring to believe that horses in training, by that fact alone, can be accepted as racing sound and in competitive shape.

To complicate the matter, truly scholarly attempts to study form, and thus provide handicappers with meaningful operational definitions of the factor, have regularly collapsed on the profit criterion. The studies have thrown losses, some considerably greater than others. So rigorous attempts to handle the form factor only have hardened the feeling that a singularly systematic reliance on form definitions could never beat the game. No wonder the mail-order system peddlers make haste to brandish their late great discoveries of form angles, form fads. After all, if nothing substantial works, why not this nonsense?

As far as the author knows, the only substantial operational definition of form that has worked under testing conditions has been a strict definition of **recent form**, supplied and tested successfully at most—but not all—major tracks by an unlikely researcher of thoroughbred form, the New York-based speed handicapper Henry Kuck. Kuck analyzed 24,687 starters at numerous tracks and found 3,668 that met his working definition of good recent form. These "form" horses represented approximately 50 percent more winners than Kuck would have expected, based on probabilities, but when they also returned a 16.8 percent loss on wagers, it looked as though the wheel had been reinvented once again.

But Kuck massaged and manipulated his data a bit more.

Thus he identified the only profitable operational definition of recent form in major racing. The decisive variable is **stage of the meeting.** The first four weeks of a meeting present handicappers armed with Kuck's definition, and accompanied by elimination and separation guidelines that are part and parcel of the full definition, an opportunity to make profits clustering at 25 to 30 percent on investment.

Of 6,490 starters Kuck studied at 10 tracks, 388 fit his operational definition, and 93 of these horses won, affording Kuck's form definition a winning probability of 218 percent its fair share of the races while tossing off a 28.3 percent profit.

Kuck's working definition of recent form, the elimination and separation guidelines that round off the operational definition in practice, and the tracks for which the findings apply, are presented below. If a local track does not appear on the list, Kuck assures handicappers the technique generalizes to 80 percent of all racetracks. Notable exceptions are the tracks on the New York circuit—where recent form horses win enough, but are so overbet they do not return a profit—Santa Anita, the winter meeting, and the Florida middle dates (Gulfstream or Hialeah), where New York shippers too frequently outclass the local horses, however sharp the locals' recent form.

Henry Kuck, "Situation Handicapping," *Woodside Associates*, New York, 1981.

Kuck's working definition of recent form:

1—Raced in last 20 days at today's track.

2—Finished no worse than 3rd last out, beaten no more than 10 lengths.

3—Must not stretch out 1/16M or longer today.

The distance stipulation protects handicappers from younger horses stretching out for the first time, a notoriously risky bet, recent form notwithstanding.

The elimination and separation guidelines depend on the type of race under consideration. Kuck identifies four categories: (1) claimers and starters for winners (2) allowance and overnight handicaps (3) stakes and (4) maidens.

The elimination guidelines apply to three categories of races, excepting maidens. There are seven. Eliminate:

1. Any maiden.

2. Any horse that hasn't raced in the last 2 months.

3. Any horse that won a maiden claimer last out, unless it drops at least $1000 in claiming price today.

4. Any horse racing with a claiming tag of $20,000 or less that drops as much as $10,000 in claiming value off its last start. Waive this stipulation if the horse switches from grass to dirt today.

5. Any horse that raced over anything other than a fast track last out, if today's race is on a fast track, UNLESS it shows a finish of 3rd or better in its past performances when facing winners on a fast track.

6. Any horse traveling a mile or farther today that picks up as much as 5 pounds to carry 120 pounds or more, UNLESS it finished 3rd or closer in a race in North America while carrying within two pounds of today's scheduled impost.

7. Any horse traveling 7f or more today and scheduled to carry as much as 123 pounds, UNLESS it finished 3rd or closer in a race in North America while carrying within two pounds of today's scheduled impost.

Just two elimination rules for maiden races.

1. Any horse entered in a maiden special weight or maiden allowance that shows 5 or more career starts.

2. Any horse that hasn't raced in two months.

Regarding the working definition, Kuck admits two exceptional situations. At Oaklawn and Fair Grounds, a last out at 5½ furlongs is acceptable if today's race is at six. In maiden races, if a horse finished 3rd last out, it must not have been beaten by more than 1½ lengths.

Horses satisfying the working definition, and not jettisoned by the elimination guidelines, should be separated by preferences that vary—again—according to type of race.

For **claiming** and **starter** races open to winners, prefer:

1. A horse with 5 wins in its money box to a horse with no wins or only 1 win.

2. The horse that won last out.

3. The horse that raced in the highest class or for the

highest selling price in its latest three starts.

(Claiming prices are only "highest" if the horse competed at least once before for a price within 20 percent of the high price.)

4. The horse scheduled to carry the least weight today. (If for 3 & up, from January to June, prefer older horses.)

For **allowance** and **overnight handicaps**, prefer:

1. The horse showing a first or second place finish in an allowance or stakes race anywhere in its past performances.

2. The horse with a win at today's track in either of its latest two starts.

3. The horse with the highest in-the-money percentage for the two years listed in the consistency box. On grass, consider the career grass record only.

For **stakes**, races, prefer:

1. A horse that won an open stakes race.

2. A horse that finished second in an open stakes race.

3. The horse with the highest in-the-money percentage for the two years listed in the consistency box. On grass, consider only the grass record. Of $100,000 purses or more, prefer horses with at least three wins in the consistency box.

For **maiden** races, prefer:

1. The horse that raced in the highest class in its latest three starts. The class hierarchy among maiden races: straight maidens, maiden claimers, state-bred straight maidens, state-bred maiden claimers.

2. The horse scheduled to carry the least weight today.

To remind handicappers, the first four weeks is the stage of the meeting at which Kuck's operational definition of recent form works as a positive handicapping factor. As with all operational definitions, **all** the rules must be followed strictly to realize success.

Here are the North American racetracks where the form technique applies effectively:

Arlington Park	Hazel Park
Atlantic City	Hollywood Park
Balmoral	Keeneland
Bay Meadows	Keystone
Bowie	Meadowlands
Churchill Downs	Monmouth Park
Detroit	Oaklawn Park
Fair Grounds	Pimlico
Golden Gate	Santa Anita (Fall)
Hawthorne	Thistledown

Having set forth to define recent form in a way that might produce positive results for handicappers, Henry Kuck learned that those results would depend on not just a workmanlike definition of form, but this in combination with the track played, stage of the meeting, and type of race. It wasn't the definition of recent form that made the difference, he determined, but several conditions that combined to present unique handicapping problems from situation to situation.

Kuck's form studies also provided five operationalized handicapping techniques, each situated to a special set of conditions at particular tracks. The second technique, for example, applies to the same tracks as Kuck's operational definition of form, but abandons form altogether, and substitutes other handicapping factors that operate more effectively from the **fifth week of the meeting and thereafter**, precisely when recent form does not matter as much. In fact, each of Kuck's final four techniques in "Situation Handicapping" abandon recent form, a positive basis for successful handicapping only during the early stages of selected meetings.

Even handicappers who do not apply Kuck's operational definition of recent form during the early stages of race meetings should learn something quite significant and fundamental from this comprehensive research. Reliance on impressive recent form as a decisive factor in handicapping, particularly during the middle and late stages of race meetings, gets to nowhere. Not only do too many horses qualify on form at those times, the contenders with more impressive recent form are largely overbet. Thus many recent form horses go postward as underlays. Even when they win, handicappers lose.

PORTFOLIOS

If the bane of successful handicapping has been rightly laid to too much action on unplayable races, a running theme of book chapters on the subject suggests that for most players highly selective betting becomes its own can of worms. Few handicappers seem willing to sit quietly on the sidelines at racetracks, awaiting the one, two, or three potentially playable horses on the card, and this day upon day. Handicappers want more action than that. Then, too, few handicappers, however regularly they attend the races, have chosen to depend on handicapping profits for a lifetime's income. This great majority mixes recreational handicapping with professional handicapping.

Tom Ainslie long ago confessed to limiting handicapping intended to maximize profits to a few weeks of the season. Andy Beyer and Steve Davidowitz each distinguished between their **prime** bets and action bets, Davidowitz admitting he expected to lose on action bets, and did, while insisting the action had important and overcompensating curative and stimulating effects. Jacada's James Selvidge bemoans the need for more action as preventing his graduation from semipro to pro. Gordon Jones encourages exotic wagering.

From practically all points of view converges the inevitable conclusion that handicappers go to the racetrack for both profits and recreation. For purposes of definition, let's agree that recreational handicapping refers to investing money in a personally entertaining way. It consists of whatever one enjoys, which normally does not include losing one's shirt. Professional handicapping refers to (a) making systematic selections that honor the fundamentals of handicapping and are consistent with known probabilities and (b) profit maximization through the most effective management of capital. That kind of money management is cut-and-dried systematic. It allows of no deviation, no sport.

A concept that appears frequently in the *Hold Your Horses* quarterly of Jacada Publications lends itself at once to recreational betting and professionalism. It is portfolio wagering. Analagous to the stock market portfolios of Wall Street investors, racetrack betting portfolios contain various and diverse kinds of investments. These range from win bets on prime selections to back-wheeling the overbet favorite in the Exacta. An essential difference from recreational betting as commonly practiced is that all bets have been planned. Having been preplanned, all kinds of bets are also monitored closely as to their continuing effectiveness, with the ineffective kind eliminated from the portfolio, even as poor performance stocks are discarded by smart Wallstreeters.

Betting portfolios, that is, are structured, and in the individualized manner that incorporates recreational bets and serious bets. Money management approaches to each kind of investment are defined, and implemented rigorously. Results are studied periodically. As results indicate, portfolios are modified, with some bets added, others eliminated. The monitoring process is nonending. As time progresses, the portfolio becomes more stabilized, consisting entirely of bets that are working well enough.

Handicappers can develop the betting portfolio easily. Only a few guidelines, as gathered from the literature, can suffice.

1. The great percentage of total capital and at least 70 percent of same must be allocated to win betting on fundamental handicapping selections that are overlays.

2. Starting capital must be at least $500 and preferably $1000 or more.

3. Betting capital must be segregated from income.

4. For each kind of bet in the portfolio a money management method must be defined and systematically applied.

5. The effectiveness of each kind of bet must be determined periodically and no later than following a series of 100 bets.

James Selvidge, "Hold Your Horses Quarterly," *Jacada Publications,* Vols. I-II-III (various), 1979-1981.

6. Ineffective bets must be eliminated from the portfolio.

7. As each new type of bet is added to the portfolio, the above guidelines apply, and the cycles continue.

Below is a hypothetical racetrack betting portfolio, starting capital of $2000.

Win betting. Amount of risk capital: $1400 (70% of bankroll). Method: optimal betting (see page 22), or fixed percentage minimum (see page 159), with 3 percent as the percentage bet, thus a first bet or minimum bet of $42.

BB + SR Flow (see page 38) on older maidens that finished 2nd last out. Amount of risk capital: $150 (five parallels, first bet of $10). Method: base bet plus square root of the profits.

Place Parlays. On prime selections that are overbet to win, or selections above 7-2 when the favorite figures to lose. Amount of risk capital: $150. Method: $10 bets, each parlayed for a series of not more than four-five races, often less, and not necessarily of a single card.

Exacta overlays. Amount of risk capital: $200. Method: $10 exactas from key selection to one, two, or three contenders, top and botton. (If risk capital is lost in full, replace in full, but not to exceed total risk capital investment of $600.)

Round Robin Win Parlays. Nonprime selections. Amount of risk capital: $100. Method: of a single card, $2 win parlays on selections of four-five relatively unpredictable races, from each selection to the others.

Portfolios can be as widely diversified as handicappers' tastes, and as risk capital permits. Almost any "angle" handicappers fancy can be tested for effectiveness cheaply, using a 15-loss base bet plus square root of the profits flow at $2 base bet, with no parallels. Risk capital of each flow amounts to $30. Whatever the type of bet, some risk capital must be allocated, as paper bets tell nothing. Profit margins can be studied monthly, or after a representative series of bets, approximately 100. Regarding profit-taking, the literature says little, but profits can be taken seasonally, monthly, or after a predetermined number of bets, perhaps 100.

The key to recreational handicapping and wagering is to structure it sensibly. Planning steps intended to structure action so that it will remain sensibly in accord with the percentages of the game, and susceptible to the most suitable betting techniques available, will absolutely limit losses, and might convert otherwise certain losses into gain. For that reason, to be sure, betting portfolios have a significant place in handicapping practice.

FULLY-INSURED INVESTMENTS IN
COMPLETELY SYSTEMATIZED HANDICAPPING

In a remarkable individual endeavor to systematize the whole of the handicapping process author William L. Scott has elaborated a system of play that has never been known to record losses for more than two consecutive days at North American racetracks. Not only that, the system invites action on almost every race. Furthermore, any race's contention is identified **before** the handicapping begins, so that Scott's rules need be applied in the vast majority of situations to just three horses. All of this has evolved from Scott's quest to find a method of betting horses so steady and dependable in its profit production it could fairly be perceived as comparable to blue chip-type investments in the stock market. Beyond the blue chip system that materialized, Scott's studies and field experiments have resulted in an operational definition of speed and class that will surely become part and parcel of the reportoire of many handicappers everywhere. He calls the concept "ability times," a measure of late speed and class. When converted to figures in Scott's fully operational handicapping, a horse's basic ability figure is modified by considerations of its form and early speed.

Yet the basis of Scott's investment system is not handicapping so much as statistics. The system depends on the invariable annual fact that the first three choices in the betting win 67 percent of all races, and Scott's discovery that one of the first three choices finishes first or second 90 percent of the time. Scott calls the latter statistic the most powerful in racing. His system is dependent on it. Further, Scott's research never shows even one day when as few as three races were won by one of the top three public choices. One of these regularly wins or runs second **in all nine**. This occurs for eight of nine races with remarkable consistency. On some days, rare, in only seven races does one of the three betting choices win or place. As Scott notes, to find only six such races on a day is nearly unbelievable. Five is unimaginable.

From these probabilities, Scott's comprehensive system emerged. The idea was to select from among the three top public choices the one that would likely beat the remaining two in two of every three races, half again as successful as would be random selection. Handicappers can appreciate that would yield four winning selections during each nine-race card. Moreover, should the selected horses not defeat the others, they will often run second, as the 90 percent statistic assures. Handicappers thus can cash numerous place tickets, and a 60 percent success rate in the two hole produces a small profit on investment.

Thus, Rule 1. Handicappers will restrict investments to one of three horses, and that horse must be one of the first three betting choices. The betting corollaries: bet to win and place, never to show; no exotics; bet the same amount of money on every race. By Scott's account, volume and percentage on statistically-sound selections equals consistent profits.

Having set the stage for investments on the likeliest of handicapping selections, all Scott needed were the rules to arrive at the likeliest of these. His method was largely trial-and-error until he determined that (a) class and form were most important, and (b) fractional times might represent more reliable estimates of true ability than do final times. He has termed his fundamental measure "ability times." Ability times estimate the basic ability of horses. Scott's measure is a fractional time of the race, adjusted for each horse by a measure of (a) lengths gained or lost between calls and (b) energy expended. Ability times are then converted to standard figures, and these are finally adjusted for early speed and form. All of this is done with a complex set of rules that allow for no deviation or personal judgment, but which are not really all that complex.

For sprints at six furlongs, ability times are derived from the final quarter-mile fractions. All other sprint distance times are converted to six-furlong equivalent times. For routes, the fractional times between the first and second calls (four furlongs to six furlongs at the frequently-run middle distances)

William L. Scott, "Investing At The Racetrack," *Simon and Schuster*, New York, 1981, Ch. 2, pp. 28-42, et. al.

have been determined the best predictor of ability, with these again converted to figures and finally adjusted for lengths gained or lost and for energy expended. The lengths-gained adjustments are finer estimates of true speed than the traditional 1/5 second per length formula. The energy adjustment depends on how fast a horse ran prior to the fractional times that measure ability. All races in a horse's past performance table are rated and the two best used to estimate ability. The final adjustments for early speed and form add or subtract to a basic ability figure in the same way conventional speed handicapping treats figures for adjusted final times. All the adjustments have been determined empirically—according to what works. Early speed adjustments, for example, derive from a method different from Bill Quirin's demonstrably-effective "speed points," but these are Scott's, and these are the points that work in this system.

The final selection is the horse with a figure advantage of two or more. That horse is bet to win and place. A horse with a one-point advantage is bet to place only. Where two horses are tied, play the one with the lower odds. The only unplayable races are (a) maiden races having three or more first-time starters, (b) turf races where none of the top three betting choices show a turf race, and (c) any race where none of the top betting choices qualify on form analysis.

In *Investing at the Racetrack* Scott deals extensively with the logic, and the numerous methodological problems and exceptions that threaten his rigorous attempts to systematize as complicated a game as handicapping. He succeeds in his persuasion. Most impressive is the rationale and stepwise logic for all that the system embraces. Unless, that is, the greater persuasion rests with the results. Below are the results the system achieved during June 1980 on a series of bets ($2) at Belmont Park and six other tracks located variously throughout the country.

Track	Days	#Bets	Wins	Cost	Gross	Profits	Dollar Return
Belmont	6	87	52	$174	$275	$101	.58
Suffolk	3	49	25	98	133	35	.36
Monmouth	4	58	32	126	160	35	.28
Arlington	3	39	18	78	105	27	.33
Churchill	3	45	20	90	108	18	.20

Hollywood	3	35	22	70	98	28	.41
Golden Gate	3	42	20	84	95	11	.13
Totals	25	355	189	$720	$974	$255	.35

Of 25 racing days, the system produced profits for 20. It had one losing day at Suffolk, at Monmouth, and at Churchill, and two losing days at Golden Gate. A $20 flat bet on each of the 355 selections (includes win and place bets) would have netted profits of $2550. At the six tracks besides Belmont the rate of return on the invested dollar was .29. After laying out the results for the testing period, Scott wonders rhetorically whether the system will attract doubtors, or investors. He reassures investors they will not at any time, any place, suffer the indignity of three consecutive days of loss.

Many handicappers will want to experiment with or invest in the ability figures earned by the top three choices in races at their place. The system rules are not reprinted here, so handicappers must consult Scott in his entirety. They will find his study illuminating, challenging, and downright confronting. Among Scott's discoveries at various stages of the experimenting was the confounding inexactitude of the daily track variant. He determined handicappers should cope with daily variants by ignoring them altogether.

THE DOSAGE INDEX

When the Cougar II colt **Gato Del Sol**, a longshot, swept from last to first and drew off to win the 1982 Kentucky Derby, the remarkable record of Steve Roman's dosage index (DI) as a predictor of classic winners was sustained further still. **Damascus** excepted, no modern horse having a ratio of speed to stamina—Dosage—in its pedigree above Roman's statistical value line of 4.00 had ever won either the Kentucky Derby or the Belmont Stakes. The 1982 pre-Derby favorites loomed as counterpoints to dosage analysts, as each had inherited much more speed than endurance, and each possessed a DI higher than the magic number, but those fast favorites perished badly in the Churchill Downs stretch, true to their pedigree prospects.

When weeks later **Conquistador Cielo**, its DI a soaring 16.0, blitzed the Belmont Stakes field, controversy swirled. Some concluded that Roman's index had been unmasked at last. Those who know statistics accepted the 1982 Belmont winner as an exception proving the rule.

In his stimulating "**Dosage: A Practical Approach**" (which appeared exclusively in **Daily Racing Form** during Spring, 1981, and to which that paper's national **Bloodlines** columnist Leon Rasmussen refers frequently and pointedly), author Steven A. Roman explained how to calculate and interpret the dosage index, which is a mathematical expression of a thoroughbred's inherent speed and endurance characteristics, and thereby predict, based on pedigree alone, which horses and stakes winners are likely to become racing's truly important horses.

Beyond educating the sport's breeders in the science of mating horses, and its auction buyers in the science of purchasing yearlings, Roman has extended a helping hand to handicappers, who are increasingly concerned about the science of picking winners. No handicapper in possession of the DIs for the 1982 Derby hopefuls should have invested a dollar in their prospects, as the prerace favorites shaped up as statistical improbables. There are other important dosage applications for handicappers, but first a basic explanation of the dosage index, one of the most inventive and scholarly contributions in the annals of the sport.

The dosage index is a statistical measure of speed and stamina in combination, calculated according to the performance aptitudes of the important sires (called "chef-de-race" sires) that appear in a horse's immediate four generation family. As students of pedigree know, but many handicappers do not, the genetic aptitudes of racehorses are five: Brilliant, Intermediate, Classic, Solid, and Professional, the five arranged in order of increasing stamina, or, in order of decreasing speed.

By simple arithmetical calculations, explained below, the index describes a horse's ratio of speed to stamina. Roman's research with the tool persuades horsemen and handicappers that horses having too great a speed quotient (above 4.00) are **not** likely to become classic winners or important sires themselves. In a sport where classic traditions have lately yielded more and more authority to speed—indeed Roman has referred to a general inflation factor towards higher DIs in contemporary pedigrees—perhaps some find solace from a scientific method that assigns a kind of ultimate authority to horses possessing greater stamina.

Roman's practical approach to dosage produces three statistics. First, a dosage profile (DP) is identified by assigning points to each of the five aptitudinal categories in a four-generation pedigree. Thus a DP looks like so: 7-5-9-1-2, where seven means Brilliant points, five means Intermediate points, 9 means Classic points, etc., etc. The dosage index (DI) and another statistic called center of distribution (CD) are merely ratios among the points, and easily calculated.

To arrive at a dosage profile, handicappers must identify the **chef-de-race** sires in each of the first four generations. The influence of each of these sires is allotted a number of points,

Steven A. Roman, "Dosage: A Practical Approach," Bloodlines, A Column By Leon Rasmussen, *Daily Racing Form*, May 1, 1982.

such that each of a preceding generation's chef-de-race sires can earn only half the points of the succeeding generation's. Thus, moving backwards, we find a possible progression of 1-2-4-8 sires in the four generations, such that these sires contribute 16-8-4-2 points each. The **chef-de-race** sires have themselves been classified by aptitudinal groups, and points for each aptitudinal group represented by the fabulous sires are totalled.

A table of current chef-de-race sires by aptitudinal groups is presented at the end of this piece.

A horse's point total in each aptitudinal group expresses its DP. **Gato Del Sol's** dosage profile is expressed as 6-3-5-2-2.

The dosage index is the ratio of the points in the speed wing to those in the stamina wing.

The speed wing is equal to the Brilliant points + Intermediate points + one-half the Classic points.

The stamina wing is equal to the other half of the Classic points + the Solid points + the Professional points.

When the speed points are divided by the stamina points, an elementary division calculation, the DI results.

What is the DI for Gato Del Sol? It is 1.77.

As the DI is directly proportional to the speed in a pedigree and inversely proportional to the stamina, a DI of 1.00 reflects a perfect balance of the two qualities. A DI of 2.00 indicates twice as much speed as stamina.

The CD of Roman's pedigree is the single point where the combined influences of all the chef-de-race sires concentrate most strongly. Its calculation requires nothing more than a sequence of addition, subtraction, and multiplication operations.

Multiply the Brilliant points by 2 and add the product to the Intermediate points.

From that sum subtract the Solid points.

Next multiply the Professional points by 2 and subtract that product from the preceding difference.

Divide the resulting number by the total number of points in the DP.

What is the CD for Gato Del Sol? It is 0.50.

Roman's research with his dosage methodology has been continuous, pragmatic, and greatly important to the production of knowledge concerning relations between bloodlines and racetrack performances. He has concentrated his studies on stakes winners, and rightly so, as the classic purpose of mating thoroughbreds, largely forgotten in the recent industrialization of the stud in numerous stateside factories thoroughout the land, has been the improvement of the breed. That improvement is most likely to occur when the highest grade of stakes winner is involved in the mating.

Consider Roman's most significant findings:

1. Champions and leading sires have significantly **lower** DIs and CDs than do the normal population of stakes winners.

2. A DI of 4.00 and a CD of 1.25 separate the classic winners and champions from the other stakes winners with astonishing reliability. In forty-two years no horse with a DI exceeding 4.00 has won the Kentucky Derby, only two the Belmont Stakes, and just one with a CD above 1.25 has won either classic.

In contrast, of stakes winners as a class, approximately 40 per cent have a DI exceeding 4.00, but these horses rarely win the sport's definitive events.

3. Studies of stakes-winning sprinters, middle distance horses, and routers have revealed a direct correlation between the DI and distance potential. The sprinters have the highest DIs, the routers the lowest, and the middle distance horses fall inbetween. The differences among the groups are statistically significant, eliminating chance as the cause of the results.

4. Although the DIs and the CDs for successive generations have been rising in general, the relative importance of stamina in top class horses, compared to the entire population, has remained stable. Breeding practices may now churn out more speed burners than ever, but these still do not often advance to the top of the class.

Of applications to handicapping, handicappers can obviously eliminate horses in the classics if their DIs exceed 4.00, and without hesitation.

A narrow application to handicapping? Perhaps.

There are at least two wider applications. Of the stakes population at any major track, horses with DIs and CDs within the classic ranges can be considered at advantage when the distance lengthens to a mile and one-quarter or farther and the quality of the competition becomes the highest. Regular, older stakes campaigners will be fairly evaluated from the past performance tables, but lightly-raced, nicely-bred four-year-olds, and similar late-blooming five-year-olds, might be moving towards the top at any time of the season. If the contest is now Grade I at a classic distance, demanding of horses the proper blend of speed and endurance, handicappers benefit if they consult the dosage indexes. Horses should qualify within the 4.00 and 1.25 limits.

Another application of dosage is far more interesting, easily more advantageous. Each season the better three-year-olds sort themselves out in increasingly-demanding stakes competition. The Roman approach helps handicappers predict which threes should go the farthest against the best. If handicappers prepare a file of DIs and CDs for stakes winners and outstanding allowance winners in the three-year-old divisions, they have accumulated useful evidence as to which hopefuls might end as sprinters, middle distance types, and routers, as well as which might be genuine graded stakes stars and classic contenders. As between sprinters and middle distance horses, Roman's research with dosage has not yet established a DI value line separating the two groups. That's an empirical problem worth its solution.

The handicapper's difficulty with Roman's practical approach to dosage is precisely the practical problem of obtaining a four-generation pedigree. The expedient sources of information are either **Daily Racing Form's** columns by Rasmussen or local pedigree services that might provide the information—for a fee. Of any season's three-year-olds, those of real distinction are quickly seized upon by Rasmussen, who dutifully reports their DPs, DIs, and CDs, along with interpretations of same. The columnist does the same for many notable older horses.

For handicappers who wish to calculate dosage statistics of their own, the chef-de-race sire table below is the basic source. The table is revised or expanded periodically, or listed sires are assigned concurrently to two aptitudinal groups, as the asterisk marks denote.

There are presently only 149 sires worth all the attention:

CHEF-DE-RACE SIRES

BRILLIANT

Abernant	Fairway	Noholme II*	Raise a Native
Black Toney*	Gallant Man*	Northern Dancer*	Reviewer*
British Empire	Grey Sovereign	Olympia	Roman*
Bold Ruler*	Heliopolis	Orby	Royal Charger
Bull Dog	Hyperion*	Panorama	Sir Cosmo
Cicero	My Babu	Peter Pan	Tudor Minstrel
Court Martial	Nasrullah	Phalaris	Turn-to*
Double Jay	Nearco*	Pharis	Ultimus
Fair Trial	Never Bend*	Pompey	What a Pleasure

INTERMEDIATE

Ben Brush	Equipoise*	Never Bend*	Star Shoot
Big Game	Full Sail	Petition	Sweep
Black Toney*	Gallant Man*	Pharos	The Tetrarch
Bold Ruller*	Havresac II	Polynesian	Ticino
Broomstick	Khaled	Princequillo*	Tom Fool*
Colorado	King Salmon	Roman*	Traghetto
Congreve	Mahmoud*	Sir Gaylord*	Turn-to*
Djebel	Nashua	Sir Ivor	T.V. Lark
Eight Thirty	Native Dancer*	Star Kingdom*	

CLASSIC

Alibhai	Gainsborough	Noholme II*	Sir Gallahad III
Aureole	Graustark*	Northern Dancer*	Sir Gaylord
Bahram	Gundomar	Persian Gulf	Star Kingdom*
Blandford	Hail to Reason	Pilate	Swynford
Blenheim II*	Herbager*	Prince Bio	Tom Fool
Blue Larkspur	Hyperion*	Prince Chevalier	Tom Rolfe
Brantome	Mahmoud*	Prince John	Tourbillon*
Buckpasser	Midstream	Prince Rose	Tracery
Bull Lea	Mossborough	Reviewer*	Vieux Manoir
Clarissimus	Native Dancer*	Ribot*	War Admiral
Count Fleet	Navarro	Rock Sand*	
Equipoise*	Nearco*	Sicambre	
Exclusive Native	Never Say Die	Sideral	

SOLID

Asterus	Discovery	Princequillo*	Tantieme
Bachelor's Double	Fair Play*	Right Royal	Teddy
Ballymoss	Graustark*	Rock Sand*	Vatout
Blenheim II*	Herbager*	Round Table	Worden
Bois Roussel	Man o' War	Sea-Bird	
Chaucer	Oleander	Sunstar	

PROFESSIONAL

Admiral Drake	Dark Ronald	Mieuxce	Spearmint
Alcantara II	Donatello II	Ortello	Sunny Boy
Alizier	Fair Play*	Precipitation	Tom Rolfe*
Alycidon	Foxbridge	Rabelais	Tourbillon*
Bayardo	Hurry On	Ribot*	Vaguely Noble
Bruleur	La Farina	Sardanapale	Vandale
Chateau Bouscaut	Le Fabeleux	Solario	Vatellor
Crepello	Massine	Son-in-Law	Wild Risk

NOTE: An asterisk following a sire's name indicates he has been placed in two separate lasses. Therefore his influence in any generation is divided equally between two classes.

EUREKA! FIXED PERCENTAGE-MINIMUM

A 100-race field study at Santa Anita Park and numerous computer simulations have revealed the racetrack money management method presented for the first time here can

(a) outperform flat betting by a significant margin,

(b) control for the profit erosion characteristic of fixed percentage wagering during losing runs, and

(c) increase in power as the number of bets increases.

Labeled fixed percentage-minimum (FP-M) by the writer, the method invests a fixed percentage of capital following a win bet, but just a minimum amount following a loss. It's an important variation of fixed percentage wagering, whereby bettors bet a fixed percentage of capital each time. As will be seen immediately and convincingly, FP-M wagering not only minimizes the losses of accumulated profits during typical losing streaks at the racetrack, but also makes it possible for handicappers to regain considerable losses quickly, or even pull ahead of previous profit margins, merely perhaps with a pair of winners.

Handicappers capable of a .35 win proficiency, at average odds of 2.6 to 1, attainable results, can expect to earn a middle management's corporate salary over a season's play. But at .30 proficiency FP-M does not perform nearly as well, and may bust once of every five times attempted.

The Problem: Fixed percentage wagering to win has long been championed as an effective money management method at the races, as bettors bet more when winning, less when losing, thereby maximizing gain and minimizing loss. At conventional win proficiency levels, the method avoids bankruptcy

James Quinn, "The Literature of Thoroughbred Handicapping, 1965-1982, *GBC Press*, Las Vegas, Nevada, 1983, pp. 151-160.

wonderfully well. As others have shown, racegoers who take $100 to the track, and bet 5 percent of it consistently, will have $45 remaining after 20 consecutive losses.

But the method suffers a fatal flaw. I call it the erosion effect. In any continuous sample of play, as of a season, even the most competent of handicappers can expect to suffer losses of 10 to 15 races in succession. When this happens, profit erosion with fixed percentage investments becomes unacceptably steep. The greater the accumulated profits, the deadlier the erosion effect. Handicappers that have begun play with a $5000 bankroll, for example, and have doubled it by betting 5 percent of capital consistently, but suddenly lose 10 straight races, will see a $5000 gain dwindle to $985, a profit reduction greater than 80 percent. If few handicappers can be found betting fixed percentage amounts, perhaps this is the explanation. Sooner or later, they experience the erosion effect.

A pleasantly inviting alternative is fixed percentage-minimum.

Rationale. The FP-M method derives from the proposition, confirmed by empirical study, that successful handicappers win and lose in clusters almost as frequently as they win and lose alternately.

Four patterns of winning and losing can be represented as follows:

Win clusters	WW WWW WWWW WW WW
Loss Clusters	LL LLL LLL LLLL LLLLLL LLLLL
Alternating Win-Loss Clusters	WW LLL WWW LLLL WW LLLLL
Alternating Wins and Losses	WLWLWLWLWLWLWLWLWLWL

The first two patterns are sensitive to fixed percentage wagering, as bettors bet more when winning, less when losing, and therefore maximize profits and minimize losses. In pattern three, of alternating win-loss clusters, losses during dry runs are further minimized using FP-M, as only the first loss in a cluster equals a fixed percentage amount, and subsequent losses equal the minimum bet multiplied by the loss N. Thus the greater number of losses in a cluster, the greater the loss reduction with FP-M. When a win cluster follows, the second bet is a fixed percentage amount, and of a capital amount that now has not decreased as much as it would have with unmodified fixed percentage wagering.

In pattern four, of alternating wins and losses, the cumulative loss is maximized using FP-M. Following a win, the higher fixed percentage amount is bet, and loses. Following a loss, the minimum is bet, and wins. To the extent this pattern is repeated, loss is maximized, gain minimized, and any cumulative profits eroded. The research question is whether FP-M investments protected during pattern three overcompensate sufficiently for the FP-M losses maximized during pattern four throughout representative betting experiences.

Two studies have supplied provocative evidence. In the Santa Anita field study, the writer won 37 of 100 plays, average win odds at 2.99 to 1. A starting bankroll of $500 was increased to $2304, an $1804 profit. The fixed percentage bet following a win was 5 percent, and the minimum bet following a loss was $25 (an original 5 percent of $500). The dollar return on investment was .57, unusually high, yet a particularly positive characteristic of FP-M, which invests considerably less than fixed percentage betting.

By comparison, a series of $25 flat bets across the 100-race sample grossed $1690.75, and $1190 profit. Return on the dollar invested was a high .47.

Interestingly, a fixed percentage bet at 5 percent of capital would have returned profits approximating $2300, exceeding FP-M by some $500, with the dollar return a healthy .36. In the Santa Anita workout of 100 races, however, the longest losing streak was seven (twice). Computer simulations of seasonal play replicated what sad experience has so often proved. With all but exceptionally conservative styles of handicapping, losing runs of 12 to 15 are absolutely normal during any season. They pop up at least once or twice, and FP-M has been designed to eliminate precisely the effects of longer losing runs.

In the example where a $5000 stake has been doubled by fixed percentage betting, but 80 percent of that profit eroded during a 10-loss sequence, the FP-M loss for the 10 races would total $2750, leaving a $7250 bankroll intact. When the next two horses win, FP-M rebounds more strongly than the fixed percentage method does. As play continues and success accumulates, these differences intensify.

To appreciate this, examine a fixed 5 percent flow of bets in contrast to FP-M where the $5000 original bankroll has swelled to $20,000 but that inevitable 10-race loss skein strikes, followed at last by two consecutive winners, each paying odds at 2.6 to 1.

Play	Fixed Percentage Bank	Loss	Fixed Percentage-Minimum Bank	Loss
1	$20,000	$1,000	$20,000	$1,000
2	19,000	950	19,000	250
3	18,050	900	18,750	250
4	17,150	858	18,500	250
5	16,292	815	18,250	250
6	15,477	774	18,000	250
7	14,703	735	17,750	250
8	13,968	700	17,500	250
9	13,268	663	17,250	250
10	12,605	630	17,000	250

Play	Bank	Gain	Bank	Gain
11	$11,970	$1,500	$16,750	$ 650
12	13,470	1,749	17,400	2,262
Totals	**$15,219**	**($4781)**	**$19,662**	**($338)**

During the 10-race slide fixed percentage wagering cost $8,030, fully 53 percent of $15,000 in profits. Alternatively, FP-M cost $3,250 for 10 straight losers, or 22 percent of previous profit.

Of the subsequent two-race win cluster, fixed percentage betting rebounds by $3,249 to $15,219, for an overall loss approximating .25. FP-M rebounds by $2,912 to $19,662, for an overall loss of .0025.

Thus during a 12-race run, consisting of 10 losers and just 2 winners, FP-M has drawn practically even with its profitable point of departure. The power of the method during win-loss clusters characterized by multiple losses can be readily appreciated.

Nonetheless, handicappers win and lose alternately as well as in clusters. As previously remarked, during these sequences the aggregate loss is intensified using FP-M. What of this?

The records of many regular handicappers indicate they win and lose in clusters almost as frequently as they alternate wins and losses. The question remained. Do the number of win-loss clusters in a handicapper's season overcompensate significantly for the number of alternating wins and losses during the season?

The field study of 100 bets proved inconclusive on the point. But computer simulations of conventional handicapping proficiency have indicated that the best of handicappers can do better by switching to FP-M. Before examining the field study in more detail, let's turn our attention to the simulations.

Computer simulations. A computer was asked to determine whether FP-M wagering gains accumulated by attainable levels of handicapping proficiency during a season overcompensated for the losses intensified by that method when alternating wins and losses occur. The criterion of success was the ability of FP-M to exceed profits yielded by flat bets at three levels of proficiency, i.e., 30 percent winners, 35 percent winners, and 40 percent winners, each at average odds of 2.6 to 1, and without busting out.

A season was defined as 440 bets, approximately one-third the races available at major tracks during a six-month calendar. The starting bankroll was $5000, and a 5 percent bet of capital was used as the FP-M bet after a win, $250 as the minimum bet following a loss. Flat bets were at $250 also.

A flat bet of $250 on each of 440 plays at the three levels of attainable results and paying 2.6 to 1 on winners yields the following:

	Investment	Profit	Dollar Return
30%	$110,000	$8,800	.08
35%	110,000	28,600	.26
40%	110,000	48,400	.44

Numerous simulations indicated the FP-M profit at the .30 proficiency level did not differ from the flat bet profits, and often fell considerably below $8,800. With FP-M at 30 percent winners handicappers might go broke in 3 of 10 replications. Losses of smaller amounts can be expected about 50 percent of the time.

Prospects brighten sharply at .35 handicapping proficiency. At that performance level FP-M profit exceeds flat bet profit by some $10,000 after 440 bets. Not only that, the simulations also show the FP-M profits exceed flat bet profits more substantially as the number of bets increases. After 2000 bets, for example, flat bet profit at .35 proficiency (2.6 to 1 odds on winners) would reach $130,000, but FP-M profit would approach $202,000, a .55 advantage to FP-M wagering.

To digress, no computer bet exceeded $1,000. Whenever the bankroll totalled $20,000, profit-taking was simulated, and the computer reverted to a $5000 bankroll and continued to play.

The computer simulations demonstrated that FP-M profit balances at .35 proficiency or better are not seriously eroded or tilted substantially backwards by the alternating wins and losses that occur during long, representative periods of betting. Thus, while winning, the method controls for the erosion effect common to fixed percentage betting. Handicappers capable of .35 proficiency at 2.6 to 1 averaged odds are encouraged to maximize profit with FP-M wagering. The method requires users to achieve a slightly higher win percentage than the general public does (.33), while avoiding those overbet favorites that lower the crowd's dollar odds ($1.60). These are attainable results, to be sure.

The field study. During the core of the Santa Anita winter racing season 1982 the writer from February 11 through April 18 (37 racing days), and starting with a $500 bankroll and betting a fixed 5 percent following a win, a $25 minimum following a loss, used the FP-M method to study 100 consecutive win bets.

At .37 handicapping proficiency, averaged win odds at 2.99 to 1, the method recorded $1804 in profits, a .57 dollar return on an investment of $3,129, far surpassing flat bet profit for the same sample of play, and surpassing the fixed percentage rate of return. Table 1 presents the dollar profits (rounded) and rate of return for the three methods during the field study of 100 races:

Table 1: Profits and rate of return for three methods during the field study

	Flat Bets	Fixed Percentage	Fixed Percentage-Minimum
Amount Invested	$2,500	$ 7,686	$3,129
Gross	$3,690	$10,986	$4,933
Profit	$1,190	$ 2,300	$1,804
Dollar Return	.47	.36	.57

The 100-race sample can be considered representative of a major racing calendar, and was unbiased by extreme odds on winning selections, unbiased by atypical winning or losing runs. Among 37 winning selections the odds range was 0.8 to 10.1. Only five winners returned odds higher than 5 to 1. The longest losing cluster was seven (twice), longest winning cluster was three (five times). Handicapping proficiency and average win odds can be accepted as representative of successful handicapping performance at the racetrack.

Regarding clusters, the field study sample contained 10 win clusters and 13 loss clusters. Alternating win-loss sequences occurred 20 times.

Of the wagers on 37 winners, 15 were at fixed percentage amounts (22 minimum bets of $25 apiece), and these overcompensated significantly for fixed percentage bets on 20 of the 63 losers.

Handicappers should examine the two seven-race losing runs, as presented in Table 2. The first, of plays 23-29, resulted in an FP-M loss of $202, while fixed percentage betting lost $332, a $130 difference. During the second, of plays 85-91, FP-M lost $260, but fixed percentage betting lost $737, a difference between the two methods of $467. Thus as pari-mutuel betting continues the loss difference between the two methods grows significantly greater, more so as the size of the bets increases and number of consecutive losses increases.

Where handicapping proficiency warrants, the Santa Anita field study indicates that FP-M not only beats flat betting, but controls for the erosion of profits incurred by fixed percentage betting during longer losing streaks, notably when bets are of higher amounts.

Summary. The studies in combination support the following assertions:

1. FP-M wagering works best for seasonal investments among handicappers whose win percentages and dollar returns exceed those of the crowd.

2. FP-M controls for the profit erosion common to fixed percentage wagering during longer losing streaks, particularly when substantial profits have accumulated and amounts to be wagered will be relatively high.

Table 2
Dollar losses as between FP-M and Fixed Percentage Wagering During Similar Losing Streaks at two Points in the Season at Santa Anita

Early Losses Bets 23 - 29		FP-M	Bank	Fixed Percentage	Bank
Feb 20	6th	(52)	$1011	(55)	$1044
	7th	(25)	986	(52)	994
	8th	(25)	961	(50)	944
Feb 21	7th	(25)	936	(47)	897
	8th	(25)	911	(45)	852
Feb 24	4th	(25)	886	(43)	809
Feb 25	5th	(25)	861	(40)	769

FP-M Loss $202
Fixed Percentage Loss $332

Later Losses Bets 85 - 91		FP-M	Bank	Fixed Percentage	Bank
Apr 9	5th	(110)	$2111	(139)	$2636
	6th	(25)	2086	(132)	2504
	8th	(25)	2061	(125)	2379
Apr 10	3rd	(25)	2036	(119)	2260
	9th	(25)	2011	(113)	2147
Apr 14	1st	(25)	1986	(107)	2040
	3rd	(25)	1961	(102)	1938

FP-M Loss $260
Fixed Percentage Loss $737

3. The power of FP-M increases as the number of bets increases.

On that point, handicappers are advised to postpone profittaking until the size of the bets arouses the kind of psychological discomfort that distorts ordinary judgment.

4. The power of FP-M increases as the **differences** between the size of the winning bets and losing bets in alternating win-loss clusters increase.

5. The method works best where frequent win-loss clusters characterize play, but this should occur normally among successful handicappers.

Limitations. The constraints of FP-M betting are apparent from its positive aspects. Handicappers should consider the following:

1. FP-M wagering requires a relatively high proficiency in selecting winners at acceptable odds. At lower levels of proficiency the more frequent occurrences of alternating wins and losses counterbalances the basic design of the method.

2. A season's play or longer generates the kind of profits the method is designed to yield. Profit-taking on a monthly or bi-monthly basis does not apply.

3. The method is most sensitive to longer losing runs. Where these do not occur, the power of the method will be counteracted. As in the Santa Anita field study, fixed percentage wagering will yield higher profits where loss clusters remain relatively small.

THE SECOND COMING OF ANDREW BEYER

Late in 1983 handicappers were served a second helping from the storied horseplaying individualist Andrew Beyer—a book on the art of "trip" handicapping, with chapters on modern betting strategy and the indispensable attitudes and work habits of racetrack winners.

Eight years after his *Picking Winners* revealed an original and effective method of adjusting the raw final times of thoroughbreds, enabling American horseplayers to estimate the true speed of racehorses more reliably and popularizing speed handicapping to an extent hardly imagined by the author, Beyer returned with new perspectives on beating his game.

Profits on speed horses have slowed to trickles, Beyer complains, with so many mathematical types, computer whizzes, and numbers merchants spewing forth speed figures and thereby lowering track odds on top figure horses everywhere, sending hundreds of them postward as underlays. The customers beating the game in the eighties, asserts Beyer, are the trip handicappers, and in *The Winning Horseplayer* he proceeds to provide handicappers with the first comprehensive, experiential treatment of that fashionable topic.

Trip handicapping should not impact as widely on the general practice of handicapping as did Beyer's speed methodology, but Beyer accomplishes something crucially important in this book that he failed to do sufficiently in *Picking Winners*. He integrates trip handicapping with the handicapping process as a whole. He combines that which is essentially a technique—i.e., evaluating horses' trips—with a basic, fully developed and demonstrably effective handicapping orthodoxy, his own speed handicapping methodology. Thus what is promoted in *The Winning Horseplayer* is not merely the technique, which, if so promoted, thousands of handicappers might wrongly substitute for the art of handicapping, but a fully formed methodology that embraces both the incidental (trips) and the fundamental (speed and pace).

In his first contribution to the handicapping literature, Beyer refused to relate adjusted final times to other important factors of handicapping. Class was ardently eschewed, pace ignored. Speed figures, standing alone, represented the truth and the way. To handicappers not particularly persuaded of numerical differences of one, two, or a few points as the means to distinguish horses competing in a complicated game characterized by a sizable error factor, Beyer's speed handicapping, though itself laborious and rigorous, could not fairly substitute for the full-dress handicapping routine. Without interpretation guidelines, applying the numbers might become something of a parlor game, and the interpretive guidance seemed too often to be missing.

Beyer speed survived and prospered nonetheless, as the methodology was sound and, more importantly, because its speed quotient *is* an intrinsic characteristic of the racehorse. But if its speed ability supplies evidence about a horse that is intrinsic and fundamental, its trips do not. Trip handicapping is situational and circumstantial, and its importance to the correct analysis of any race may be incidental, not fundamental. The handicapper's capitulation to trip handicapping as a first and last resort can therefore be terribly misleading, unless trip analyses can be carefully entwined in a broader context of fundamental handicapping.

Beyer handles these issues impressively. Not only are trip analyses related to other crucial situational variables, notably track biases and pace, but in the book's most influential chapter Beyer cleverly interweaves trip information and speed figures. The lesson for handicappers of all persuasions should not be lost—trip information must be integrated with a handicapping orthodoxy that is far more fundamental, much more encompassing. Beyer makes that case well. This point of view might become his second book's most valuable legacy.

As Beyer says, trip handicapping involves a scheduled observation of horses in competition. The schedule of observations does not include watching the horses one has bet from flagfall to finish, a deeply ingrained tendency handicappers will have a devilish time changing. Beyer provides handicappers with tested procedures for watching races effectively, along with surprisingly simple notation for recording what has been systematically observed. The notation should not be underestimated. It is crucial to effective trip handicapping, which relies not only on observation skills but also on the efficient recording of all the combustion. Beyer's notation can be found at the conclusion of this piece. Surprising too, and happily so, is the lack of emphasis on the kinds of racing trouble that regularly beset horses and jockeys—stumbling at the start, taking up, checking, shuffling back, altering course, getting blocked, etc. Beyer instead concentrates more on running position, especially on the turns and entering the stretch.

When position is related to the presence or absence of a track bias, and in turn to considerations of pace, handicappers can readily appreciate the advantages trip handicapping promises. In a typical illustration, the notation 3B, 4T, 5E of a horse racing in outside paths down the backside, around the far turn, and into the stretch can denote either a positive or negative trip, depending on the bias, or perhaps on the pace set by frontrunners.

Beyer does something else in *The Winning Horseplayer* perhaps unexpected by his legions of speed fanciers. He achieves a point of view about trips vis-a-vis speed that handicappers everywhere might usefully ponder. In contrasting the two methods he now employs in combination, Beyer notes that whereas speed handicapping is mainly objective, trip handicapping is subjective; whereas speed handicapping is analytical, trip handicapping is visual; whereas speed handicapping is quantitative, trip handicapping is qualitative. Beyer avoids the temptation to translate into numbers information that is inherently descriptive. Beyer does not modify his speed figures with trip adjustments. He illustrates how those who do so might go badly astray and implores handicappers not to descend into those well-concealed traps.

Instead, Beyer recommends handicappers ask a series of logical questions about the trip information at hand. He lists the questions. Drawing on his extensive experience with trip information, Beyer then profiles the kinds of horses he most prefers and those he most strongly resists when trips have been juxtaposed to biases, pace, and speed figures. All of it adds up to a powerful methodology that combines vital information from past performances and vital information obtainable during the actual races.

Moreover, the practical problems many might expect to limit the successful practice of trip handicapping—notably getting to the racetrack daily—have been vastly overdrawn in Beyer's view. Indeed, handicappers hesitant to embrace trip handicapping because they cannot attend the races every day should not be so put off. Beyer shows that by attending the track twice a week, handicappers are able to see 80 percent of a week's trips. They just have to arrive in time to see the previous day's replays. In this way two days' attendance equals four days' trips.

With respect to modern betting strategy, Beyer promotes the advantages of exotic wagering, whereby handicappers can scramble key selections and the other contention of decipherable races. By this approach big money may more often result at small risk. Underlays in the win pools might become overlays in exotic combinations. Even prime selections bet seriously to win might be protected in the exotics, with smaller wagers on marginal horses that Beyer refers to as "savers," meaning of one's capital.

What Beyer espouses most is flexibility in betting strategy, counseling handicappers to free themselves of practices that demand comparable amounts be bet on each selection, i.e., fixed percentage wagering. Beyer contends handicapping selections reflect an array of opinions having numerous gradations of strength, such that the size of the wagers should be proportionate to the differences of one's opinions.

When betting seriously to win, Beyer advises handicappers to ask what would be the largest amount they could comfortably risk in the best of situations, i.e., when the prime selection and all the attending circumstances of the race appear to be ideal. From that threshhold handicappers are urged to downscale win bets in accord with the rigor of their opinions. Beyer's personal ceiling is $3000, an amount he invests a few times a season. Thus for him $100 spent on exotics represents 1/30th or 3 percent of his maximum, a comfortable risk.

Beyer does not expect others to implement his betting strategy as he does, but he cautions that risk capital should be relatively sizable to begin. In recounting how an acquaintance having a $2000 bankroll to start soon lost confidence and was forced to quit the game, Beyer concludes the man's bankroll was too thin to begin.

To be sure, $100 equals 5 percent of a $2000 stake, a relatively bold investment strategy, as computer simulations have shown. Studies also having revealed that handicappers are mostly spinning wheels with bets to win on horses at 3 to 1 odds or lower, Beyer's more aggressive strategy offers handicappers an alternative for backing all those properly bet or overbet horses that do figure.

Beyer concludes his resurrection by noting that winning attitudes belong to those who can deal effectively with (a) anger and (b) self-pity. He maintains that winning horseplayers are most likely to be those who collect the most meaningful information and work the hardest to interpret it smartly.

Those of us who have enjoyed opportunities to play the races for a time with Andy Beyer usually have chronicled the experiences to friends and others by adding to the man's legend as a big bettor and aggressive gambler. So be it. But few make the effort to point out, as Beyer gently does in *The Winning Horseplayer,* that his big bets are carefully structured and are based not only on considerable and fundamental information, but also on comprehensive skill in interpreting it.

And almost no one stops to mention that Andy Beyer collects more information and works harder with it than just about anybody else playing this difficult, challenging parimutuel game. If anyone doubts this or cares to dispute the point, let them read in this book how deliberately and painstakingly Beyer prepared for his 1983 attack on Santa Anita, beginning a year earlier in Washington, D.C. Beyer is a serious, studious, rigorous professional. When handicapping for profit, he's hard at work for long, long hours, to be sure. His books prove the point unmistakably.

A Notation System for Trip Handicapping

Stages of the Race

G   The gate; anything that happens at the start of a race
FT   First turn
B   Backstretch
T   Turn
E   Entering the stretch
S   Stretch

The Pace

Duel	A horse fighting for the lead
Stalk	A horse sitting behind a duel for the lead
Move	A horse accelerates strongly in a way that almost makes his rivals look as if they are standing still.
MIHP	Move into hot pace. A horse makes a strong move, but does it at a time when the leaders are accelerating, too.
Inherit	A horse gets the lead by taking over from rivals who have collapsed.

Types of Trouble

Slo	A horse breaks from the gate behind the field.
Rush	A horse rushes into contention suddenly after breaking slowly.
Steady	Mild trouble, caused by a lack of running room
Alter	A horse is forced to alter his course sharply.
NP	No push; the jockey is not asking his horse to run at some stage of a race.
Stiff	A jockey has not asked his horse to run at any stage of a race.
V	Vise; a horse is in heavy traffic without encountering actual interference.
GP	Good position; a horse is in the clear with no rivals inside or outside him.

Positions on the Track

Rail   A horse on the innermost part of the track. Each successive horse width from the rail is described as the 2-path, the 3-path, and so on. A notation of 3T would indicate a horse in the 3-path of the far turn.

Track Biases

GR	Good rail
GR+	Very strong good rail
BR	Bad rail
BR+	Very strong, bad rail
S	Speed-favoring track
S+	Very strong speed-favoring track
C	Track that favors closers

INTERNATIONAL RACING AND THE HANDICAPPER'S NEW BIG EDGE

Thoroughbred handicappers prosper to the extent they have useful information that other racegoers do not have. Information frontiers have receded rapidly in recent years. In the mid-seventies speed methods displaced more classical handicapping. Since then speed handicapping has lost ground to methods emphasizing trainer intentions and trip information. The idea behind all this change is to isolate overlays, horses sent off at odds greater than real abilities warrant. It is only by betting on true overlays that talented handicappers prosper.

In this context there is one relatively new and vital information frontier that has hardly been explored. Foreign-bred and foreign-raced horses have been competing in the United States in increasingly notable numbers during the past few seasons. When Santa Anita opened its doors for 1983–84, more than 500 foreign horses had a place in the track's 2100 stalls. Several competed every racing day—in stakes, in classified races, and in the nonwinners allowance series.

The handicapper's basic need is always information—in this case information about the group stakes and other stakes races the invaders have been contesting. How do the foreigners compare to their American counterparts? How do they compare to other foreign imports? In particular, handicappers need to know the relative quality of the stakes races foreign-bred and foreign-raced horses have won or almost won, including details on purse values and eligible age groups. Grade designations of foreign stakes are also vital, but the *Racing Form*'s past performance tables provide that information. Significantly, the *Form* does not provide the grade designations or purse values of the U.S. stakes, rendering key comparisons impossible for handicappers without charts. Even handicappers well-equipped with local charts are often adrift when confronted with shippers.

As one very remarkable illustration of the overlays this kind of information can illuminate, handicappers need only consider the 1983 Arlington Million, in which the favorite, **John Henry,** finished second. The upset winner was the three-year-old English invader **Tolomeo.** The colt paid $78.40 to win, sent off at odds of 38 to 1. The $2 Exacta at Arlington Park for the Million returned $439.20. Those payoffs are preposterous when handicappers consider that **Tolomeo** was a 4 to 1 shot in England.

What did the British players know that the Americans did not? Well, for one thing they knew **Tolomeo** was a "group" stakes winner that had recently placed in England's Grade 1 Sussex stakes. They knew, too, that the Sussex stakes was open to older horses as well and carried England's sixth highest purse value, the equivalent of $115,500. Now, did American horseplayers make **Tolomeo** their 38 to 1 shot in the Million? Did they couple the horse with **John Henry** to make the Exacta possibility, worth $439 for every two-spot? No, they didn't. They were blind to essential details, because these were not readily available.

To carry this illustration to an almost ridiculous conclusion, in early 1984 I received a letter from a gentleman named Winford J. Mulkey, of Siloam Springs, Arkansas. Mulkey had just purchased, if you will, *Quinn's International Stakes Catalogue,** a reference guide for handicappers that contains the vital information for every important stakes race in the world, and he was prompted to recall his experience at Louisiana Downs on Arlington Million day.

"I am wondering if you are aware that on the simulcast of the Arlington Million to Louisiana Downs at Bossier City, Louisiana, **Tolomeo** paid over $200.00 to win per $2.00 ticket

---

Quinn's International Stakes Catalogue ($19.95) is available from Foothills Publications, 30 South 1st Street, Suite 291, Arcadia, CA 91006. Add $1 for postage and handling.

and the [$3] Exacta paid over $6,000.00. I thought this might be of interest."

By remarking that "this might be of interest" to handicappers, Mulkey proves himself a master of understatement. He could also have observed that a $20 Exacta from a legitimate 4–1 horse to **John Henry** in the two hole would have netted handicappers $60,000.00 in one swoop. Can the handicapper's need for information about foreign horses and stakes races be dramatized any more convincingly than that? With simulcasting and local pari-mutuel pools now entrenched at many tracks throughout the country, similar opportunities are certain to arise in the near future. Only handicappers possessed of the appropriate information will be in a position to grab the advantage offered.

The *International Stakes Catalogue*, prepared by this writer, contains more than 1,000 listings and reveals the grade designations, purse values, and eligible ages for all the graded and listed stakes in Canada, England, France, Germany, Ireland, Italy, and the United States. It supplies some information about the Grade 1 stakes of Argentina and Chile and provides specific handicapping guidelines for interpreting the information accurately and using it effectively.

Regarding "listed" stakes, this is a new category of stakes in the United States but has existed in Europe for years. The stakes are considered just below the status of graded stakes in competitive quality and are judged important enough to be listed on the pages of international sales catalogues. Handicappers will soon learn that victories and close finishes in listed stakes signal a level of class superior to winners of unlisted stakes. Where one horse has won listed stakes and another has lost unlisted stakes, the class difference is often outstanding.

An illustration is in order. At Santa Anita's 1984 winter meeting, in the advanced nonwinners allowance competition, handicappers on February 11 confronted a turf sprint for nonwinners of four races of allowance grade or better. Two sharp-working foreign-raced colts made their first starts in the States in this particular contest. Can you tell the winner from the loser?

Orixo

Ch. c. 4, by Our Native—Bold Fluff, by Boldnesian
Br.—Kohler C F (Va)
Own.—Plesch Maria (lessee)   **113**   Tr.—Gosden John H M

					1983	3 1 0 0	$6,469
					1982	4 1 1 0	$30,206
	Lifetime	7 2 1 0	$36,675		Turf	7 2 1 0	$36,675

25Jun83 ◊ 3Newmarket(Eng) 7f	1:26⁴gd *9-5 122	① 11	Carson W	Van Geest	Thug, Lindas Fantasy, Montelin	12
14Jun83 ◊ 3Ascot(Eng) 1	1:40 gd *3½ 126	① 7	CrsonW	St Jms Plce(Gr2)	Horage, Tolomeo, Dunbeath	7
8Jun83 ◊ 2Newbury(Eng) 1	1:38⁴gd *4-5 114	① 14	Carson W	Hermitage	Orixo,HungrinPrince,LordProtctor	10
30Sep82 ◊ 4Newmarket(Eng) 6f	1:13¹gd 16 126	① 22½	CrsnW	Middle Park(Gr1)	Diesis, Orixo, Krayyan	5
10Sep82 ◊ 2Doncaster(Eng) 6f	1:14¹gd 3½ 123	① 12½	CrsonW	Mining Supply	Orixo, Coquilos Friend, Sharpish	25
24Jun82 ◊ 3Salisbury(Eng) 6f	1:15³gd 5 123	① 46½	CrsonW	Champagne	LyphrdsSpcl,GrnNrmndy,WhskTlk	13
10Jun82 ◊ 7Newbury(Eng) 6f	1:13¹gd 4 126	① 6¹⁰	CrsonW	Kennett(Mdn)	Talibah,HarvestBoy,BahrainPearls	18
Feb 6 SA 6f ft 1:14² h	Feb 1 SA 6f ft 1:12¹ h		● Jan 27 SA 7f ft 1:25 h	● Jan 22 SA 5f ft 1:12 h

Ice Hot

B. c. 4, by Icecapade—Beau Fabuleux, by Le Fabuleux
Br.—On The Rocks Farm (Ky)
Own.—Paulson A E   **113**   Tr.—McAnally Ronald

					1984	11 3 0 4	$52,832
					1983	3 1 1 0	$12,278
	Lifetime	14 4 1 4	$65,171		Turf	14 4 1 4	$65,171

9Oct83 ◊ 3Longchamp(Fra) a7f	1:19²fm 5½ 127	① 1½	DubrocqG	Px du Pin	IceHot, Lichine, AfricanJoy	18
22Sep83 ◊ 5MLaffitte(Fra) a1	1:36³gd 23 126	① 1²	AsssnC	Hcp de laTamise	Ice Hot, Mauve Lilas,WaterMelon	20
4Sep83 ◊ 3Longchamp(Fra) a1¾	2:05³gd 23 122	① 32½	PiggottL	Px del Table H	Port Franc, Regal Step, Ice Hot	24
24Aug83 ◊ 6Deauville(Fra) a1	1:43 gd 8½ 122	① 3½	GibertA	Px de Varavle	Dayzaan, Conerton, Ice Hot	7
15Aug83 ◊ 3Deauville(Fra) a1	1:39²gd 10 118	① 13	Head F	GrdHcp deDeville	BellTempo,FiddlersGreen,Relayeur	17
2Jly83 ◊ 5Evry(Fra) a1½	1:59²gd 17 128	① 44½	DbrcqG	Px Daphnis(Gr3)	Glenstal, Luderic, Redmead	7
Feb 8 SA 5f ft 1:04⁴ h		● Jan 27 SA 5f ft :59¹ h		Jan 20 SA 6f ft 1:12² h		Jan 14 SA 6f ft 1:14 h

Those who picked **Orixo** were sadly wrong. Its Hermitage win at 3 June 83 is unlisted; it finished dead last when favored in England's Grade 2 St. James Place, a $49,500 stakes restricted to three-year-olds, and subsequently ran badly in the unlisted Van Geest stakes. After winning the unlisted Mining Supply stakes at 2, **Orixo** finished second of five in a Grade 1 event, as a longshot. But the full record hardly supports this placing in a five-horse field and, as handicappers should appreciate, two-year-olds' performances not repeated at three do not translate readily into the four-year-old season.

Ice Hot's record tells a different tale. Last out the colt won the Pin stakes, a listed race run at Longchamp, France's flagship oval. The Pin purse was only $22,500, but the race was open to older horses. **Ice Hot** also placed in the listed Table stakes, a $33,150 race open to older horses, and was beaten only four lengths in the Grade 3 $38,250 Daphnis stakes for threes. Its single poor performance was a thirteenth in the listed Deauville stakes. Entered in two unlisted stakes, it won one, was beaten three-quarters in the other. All of this was accomplished at age three.

Having won a listed stakes in France, placed in another, and finished close in a Grade 3 stakes, the consistent **Ice Hot** looked more tempting than **Orixo**, notably so at the odds, and **Ice Hot** won handily at Santa Anita, paying $12.80. **Orixo**, the 5 to 1 favorite under Chris McCarron, was no factor in the race.

In three other 1984 Santa Anita examples, an English colt named **Airfield** was sent out by leading trainer Charles Whittingham against horses that had never won two allowance races. In its most recent races on the Continent, **Airfield** had finished second twice in listed stakes in England. The colt might just as well have dropped into the Santa Anita allowance race from a listed stakes in the United States. It won smashingly, paying $18.60.

In an especially notable situation, an Irish-bred horse, **Minnelli**, paid $13.60 at Santa Anita after beating sprinters that had not yet won even one allowance race. **Minnelli** had finished second of fifteen in Ireland's Moyglare stakes, now a Grade 1 sprint no less, having the second highest purse in that country. In the minor Santa Anita sprint, the Irish colt was nothing less than a standout.

And finally, in an extraordinary overlay, the filly **Bid for Bucks**, which had finished fifth of seventeen (beaten by just four lengths) in France's important Grade 1 Diane stakes, with a purse equivalent of $204,000, and had placed in another listed French stakes to boot, was sent to the post at Santa Anita versus nonwinners of two allowance races at 16 to 1. Under Bill Shoemaker, the stakes-placed French filly won in a breeze, returning $35.00

The key to unlocking all of the above is information that reveals relative class. Handicappers need to know the grade designations, purse values, and age restrictions of the foreign races. They need to know which stakes are listed and which are not. That information is not found in the *Daily Racing Form*'s past performance tables, thus it's the player's newest, biggest edge. To be sure, even when foreign horses figure on class, they sometimes lose, either because they have not raced recently and form is short or because the U.S. distance or footing is uncomfortable. So be it. Foreign horses that do win regularly pay mutuels large enough to overcompensate for the losers.

Well-informed handicappers finish comfortably in the black.
International racing is a sign of the times. It's happening
everywhere. Handicappers who have until now been flying by
the seat of their pants when it comes to evaluating foreign
horses need to adapt, to prepare to seize the moment. They
need the information that helps them differentiate one stakes
race from another, the few hundred important stakes from the
other thousands. That information is the new big edge. Smart
handicappers will want to take that edge.

FORM DEFECTS, FORM ADVANTAGES

The latest research on thoroughbred form indicates that horses can be absent from the races for six months or more, but if they have worked five furlongs or longer within fourteen days of today's race, they are acceptable. In 1968, Ainslie's classic chapter on form advised handicappers that horses that did not show a race and a workout within the past seventeen days, or if unraced had not worked out within the past twelve days, should be eliminated.

The divergent views reflect the most significant trend in form analysis across the past decade at least, a dramatic shift from conservative to liberal interpretations of form information. If the publication in 1984 of William L. Scott's *How Will Your Horse Run Today?* means anything, it is this: Handicappers will get more from their wagering dollars as soon as they begin to liberalize their standards of acceptable form. Remaining rigid or even strict with traditional form guidelines means eliminating too many winners, many of them at juicier prices than "good form" horses have normally returned.

Scott's intention with his form research was to identify more specific handicapping guidelines than previously had been clarified, a purpose at which he succeeded impressively, but the specifics speak volumes about the more general trends that all smart handicappers must abide.

Besides the warning to loosen the grips on firmer form standards, handicappers need to be cautioned more specifically that recency has been overrated and the positive stretch gain has also been greatly overrated. Handicappers have known for years now, since the first national probability studies hit the market in the mid-seventies, that powerful stretch performers won no more than the expected share of their next starts. Often they were overbet. Scott's descriptive data support the probabilities. The book awards pluses to four of the five form factors its author studies, but no matter what, horses cannot be considered at advantage next time due to outstanding performance in the stretch.

Before summarizing Scott's specific findings, it is important to understand the evolutionary context. Historically, the American horseplayer has confronted two persistent, fundamental problems with form analysis. First, operational definitions of good and bad form were practically nonexistent prior to 1968. Because the horse populations and racing calendars were so different, Robert Saunders Dowst, the leading handicapping author of the thirties and forties, virtually ignored the form factor. No one else much bothered with the matter until Ainslie set forth his numerous elimination and selection guideposts. Since then, more rigorous examinations of specific "good" and "bad" form standards have crystallized the second historical problem—horses having "good" form regularly collapse on the profit criterion. Positive form horses win more races than probability estimates would expect, but they also toss considerable losses while winning. The probability studies of form proved mainly that the public bets too much money on good form prospects. These go postward as underlays and are often favored to win.

What has been needed by students of the *Daily Racing Form* are carefully observed empirical studies of highly specific form indices that operate within the well-established parameters of recent action and acceptable performance. Author Scott has contributed exactly that kind of research, precisely those kinds of results, concentrating first in 1981 on a 433-race sample encompassing Belmont Park, the Meadowlands, Keystone, and Bowie racetracks, next testing initial discoveries variously at selected tracks around the nation, culminating with a 500-race national replication during 1982.

A key result has been designated the "form defect," or a disadvantage on form that predicts reliably which horses will probably lose. As form defects are often characteristic of favorites and low-priced underlays, those eliminations open the handicapping decisions to solid prospects at better prices, the overlays by which handicappers make their way. Horses were also found to enjoy form advantages, and these can be incorporated into the rating processes of whatever methods handicappers of varying persuasions might prefer. A third rating category has been called "neutral." Neutral ratings are acceptable, but inconclusive.

Scott explored five topics of interest, after his original investigations identified these as the directions of most promise. The five include recency, the last usable running line, stretch performance, last race winners, and declining-improving cycles of performance. There are four rating symbols:

0   Form defect; eliminate.
N   No significant impact, or neutral; accept.
+   A plus factor; give extra credit.
U   Unknown; do not rate.

It's instructive to list Scott's crucial results in regard to recent action. The first plus factor will be familiar to handicappers, but the second will not, and the remaining four findings suggest that in the future more horses than ever will be acceptable on recency.

+   Has run within seven days or less than today
+   Has run within twenty-one days of today and has either:
    a. a 5f bullet workout within fourteen days, or
    b. a 5f workout that is exceptionally fast, i.e., in the East or Midwest at :59⁴⁄₅ or less; in the West at :58⁴⁄₅ or less
N   Has run within twenty-one days of today's race
N   Has run within twenty-eight days of today's race and has worked 4f within the past week
N   Regardless of layoff time, has worked 5f or longer within fourteen days.
0   Has not run in twenty-one days, without a qualifying workout.

Scott has labeled his plus factor for exercise in the morning "the fabulous five-furlong workout," explaining the move is both unusual and tremendously impactful at all tracks below the rank of New York and Southern California. Scott makes clear that sharp recent action is more of an advantage to racehorses than dull recent form is a disadvantage.

Scott shows handicappers how best to evaluate what he

calls "the last usable running line," which is normally the last race, provided it was run within the past twenty-eight days and was not unrepresentative due to class or footing differences or to notable trouble lines. The rating depends on the presence or absence of "up close" position, usually at the stretch call. Being "up close" is defined variously, in relation to distance, as follows:

a. sprints up to 6½ furlongs   2¾ lengths
b. races at 7f and 1M   3¾ lengths
c. races at 1¹⁄₁₆ miles or farther   4¾ lengths

Horses are generally acceptable on performance if they were "up close" at the stretch call, but horses dropping in class can be up close at any call, and horses shortening distance by a furlong or more can be up close at the pre-stretch call. A well-defined fall back–gain again pattern is also acceptable. A plus is awarded only to horses "up close" at every call of the last race, provided that race is "usable."

All horses that do not qualify for the plus or neutral ratings receive a "0," a form defect, to be eliminated. The exceptions are "U" horses, including first starters, first starters on grass, and foreign horses in their first United States race.

This research recommends handicappers attend more to recent performance patterns than to recent action of itself. That is, performance indices surpass training indices.

Horses get no pluses for stretch performance, as mentioned. If they were "up close" at the stretch call last out in a ratable race and lost one length or more in the stretch, handicappers are urged to give them a form defect.

Which horses that won last out are likely to repeat today?

In general, and absolutely for horses rising in class, it's the horses graduating from a "big win," or victory by at least three lengths, and having another plus factor for form. Maiden graduates must satisfy those twin conditions as well, but horses not moving ahead in class can show two form pluses of any kind, or even a single plus factor if they also reveal high consistency. The material on last-out winners is a vital and new wrinkle to unlocking the class-form interplay that has bedeviled handicappers for years. Scott cautions that as many as nine of ten last-out winners do not repeat, and he sets up strict repeat-win conditions to protect handicappers from that downside.

In the book's most complicated and technical sections, Scott presents an arithmetical technique for identifying declining and improving form. The procedure relies on information provided by the *Form*, final times and speed ratings, but three preconditions must coexist before the ratings can be calculated. To be eligible, horses must show at least a length gain (closer to the leader) at the stretch calls of their previous two races, and the races must represent the same class and distance. Where those conditions are present, handicappers will apply a handy technique for evaluating declining and improving form numerically. It's a convenient and valid advance.

Scott's kind of research is empirical—descriptive, iterative, laborious, and a function of scheduled observations involving numerous reexaminations of the same data, until plausible patterns apparent on first observations have been confirmed for the total sample of races. The research method does not examine prearranged hypotheses but instead follows a kind of intuitive search for what works, in this case the specific characteristics of the form cycle associated with relatively large numbers of winners.

Because the research is descriptive, it intends to describe a group or class of predefined populations, or races. These have not been sampled randomly. This reduces the generalizability of the findings, not in any essential way, but in particular variations that may differ from track to track, notably at racetracks with different horse populations and racing programs from the five that comprised this study, including its application for a day at Golden Gate Fields. Minor tracks are not well represented here, and handicappers there and elsewhere are recommended to conduct local replications.

It's rather easy, to be sure. As one interesting approach, if the percentage of winners having form defects were divided by the percentage of starters having form defects, say for a group of 250 to 400 races, the resulting quotient would be an impact value (I.V.), or probability index. That value should be 0.50 or lower.

In short replications of two weeks or less, this writer applied the book's findings to Hollywood Park, Keystone, Santa Anita, Golden Gate Fields, and Arlington Park. They worked, impressively. They did not work as well for three days at Longacres, a small track near Seattle.

At the end of his exposition, characterized by the same logical progression of thought and inquiry that marked his *ability times* research in *Investing at the Racetrack,* all of it exceptionally well qualified and illustrated, Scott elaborates four methods handicappers might use to apply the information. Three concentrate on favorites and low-priced choices. The fourth opens itself to fundamental handicapping and allows its practitioners to fasten on overlays, even longshots. Recreational handicappers can rightfully be expected to concentrate their personal energies at method four.

IDEAS THAT NO LONGER APPLY

The monumental probability studies conducted by researchers Fred Davis and William Quirin have alerted handicappers at all major tracks as to the traditional practices in need of revision or abolition. That laundry list appears immediately below. Where local studies contradict the national samples, local results can apply, provided (a) the research questions are identical, (b) local samples are sufficiently large and representative, such that random samples contain at least 200 races and nonrandom samples contain at least 500 races, (c) the local statistical methods obtained probability values by dividing the percent of winners having a pp characteristic by the percent of starters having the characteristic, and (d) the local samples are not subjectively biased, i.e., only represent the selections or winning selections of a particular public selector or small group of same.

Handicappers whose methods of selection, or methods of separating contenders, or rating methods, or methods of making figures are influenced by the past performance characteristics reflected in the scientific findings reported here can improve their effectiveness either by eliminating the factor or by doing the opposite, whichever the data suggests.

Horses with a blowout on the day preceding a race enjoy no statistical advantage. All studies demonstrate that a recent race is more influential than a recent workout.

Inconsistency is no basis for eliminating horses as contenders. Although consistent horses win more than a fair share of their races, inconsistent horses win enough, and horses that only have won one of their previous 10 starts win almost their fair share of the races they enter. This is particularly true in claiming races.

The stretch gain is overrated as an impending sign of victory. Horses able to pass 1-2 others inside the stretch call or gain 1-2 lengths at that point usually retain the sharp form, but are at no significant advantage.

Points for less weight, points off for higher weight, turns reality upside down. Higher-weighted horses race at such a statistical advantage, the researchers argue that racegoers that have no time for handicapping might as well support the top weight in each field. In stakes and handicaps it is risky to bet against the heavyweights.

Favorites on the turf win at approximately the same rate as their counterparts on dirt, but their rate of loss on a series of wagers is half-again as great.

Apprentice jockeys perform almost as well as journeymen, even at the route. Horsemen that have long held the horse makes the rider have been statistically sustained.

Excepting inside posts on grass or in certain route races, post position has incidental effect on race outcomes.

Leading claiming trainers win more than their share of the races, but are overbet. Handicappers should require their horses deserve the odds the crowd allows.

Speed duels do not ruin the chances of the horses that engage in them, particularly in sprints. Early speed is so important horses are not fairly eliminated because they figure to contest another horse early.

The inside horse in speed duels has no real advantage.

Almost every North American racetrack, under normal racing conditions, favors horses with good early speed. Quirin has referred to early speed as the universal track bias.

On drying tracks early speed horses do not tire enough to lose their customary advantage to come-from-behind types. Early speed does best on sloppy tracks, but statistics suggest tiring tracks tire the other horses as much as they do the speed burners.

At mile tracks the number one post position is at no disadvantage in sprints. The one post in fact is the most powerful. It is less potent in one-turn routes (mile or longer), but still at slight advantage.

Frederick S. Davis, "Thoroughbred Racing: Percentages and Probabilities," *Millwood Publications*, New York, 1974 (various), and

William Quirin, "Winning At The Races: Computer Discoveries in Thoroughbred Handicapping," *William Morrow and Company*, New York, 1979 (various).

Routers dropping back to sprints do not win nearly their fair share, but sprinters stretching out do. The likeliest sign of success is a recent sprint finish in-the-money or within two lengths of the winner.

Impressive maiden special winners do move into nonwinners allowance competition successfully, winning half again their rightful share of the allowance starts.

In sprints, freshened horses fare better in the second start after a layoff, but only if the first start reveals a good and not overexerting performance.

Freshened routers do best if they return to competition in a pair of sprints before stretching out. Only one sprint warm-up has deteriorating effects.

Allout stretch drives from the quarter pole or eighth pole do not sap horses' energy reserves. These competitors win better than expected next out. The data holds for sprints and routes.

Better than the stretch gainers are horses that bid at the second or third calls, but hung in the drive, losing, yet finishing in the front half of the field.

Horses that flash surprise early speed, which they usually lack, are not good bets next time. Typically, these simply revert to their familiar style, which does not include early speed.

Weight shifts are of little importance, in either sprints or routes.

When entered in races limited to their sex, females can repeat previous victorious as often as males, can carry high weight as effectively, and can withstand allout stretch drives just as well.

Recent action is unimportant in two-year-old racing.

Early speed does not stand up on turf as on dirt. The single exception is the lone frontrunner, capable of securing the clear lead. These win, pay 20 percent on the dollar.

AINSLIE'S COMPLETE GUIDE
TO THOROUGHBRED RACING

The literature of handicapping passed the high-water mark in 1968 when Simon and Schuster of New York published *Ainslie's Complete Guide To Thoroughbred Racing*, by Tom Ainslie, also of New York. The substance and exposition of this work proved so influential in their effects the publication's impact far exceeded giving racegoers the most complete codification of handicapping theory and method yet elaborated. There would be enormous external rippling effects, the most important of which was that the intellectual character of racing and handicapping had been persuasively and gracefully communicated to interested publics as not before, and these publics would come to accept the ideas as they never had. Playing the races became legitimized, intellectually, and not just to horseplayers who suddenly became handicappers, but also to book publishers, the marketplace, and even the racing Establishment. With sales in excess of 100,000 and still selling strongly in 1982, 'The Complete Guide has established itself as the undisputed leader and classic in the dubious field of handicapping instruction. The content and integrity of the book mark it at once as the fundamental source for newcomers as well as an advanced and fully integrated kind of handicapping for professionals. To be sure, all who read the book end the experience with a deeper respect for the sport of racing and the joys of handicapping, hardly an inconsequential legacy.

Of effects that go beyond the practice of handicapping, handicappers might consider these:

1. Tens of thousands of reasonably bright racegoers came to understand their sport in its participative aspects, thereby enhancing their personal pleasure and satisfaction when playing the game, even while thousands more took up the pursuit

of a game that had been fully exposed as a stimulating and rewarding pastime.

2. The market for handicapping literature of substance opened widely and expanded fantastically. Thus came to die the ancient but much-revered myth that horseplayers can't read. The message had been sounded loudly, clearly. Racing is formful, skillful players can beat the game, and here's practically everything you need to know. It was all absolutely so.

3. In consequence of one and two, publishers of books discovered a market surprisingly large for handicapping instruction. The several important books that have come to life since trace directly or indirectly to the commercial success of 'The Complete Guide. Publishers now appreciate the handicapping market can be at least 100,000 strong, with annual sales remaining brisk for those works perceived by the market to be standards.

4. The comprehensive and integrated body of knowledge about the nature of racing and handicapping contained in 'The Complete Guide became the hypotheses and propositions stimulating the first truly scientific investigations of handicapping ever conducted. The probability studies of Fred Davis and Bill Quirin, conducted on a national scale, were completed and published, affording handicapping a scientific basis at last. There followed numerous local, smaller-scale studies, and countless personal studies conducted most seriously by individuals in quest of handicapping's profits. In the subsequent findings of these studies, for the most part 'The Complete Guide was sustained. Portions that science indicated to need revision received precisely such revisions in 1979, when Ainslie refined parts of the content.

5. At least seven of the prominent handicapping authors for the seventies and eighties trace in lineage to 'The Complete Guide, or to its author, in writer Ainslie's various capacities as publisher, editor, and co-author of handicapping works of merit. To wit: Fred Davis, Steven Davidowitz, William Quirin, Henry Kuck, Bonnie Ledbetter, James Quinn, and lately William L. Scott. Authors that might never be published

---

Tom Ainslie, "Ainslie's Complete Guide To Thoroughbred Racing," *Simon and Schuster*, New York, 1968, 21 Chapters, 470 pages.

otherwise, or if they had been, would otherwise have found a much more restricted market for themselves, owe 'The Complete Guide a nod for their own special place in this specialized field.

6. The attitudes, values, and personal qualities attached by the book to successful handicappers, to handicapping, and to racetrack participation, of the deliberate, informed, and goal-directed kind, were of an ambience widely and happily reinforced by anyone professionally concerned with the substance, integrity, and professional conduct of the sport. This was a book indeed men of such stature as Santa Anita director of racing Jimmy Kilroe could applaud and promote as representing the best of the sport. No unimportant matters, these.

7. Author Ainslie established himself as a leading authority on handicapping. The skill of handicapping and its instruction enjoyed a contemporary figurehead, such that others might establish themselves as figures in the field as well. And others did. In this important role Ainslie has continuously conducted himself as a model that serves the field and all that are a part of it. As this is written an already well-represented field of study grows larger and stronger still, with the hucksters and quick-fix artists losing ground every season, with much of the expansion a part of 'The Complete Guide's not inconsiderable legacy.

Of handicapping as an art and a game, the book's contributions are many and lasting. A few of the larger gifts:

1. The theory and method of comprehensive handicapping, a method which encompasses all the handicapping factors, their interrelations, and the priorities these obtain under various conditions of racing.

2. Guidelines for distinguishing playable-unplayable races.

3. Criteria and guidelines for evaluating the past performance records of horses specifically as well as comprehensively, notably numerous elimination guidelines that reliably crystallize the real contention of any race.

4. A conceptual and practical framework for exploring the critical dynamics of class-form and speed-pace. A

preponderance of the important work that has followed has greatly concerned itself with deeper investigations of these crucial elements.

5. A classic chapter on the variations of thoroughbred form, and unprecendented operational definitions of same.

6. Pointedly clear perspectives on the arithmetic of racing and the economics of the sport, and how each affects the lives of handicappers.

7. A definitive glossary and index, a framework for evaluating systems and methods, guidelines for paddock and post parade inspections, and a who's who of racing's jockeys and trainers.

Surely this was a bellwhether book.

SECRETARIAT

Let horsemen, owners, racing officials, and racing fans quarrel about the history of events if they must, but handicappers have united on the argument as to which horse is the greatest of them all. It is **Secretariat**, the phenomenal son of the great Bold Ruler. The red colt raced only at two and three, in that second season altering for all times the conduct of the sport and its business by contributing within the six months from May 5 to October 28 of 1973

(a) the first Triple Crown sweep in 25 years and in such consummate style that new and standing classic and racetrack time records were erected for the Kentucky Derby, the Preakness, and the Belmont Stakes,

(b) the ground-shattering breeding syndication price of six million dollars, for services at stud,

(c) the most devastating series of six consecutive Grade 1 stakes triumphs ever witnessed at American racetracks, and

(d) the single greatest racing performance yet delivered in the history of Thoroughbred racing.

To the testament of others it is greatly appropriate to conclude a first comprehensive review of the handicapping literature by adding to the praise of the horse, as Secretariat has left to handicappers the very real time model of Thoroughbred class and speed. When Secretariat's name appears in the literature of handicapping, it is invariably invoked as a simile or metaphor that illuminates the author's point about class. At those moments the horse and his races return vividly to the mind, almost 10 years afterwards.

Of the single greatest performance of them all, Secretariat's glorious dance in The Belmont Stakes of 1973, handicapping authors Andy Beyer and Steve Davidowitz have borrowed from the virtuoso act to illustrate special considerations in handicapping. Beyer asserts that speed handicappers enjoyed the earliest insight as to the horse's special dimensions. For Secretariat at two, Beyer had recorded a speed figure of 129, by far the highest figure ever accorded a two-year-old, and almost the highest figure ever accorded any horse. On the Monday following the 1973 Belmont Stakes, Beyer sat down to record his figures for that day's races in New York. He writes:

> "Secretariat earned a figure of 148 that day—so much higher than any race I had ever seen that the horse had seemed to step into a different dimension. . .
>
> Romanticists could appreciate Secretariat for his strength, his grace, his exciting style of running. But for me the most awesome moment of his career came two days after the Belmont Stakes, when I sat down with my paper, my pencil, and the Belmont charts, calculated my track variant and wrote down the number 148 for the eighth race that day. For a true addict, speed figures ar the most beautiful part of the game."

Steve Davidowitz experienced a different kind of peak on that exciting Saturday in New York. He recalls the remarkable Sham's valiant efforts to beat the great horse in The Kentucky Derby and The Preakness.

> "In the Derby Secretariat went very wide on both turns and with power in reserve outdrove Sham from the top of the stretch to the wire. . .
>
> In The Preakness, while under no special urging, Secretariat made a spectacular move around the clubhouse turn—from last to first—passing Sham in the back-stretch. For the final half of the race Pincay slashed his whip into Sham with wild fury. Turcotte, aboard Secretariat, never moved a muscle. But Sham never gained an inch. At the wire he was a tired horse."

As the Belmont Stakes approached, Davidowitz focused on the Exacta. Secretariat was coming to the race of his life, while Sham was a tired and already-beaten horse. Given an overbet second choice in small fields, where one horse figures a legitimate standout, Davidowtiz tells how to benefit from Exacta overlays. Merely eliminate the overbet second choice. Wheel the prime selection to the nondescript others. When Sham disappeared in the Belmont, Secretariat ran off into history, and Steve Davidowitz not only revelled in the moment, but also cashed a $2 Exacta worth $35.

Here for the reading pleasure of handicappers are reprints of the results charts for the six consecutive Grade 1 stakes races in which Secretariat astonished the racing world. During the series this incredible racehorse erased five racetrack time records at five different distances, from one and one-eighth miles to one and one-half miles. Against older horses in the inaugural running of The Marlboro Cup at Belmont Park in New York, Secretariat set the standing world record for a mile and one-eighth. Given just two attempts on grass, Secretariat demonstrated that he was also the greatest turf runner of all time. As the charts and the races they signify are recalled, handicappers should remember too that in 1973 both the three-year-old and older handicap divisions luxuriated in a surplus of some of the finest racing talent of the decade. In none of the races was Secretariat fully extended.

NINTH RACE CD May 5. 1973

1¼ MILES. (2:00). Ninety-ninth running KENTUCKY DERBY. SCALE WEIGHTS. $125,000 added. 3-year-olds. By subscription of $100 each in cash, which covers nomination for both the Kentucky Derby and Derby Trial. All nomination fees to Derby winner, $2 500 to pass the entry box, Thursday, May 3, $1,500 additional to start, $125,000 added, of which $25,000 to second. $12,500 to third, $6,250 to fourth. $100,000 guaranteed to winner (to be divided equally in event of a dead-heat). Weight, 126 lbs. The owner of the winner to receive a [gold] trophy. Closed with 218 nominations.
Value of race, $198,800. Value to winner $155,050; second, $25,000; third, $12,500; fourth, $6,250.
Mutuel Pool, $3,284,962.

Last Raced	Horse	EqtAWt	PP	¼	½	¾	1	Str	Fin	Jockeys	Owners	Odds to $1
4-21-73^{7} Aqu^{3}	Secretariat	b3 126	10	11^{h}	$6^{½}$	5^{1}	$2^{1½}$	$1^{½}$	$1^{2½}$	RTurcotte	Meadow Stable	a-1.50
4-21-73^{7} Aqu^{2}	Sham	b3 126	4	5^{1}	3^{2}	2^{1}	$1^{½}$	2^{8}	2^{8}	LPincayJr	S Sommer	2.50
4-26-73^{6} Kee^{2}	Our Native	b3 126	7	$6^{½}$	$8^{1½}$	8^{1}	5^{h}	3^{h}	$3^{½}$	DBrumfield	Pr'ch'd-Thom's-R'q't	10.60
4-26-73^{6} Kee^{5}	Forego	3 126	9	$9^{1½}$	$10^{½}$	$6^{½}$	6^{2}	$4^{½}$	$4^{2½}$	PAnderson	Lazy F Ranch	28.60
4-28-73^{7} CD^{2}	Restless Jet	3 126	1	$7^{1½}$	7^{h}	$10^{1½}$	$7^{1½}$	$6^{1½}$	$5^{2½}$	MHole	Elkwood Farm	28.50
4-28-73^{7} CD^{1}	Shecky Greene	b3 126	11	$1^{1½}$	1^{3}	$1^{1½}$	3^{3}	5^{4}	$6^{1½}$	LAdams	J Kellman	b-5.70
4-26-73^{6} Kee^{6}	Navajo	b3 126	5	$10^{1½}$	10^{1}	11^{4}	$8^{1½}$	8^{2}	7no	WSoirez	J Stevenson-R Stump	52.30
4-26-73^{6} Kee^{7}	Royal and Regal	3 126	8	3^{1}	4^{3}	4^{3}	4^{1}	$7^{1½}$	$8^{3½}$	WBlum	Aisco Stable	28.30
4-26-73^{6} Kee^{1}	My Gallant	b3 126	12	8^{h}	$11^{1½}$	12^{3}	11^{2}	$10^{½}$	9^{h}	BBaeza	A I Appleton	b-5.70
4-21-73^{7} Aqu^{1}	Angle Light	3 126	2	4^{h}	$5^{1½}$	7^{1}	$10^{1½}$	$9^{1½}$	$10^{1½}$	JLeBlanc	E Whittaker	a-1.50
5- 1-73^{8} CD^{5}	Gold Bag	b3 126	13	2^{h}	2^{h}	$3^{½}$	9^{1}	11^{1}	11no	EFires	R Sechrest-Gottdank	68.30
4-28-73^{7} CD^{6}	Twice a Prince	b3 126	6	13	13	13	13	12^{2}	$12^{1½}$	ASantiago	Elmendorf	62.50
4-26-73^{6} Kee^{3}	Warbucks	3 126	3	12^{1}	12^{3}	9^{h}	$12^{1½}$	13	13	WHartack	E E Elzemeyer	7.20

a-Coupled, Secretariat and Angle Light; b-Shecky Greene and My Gallant.
Time, :23⅖, :47⅖, 1:11⅘, 1:36⅕, 1:59⅖ (new track record). Track fast.

$2 Mutuel Prices:			
1A-SECRETARIAT (a-Entry)	5.00	3.20	3.00
5-SHAM		3.20	3.00
8-OUR NATIVE			4.20

Ch. c, by Bold Ruler—Somethingroyal, by Princequillo. Trainer, L. Laurin. Bred by Meadow Stud, Inc. (Va.).
IN GATE—5:37. OFF AT 5:37 EASTERN DAYLIGHT TIME. Start good. Won handily.

SECRETARIAT relaxed nicely and dropped back last leaving the gate as the field broke in good order, moved between horses to begin improving position entering the first turn, but passed rivals from the outside thereafter. Turcotte roused him smartly with the whip in his right hand leaving the far turn and SECRETARIAT strongly raced to the leaders, lost a little momentum racing into the stretch where Turcotte used the whip again, but then switched it to his left hand and merely flashed it as the winner willingly drew away in record breaking time. SHAM. snugly reserved within striking distance after brushing with NAVAJO at the start, raced around rivals to the front without any need of rousing and drew clear between calls entering the stretch, was under a strong hand ride after being displaced in the last furlong and continued resolutely to dominate the remainder of the field. OUR NATIVE, reserved in the first run through the stretch, dropped back slightly on the turn, came wide in the drive and finished well for his placing. FOREGO, taken to the inside early, veered slightly from a rival and hit the rail entering the far turn, swung wide entering the stretch and vied with OUR NATIVE in the drive. RESTLESS JET saved ground in an even effort. SHECKY GREENE easily set the pace under light rating for nearly seven furlongs and faltered. NAVAJO was outrun. ROYAL AND REGAL raced well for a mile and had nothing left in the drive. MY GALLANT, outrun at all stages, was crowded on the stretch turn. ANGLE LIGHT gave way steadily in a dull effort and was forced to check when crowded by GOLD BAG on the stretch turn. GOLD BAG had good speed and stopped. TWICE A PRINCE reared and was hung in the gate briefly before the start and then showed nothing in the running. WARBUCKS was dull.

EIGHTH RACE
Pim
May 19, 1973

1$\frac{3}{16}$ MILES. (1:54). Ninety-eighth running PREAKNESS STAKES. SCALE WEIGHTS. $150,000 added. 3-year-olds. By subscription of $100 each, this fee to accompany the nomination. $1,000 to pass the entry box, starters to pay $1,000 additional. All eligibility, entrance and starting fees to the winner, with $150,000 added, of which $30,000 to second, $15,000 to third and [illegible] to fourth. Weight, 126 lbs. A replica of the Woodlawn Vase will be presented to the winning owner to remain his or her personal property. Closed Thursday, Feb. [illegible] with 194 nominations.
Value of race $182,400. Value to winner $129,900; second, $30,000; third, $15,000; fourth, $7,500.
Mutuel Pool, $922,989.

Last Raced	Horse	EqtAWt	PP	St	¼	½	¾	Str	Fin	Jockeys	Owners	Odds to $1
5- 5-73^{9} CD^{1}	Secretariat	b3 126	3	6	$4\frac{1}{2}$	$1\frac{1}{2}$	$1^{2\frac{1}{2}}$	$1^{2\frac{1}{2}}$	[illegible]	[illegible]Turcotte	Meadow Stable	.30
5- 5-73^{9} CD^{2}	Sham	b3 126	1	4	$3^{1\frac{1}{2}}$	4^{3}	$2^{1\frac{1}{2}}$	2^{5}	[illegible]	[illegible]PincayJr	S Sommer	3.10
5- 5-73^{9} CD^{3}	Our Native	b3 126	4	5	5^{h}	5^{8}	4^{3}	3^{3}	[illegible]	[illegible]Brumfield	Mrs M J Pritchard	11.90
5-12-73^{6} Pim^{1}	Ecole Etage	b3 126	6	1	$1^{1\frac{1}{2}}$	2^{2}	$3\frac{1}{2}$	4^{10}	[illegible]	[illegible]Cusimano	Bon Etage Farm	11.30
5- 5-73^{7} Pen^{1}	Deadly Dream	b3 126	2	3	6	6	6	6	[illegible]	[illegible]SBlack	Wide Track Farms	35.50
5-12-73^{6} Pim^{5}	Torsion	3 126	5	2	$2\frac{1}{2}$	3^{h}	5^{14}	5^{3}	[illegible]	[illegible]MFeliciano	Buckland Farm	39.00

Time, :24⅖, :48⅕, 1:11⅖, 1:35⅘, 1:5[illegible]. Track fast.
(Daily Racing Form Time 1:53⅖ New Track Record).

$2 Mutuel Prices:			
3-SECRETARIAT	2.60	2.20	2.10
1-SHAM		2.20	2.20
4-OUR NATIVE			2.20

Ch. c, by Bold Ruler—Somethingroyal, by Princequillo. Trainer, [illegible] Laurin. Bred by Meadow Stud Inc. (Va.).
IN GATE—5:40. OFF AT 5:40 EASTERN DAYLIGHT TIME. Start good. Won handily.

SECRETARIAT broke well and was eased back and relaxed nicely as the field passed the stands the first time. He was guided outside two rivals entering the clubhouse turn and responding when Turcotte moved his hands on the reins, made a spectacular run to take command entering the backstretch. SECRETARIAT was not threatened thereafter and was confidently hand ridden to the finish. SHAM broke to the right and brushed with DEADLY DREAM leaving the gate, then drifted in and hit the rail entering the clubhouse turn. Pincay swung SHAM out entering the backstretch and roused him in pursuit of the winner but he could not threaten that rival in a game effort. OUR NATIVE, reserved between rivals early, rallied to gain the show. ECOLE ETAGE, hustled to the lead, gradually weakened after losing the advantage. DEADLY DREAM stumbled then was brushed by SHAM just after the break and was outrun thereafter. TORSION, stoutly rated early, could not menace when called upon.

(The :25, :48⅘, 1:12, 1:36⅕ and 1:55 as posted by the electric timer during the running was invalidated after a 48-hour interval by a stewards' ruling, and the above time reported by official timer E. T. McLean Jr. was accepted as official. Scratched—The Lark Twist.

EIGHTH RACE
Bel
June 9, 1973

1½ MILES. (2:26⅗). One Hundred-fifth running BELMONT. SCALE WEIGHTS. $125,000 added. 3-year-olds. By subscription of $100 each to accompany the nomination; $250 to pass the entry box; $1,000 to start. A supplementary nomination may be made of $2,500 at the closing time of entries plus an additional $10,000 to start, with $125,000 added, of which 60% to the winner, 22% to second, 12% to third and 6% to fourth. Colts and geldings. Weight, 126 lbs.; fillies, 121 lbs. The winning owner will be presented with the August Belmont Memorial Cup to be retained for one year, as well as a trophy for permanent possession and trophies will be presented to the winning trainer and jockey. Closed Thursday, Feb. 15, 1973, with 187 nominations.
Value of race $150,200. Value to winner $90,120; second, $33,044; third, $18,024; fourth, $9,012.
Mutuel Pool, $519,689. Off-track betting, $688,460.

Last Raced	Horse	EqtAWt	PP	¼	½	1	1¼	Str	Fin	Jockeys	Owners	Odds to $1
5-19-73^{8} Pim^{1}	Secretariat	b3 126	1	1^{h}	1^{h}	1^{7}	1^{20}	1^{28}	1^{31}	RTurcotte	Meadow Stable	.10
6- 2-73^{6} Bel^{4}	Twice a Prince	3 126	4	4^{5}	4^{10}	3^{h}	2^{h}	3^{12}	$2\frac{1}{2}$	BBaeza	Elmendorf	17.30
5-31-73^{6} Bel^{1}	My Gallant	b3 126	3	3^{3}	3^{h}	4^{7}	3^{2}	2^{h}	3^{13}	ACorderoJr	A I Appleton	12.40
5-28-73^{8} GS^{2}	Pvt. Smiles	b3 126	2	5	5	5	5	5	$4\frac{3}{4}$	DGargan	C V Whitney	14.30
5-19-73^{8} Pim^{2}	Sham	b3 126	5	2^{5}	2^{10}	2^{7}	4^{8}	$4^{1\frac{1}{2}}$	5	LPincayJr	S Sommer	5.10

Time, :23⅗, :46⅕, 1:09⅘, 1:34⅕, 1:59, 2:24 (new track record) (against wind in backstretch). Track fast.

$2 Mutuel Prices:			
2-SECRETARIAT	2.20	2.40	...
5-TWICE A PRINCE		4.60	...

(NO SHOW MUTUELS SOLD)

Ch. c, by Bold Ruler—Somethingroyal, by Princequillo. Trainer, L. Laurin. Bred by Meadow Stud, Inc. (Va.).
IN GATE—5:38. OFF AT 5:38 EASTERN DAYLIGHT TIME. Start good. Won ridden out.

SECRETARIAT sent up along the inside to vie for the early lead with SHAM to the backstretch, disposed of that one after going three-quarters, drew off at will rounding the far turn and was under a hand ride from Turcotte to establish a record in a tremendous perfomance. TWICE A PRINCE, unable to stay with the leaders early, moved through along the rail approaching the stretch and outfinished MY GALLANT for the place. The latter, void of early foot, moved with TWICE A PRINCE rounding the far turn and fought it out gamely with that one through the drive. PVT. SMILES showed nothing. SHAM alternated for the lead with SECRETARIAT to the backstretch, wasn't able to match stride with that rival after going three-quarters and stopped badly. Scratched—Knightly Dawn.

Exacta (2-5) Paid $35.20; Exacta Pool, $274,110; Off-Track Betting, $334,273.

SEVENTH RACE 1⅛ MILES (chute). (1:46⅕). First running MARLBORO CUP. HANDICAP. By invitation. Purse $250,000. Purse to be divided 60% to the winner, 22% to second, 12% to third and 6% to fourth. Trophies to be presented to the winning owner, trainer and jockey.

Bel

September 15, 1973

Value of race, $250,000. Value to winner $150,000; second, $55,000; third, $30,000; fourth, $15,000.
Mutuel Pool, $595,169. Off-track betting, $325,311.

Last Raced	Horse	EqtAWt	PP	St	¼	½	¾	Str	Fin	Jockeys	Owners	Odds to $1
8-4-73^{7} Sar^{2}	Secretariat	b3 124	7	6	5^{4}	5^{4}	3^{2}	1^{2}	1^{3}½	RTurcotte	Meadow Stable	b-.40
8-21-73^{7} Sar^{1}	Riva Ridge	b4 127	6	2	2^{1}	2^{1}	1½	2^{6}	2^{2}	EMaple	Meadow Stable	b-.40
7-23-73^{8} Hol^{1}	Cougar II.	7 126	2	7	7	7	7	3^{1}	3^{6}½	WShoemaker	Mary F Jones	a-4.00
9-8-73^{7} Bel^{7}	Onion	4 116	3	4	1½	1h	2h	4½	4^{2}½	JVelasquez	Hobeau Farm	14.30
8-25-73^{8} Mth^{2}	Annihilate 'Em	3 116	4	3	4^{1}½	3h	4h	5^{2}	5½	ACorderoJr	Patricia Blass	21.70
8-18-73^{7} Dmr^{1}	Kennedy Road	5 121	5	1	3^{1}	4h	5^{5}	6^{1}½	6^{2}	DPierce	Mrs A W Stollery	a-4.00
7-21-73^{7} Aqu^{1}	Key to the Mint	b4 126	1	5	6^{6}	6^{4}	6^{1}	7	7	BBaeza	Rokeby Stable	3.50

b-Coupled, Secretariat and Riva Ridge; a-Cougar II. and Kennedy Road.
Time, :22⅗, :45⅘, 1:09⅕, 1:33, 1:45⅖ (new American and world record) (against wind in backstretch). Track fast.

$2 Mutuel Prices:

2B-SECRETARIAT (b-Entry)	2.80	2.80	2.40
2-RIVA RIDGE (b-Entry)	2.80	2.80	2.40
1-COUGAR II. (a-Entry)			3.00

Ch. c, by Bold Ruler—Somethingroyal, by Princequillo. Trainer, L. Laurin. Bred by Meadow Stud, Inc. (Va.).
IN GATE—4:50. OFF AT 4:50 EASTERN DAYLIGHT TIME. Start good. Won ridden out.

SECRETARIAT, unhurried away from the gate, moved around horses to reach contention after going the half, drifted out a bit leaving the turn, headed RIVA RIDGE with three sixteenths remaining and drew away under brisk handling. RIVA RIDGE, prominent from the outset, took over when ready racing into the turn, remained well out in the track while making the pace into the stretch but wasn't able to stay with SECRETARIAT while holding COUGAR II. safe. COUGAR II., off slowly, settled suddenly approaching the stretch, altered course when blocked attempting to split horses nearing midstretch and finished with good energy. ONION showed good early foot while racing well out from the rail but had nothing left for the drive. ANNIHILATE EM made a run along the inside approaching the end of the backstretch and was finished soon after going three quarters. KENNEDY ROAD, steadied along while between horses on the backstretch, gave way approaching the stretch. KEY TO THE MINT showed nothing.

SEVENTH RACE 1½ MILES (turf). (2:25⅘). Fifteenth running MAN O' WAR. Weight For Age. $100,000 added. 3-year-olds and upward. By subscription of $200 each, which shall accompany the nomination; $500 to pass the entry box; $500 to start, with $100,000 added. The added money and all fees to be divided 60% to the winner, 22% to second, 12% to third and 6% to fourth. Weight for age. 3-year-olds, 121 lbs.; older, 126 lbs. The N.Y.R.A. to add The Man o' War Bowl to be won three times, not necessarily consecutively, by the same owner before becoming his or her property. The owner of the winner will also receive a trophy for permanent possession and trophies to the winning trainer and jockey. Closed with 23 nominations.

Bel

October 8, 1973

Value of race $113,600. Value to winner $68,160; second, $24,992; third, $13,632; fourth, $6,816.
Mutuel Pool, $428,256. Off-track betting, $188,300.

Last Raced	Horse	EqtAWt	PP	¼	½	1	1¼	Str	Fin	Jockeys	Owners	Odds to $1
9-29-73^{7} Bel^{2}	Secretariat	b3 121	3	1^{1}½	1^{3}	1^{3}	1^{1}½	1^{3}	1^{5}	RTurcotte	Meadow Stable	.50
9-27-73^{8} Atl^{1}	Tentam	b4 126	1	3^{1}½	3^{3}	2^{2}	2^{8}	2^{10}	2^{7}½	JVelasquez	Windfields Farm	3.60
9-22-73^{7} Bel^{2}	Big Spruce	b4 126	7	7	7	7	7	5^{2}	3½	ASantiago	Elmendorf	6.90
9-22-73^{7} Bel^{3}	Triangular	6 126	4	5h	6^{5}	6^{2}	4½	3½	4^{2}½	RCSmith	Hobeau Farm	25.40
9-22-73^{7} Bel^{1}	London Company	3 121	6	6^{4}	5^{1}	5^{1}	3½	4^{2}	5^{7}	LPincayJr	Chance Hill Farm	8.40
8-4-73^{7} Sar^{5}	West Coast Scout	b5 126	5	4^{2}	4^{2}	4^{1}½	6^{3}	6^{3}	6^{6}	ACorderoJr	Oxford Stable	25.90
9-21-73^{7} Bel^{1}	Anono	b3 121	2	2^{1}	2^{1}½	3^{1}½	5h	7	7	MVenezia	A D Schefler	38.60

Time, :23⅘, :47, 1:11⅗, 1:36, 2:00, 2:24⅘ (new course record) (against wind in backstretch). Track firm.

$2 Mutuel Prices:

1A-SECRETARIAT	3.00	2.40	2.20
2-TENTAM		3.00	2.60
7-BIG SPRUCE			3.20

Ch. c, by Bold Ruler—Somethingroyal, by Princequillo. Trainer, L. Laurin. Bred by Meadow Stud, Inc. (Va.).
IN GATE—4:48. OFF AT 4:48 EASTERN DAYLIGHT TIME. Start good. Won ridden out.

SECRETARIAT, away in good order, moved to the fore from between horses nearing the finish line the first time, saved ground after opening a clear lead around the first turn, responded readily to shake off a bid from TENTAM after going three-quarters, turned back another bid from that rival approaching the stretch and drew away under a hand ride. TENTAM, never far back while saving ground, eased out to go after SECRETARIAT entering the backstretch, wasn't able to stay with that one after going three-quarters, made another run midway of the far turn but was no match for the winner while besting the others. BIG SPRUCE, outrun to the stretch, passed tired horses. TRIANGULAR was always outrun, as was LONDON COMPANY. WEST COAST SCOUT was finished at the far turn. ANONO showed good early foot but had nothing left after going a mile.

Scratched—Dendron, Star Envoy, Apollo Nine, Riva Ridge.

EIGHTH RACE 1 5-8 MILES, MARSHALL COURSE (2:41). Thirty-Sixth Running CANADIAN INTERNATIONAL CHAMPIONSHIP STAKES. $125,000 Added. 3-year-olds and upward. Weight for age (European scale). 3-year-olds, 117 lbs.; older, 126 lbs. Fillies and mares allowed 3 lbs. (No Canadian-bred allowance). By subscription of $150 each which shall accompany the nomination and an additional $750 when making entry. The added money and all fees to be divided 65% to the winner, 20% to second, 10% to third and 5% to fourth. Closed Saturday, September 15, 1973, with 58 nominations

Woodbine

October 28, 1973

Gross value of race, $142,700. Value to winner, $92,755; second, $28,540; third, $14,270; fourth, $7,135. Mutuel Pool, $ 81 485.

Last Race	Horse	Eqt	A	Wt	PP	¼	½	1	$1\frac{3}{8}$	Str	Fin	Jockey	Owner	Odds $1
10- 8-73 ^{7}Bel^{1}	Secretariat	b	3	117	12	$2^{4\frac{1}{2}}$	2^{8}	2^{6}	1^{5}	1^{12}	$1^{6\frac{1}{2}}$	MapleE	Meadow Stable	.20
10- 8-73 ^{7}Bel^{3}	Big Spruce	b	4	126	4	12	11^{h}	10^{6}	5^{h}	4^{1}	$2^{1\frac{1}{2}}$	SantiagoA	Elmendorf	13.45
10-13-73 ^{8}Spt^{3}	Golden Don	b	3	117	6	11^{1}	9^{h}	8^{2}	8^{5}	$5^{2\frac{1}{2}}$	$3^{\frac{3}{4}}$	Mang'n'lloM	Donaldson-Goldchamp	28.90
10-20-73 ^{7}WO^{3}	Presidial		4	126	9	$3^{1\frac{1}{2}}$	3^{h}	$4^{1\frac{1}{2}}$	$3^{\frac{1}{2}}$	3^{h}	4^{4}	HawleyS	Windfields Farm	23.15
10-20-73 ^{7}WO^{1}	Fabe Count		5	126	8	4^{1}	$5^{\frac{1}{2}}$	6^{5}	6^{h}	6^{h}	$5^{\frac{3}{4}}$	DuffyL	Parkview Stable	24.40
10- 8-73 ^{7}Bel^{4}	Triangular		6	126	1	8^{1}	8^{4}	5^{1}	7^{2}	8^{3}	6^{nk}	SmithRC	Hobeau Farm	32.55
10-20-73 ^{7}WO^{4}	Top of the Day		3	117	2	10^{1}	12	$11^{1\frac{1}{2}}$	9^{h}	9^{5}	$7^{1\frac{1}{2}}$	PlattsR	Gardiner Farm	85.10
10-20-73 ^{7}WO^{2}	Twice Lucky	b	6	126	7	$7^{\frac{1}{2}}$	4^{2}	$3^{2\frac{1}{2}}$	4^{3}	7^{1}	$8^{\frac{1}{2}}$	DittfachH	C Smythe	45.40
10-21-73 ^{8}WO^{1}	Kennedy Road		5	126	5	$1^{1\frac{1}{2}}$	$1^{1\frac{1}{2}}$	$1^{\frac{1}{2}}$	2^{7}	2^{h}	9^{5}	GomezA	Mrs A W Stollery	9.25
10-21-73 ^{7}WO^{2}	Tico's Donna		5	123	10	5^{1}	6^{h}	$7^{\frac{1}{2}}$	10^{5}	10^{3}	$10^{3\frac{1}{2}}$	McMahonW	F Stronach	57.65
10-20-73 ^{7}WO^{5}	Roundhouse	b	5	126	3	9^{1}	10^{h}	12	11^{4}	11^{8}	11^{11}	GrubbR	M Resnick & W Walsh	121.70
10-20-73 ^{7}WO^{6}	Fun Co K.	b	4	126	11	6^{h}	7^{3}	9^{h}	12	12	12	VasquezJ	Mrs M D Keim	90.70

Time, :24, :47⅗, 1:11⅗, 1:37⅗, 2:41⅘. Course firm.

$2 Mutuel Prices:			
12-SECRETARIAT	2.40	2.50	2.10
4-BIG SPRUCE		4.40	2.90
6-GOLDEN DON			4.50

Ch. c, by Bold Ruler—Somethingroyal, by Princequillo. Trainer, L. Laurin. Bred by Meadow Stable Inc. (Va.).
IN GATE—4:52. OFF AT 4:52 EASTERN STANDARD TIME. Start good. Won ridden out.

SECRETARIAT stalked the early pace while under restraint, came outside KENNEDY ROAD in the backstretch, dueled with that one to the far turn, took command thereafter to open up a long lead a furlong out and was under mild intermittent pressure to prevail. BIG SPRUCE, well back early, closed willingly. GOLDEN DON came outside into the home lane and outfinished the balance. PRESIDIAL saved ground early while stalking the leaders but never threatened. FABE COUNT could not keep up. TRIANGULAR was never a serious threat. TWICE LUCKY, a contender at the mile, faded thereafter. KENNEDY ROAD set the early pace under restraint, dueled with SECRETARIAT in the backstretch but could not stay into the far turn.

Exacta (12-4) Paid $7.60—Exacta Pool, $129,545

EPILOGUE

GOLDEN SHOE

An extended tribute to jockey William Shoemaker, of Southern California, who turned 50 August 19, 1981, and eleven days later delivered still another unlikely ride, this time to win the inaugural Arlington Million by a nose.

To call him the best of his time is obvious, but obligatory. That his time endures after 33 seasons may not be altogether surprising. That it endures at the sport's apex, without trace of diminishing skill or desire, is unique.

Thoroughbred racing awarded Shoemaker its 1981 Eclipse for outstanding achievement by a jockey, the sport's highest honor, and until now the only tribute to have eluded him. It was richly deserved.

He has been Wee Willie, Silent Shoe, Willie the Shoe, The Shoe, and simply Shoe.

Henceforth he shall be Golden Shoe.

by James Quinn

(**Author's introduction.** *In 1970, when first I followed the thoroughbreds on the Southern California circuit, jockey William Lee Shoemaker was 39 years old. By large consensus he was past his prime. Racing people who sensed in me a keen, continuing interest in the sport sympathized greatly when the conversation turned to Shoemaker. Too bad you missed his great years, they would say. Shoe was really something, back then.*

Five seasons passed before I had begun at last to appreciate what Shoemaker actually does atop a thoroughbred during a race. Riding ability is a multifaceted thing. It remains darkly obscure to most customers and insiders alike of this widely misunderstood sport.

In 1978, when he started briskly, I decided to follow the Shoemaker style closely, using binoculars and the experience I felt had prepared me well enough for the task. By coincidence I selected a season that stands as one of his best, perhaps his best ever. Two important rides remain indelible in the memory, and forever shall. Only a truly great rider could have won either race. Because the races represent two of the most important of the racing calendar, one in California, the other in New York, I choose to lead with them for this extended tribute.

It was in 1978 too that leading handicapping authority Tom Ainslie, of New York, wrote than handicappers of Southern California were privileged to watch Shoemaker guide his horses day after day. That has been my privilege for a decade now. By any standard this is one of the most remarkable athletes of the century.

The following attempts to capture the talents and qualities that combine to make the 4'11", 100-pound, 50-year-old Shoemaker so extraordinary.)

Vigors, the Great White Tornado of Santa Anita's 1978 winter season, to recall, became a legend in his time by falling behind the best horses in training, by as many as 30 lengths, and then unleashing a long late run of such devastating speed and power he would win by daylight. When in the Santa Anita Handicap **Vigors** repeated the spectacular run for the third time within months, some veteran horsemen were moved to acclaim the horse the best stretch-runner of all time.

What must not be conveniently forgotten in the tale is that **Vigors** of 1978 was a five-year-old. The horse had raced for two seasons previously, on turf, a footing its breeding promised would be its best, with no distinction. But it rained relentlessly during Santa Anita 1978. The turf course was closed down. Among many other turf specialists **Vigors** was switched to the main track. That he was fast becoming a champion on dirt surprised everyone, including the horse's owner, trainer, and jockey. The vicissitudes of racing can be pleasantly surprising too.

Vigors jockey that Santa Anita was Darrel McHargue, one of the nation's best, and eventually the 1978 winner of racing's jockey Eclipse, for overall outstanding performance. McHargue was 23 years old. He happened to be aboard for the first of **Vigors** unexpected rampages. He stayed up, naturally, as the stretch runs were repeated. Naturally too turf reporters noted that McHargue, of the patient, sit-still style, fit this late-running monster perfectly.

No one will deny McHargue rode **Vigors** perfectly that Santa Anita. Then too most often McHargue and jockeys of that high caliber ride any horse in the barns correctly. As the horse was not expected to do so, McHargue rode under no pressure to win. Even in the rich, prestigious Santa Anita Handicap, whatever pressures had accumulated remained squarely on the horse, not its jockey. Everyone wondered still whether the Great White Tornado would turn loose his wild charge again. The horse did, coming from farther back than before, and under the patient, poised direction of Darrel McHargue.

Now it's two months later at Hollywood Park. That track's rich, prestigious Hollywood Gold Cup has arrived. Darrel McHargue will ride **Vigors**, who is now not only a heavy pre-race favorite, but absolutely expected to win. Even more. By this time **Vigor's** owner W. R. Hawn has announced the horse will be shipped East following the big Hollywood race, to compete in New York's Fall championship series. The objective is Horse-of-the-Year honors. The pressure has increased, terrifically.

The 1978 Hollywood Gold Cup was unusually star-studded. Three horses were divisional champions, another a near-champion. Bill Shoemaker was named on the marvelous handicap star **Exceller**, owned by Nelson Bunker Hunt, and the best racehorse that sportsman-industrialist has ever campaigned. Oddly, as had **Vigors**, **Exceller** had raced exclusively on turf until that year's rains forced him to try the dirt. As did **Vigors**, **Exceller** completed the transition remarkably well, retaining top handicap form. Although versatile as to running style, **Exceller** too was best when permitted to lag behind the pace and complete one long late run. Accordingly, **Exceller** was not expected to win the 1978 Hollywood Gold Cup. To out-finish perhaps the best stretch-runner of all time?

In the field too was **J.O. Tobin**, champion sprinter of 1978,but best remembered for having slaughtered champion **Seattle Slew** in Hollywood Park's Swaps Stakes at one mile and one-quarter when both horses were three-year-olds. Now four, **J. O. Tobin** had not repeated that smashing style in races prior to the Gold Cup, especially at longer distances against top-rank competition. His habit of spending too much of his blazing speed and tiring in the final stages should help **Vigors'** Gold Cup, in the handicapping sense, but a **J.O. Tobin** on a faraway lead sure can put the scare into a jockey whose horse is 30 lengths behind.

As events proceeded, **Vigors** lost the Hollywood Gold Cup, a race he had to win, and a race he should have won. He finished third, beaten a neck and a head. The finish proved hotly controversial, as **Vigors** was "floated" wide in midstretch by a tiring **J.O. Tobin**.

The winner on the deep inside was **Exceller**. It was one of Shoemaker's greatest rides, characterized by a combination of timing, patience, and poise that few athletes can summon and maintain consistently in the tensest moments of the strictest competition, when the slightest lapse means sure defeat. In this important race Shoemaker kept his mount three to five lengths **behind Vigors** as the horses raced down the back-stretch. To imagine that another horse should race behind one of the greatest stretch runners of all time and beat that fabled finisher at the wire would have been unthinkable prior to the race.

That it happened just that way remains a sweet testimonial to Shoemaker, who on that day demonstrated once again that which is the greatest asset of the champion athletes, the highest order of performance under the severest of pressures. Shoemaker's timing, patience, and poise would not have mattered in that Gold Cup had jockey McHargue not lost his in the heat of the moment. The floating incident bothered **Vigors**, all right, but it did not cause the horse to lose. **Vigors** actually regained the lead, briefly, following the incident, but as the race's result chart accurately noted, ". . . **Vigors**. . . hung at the wire," meaning the horse had lost its acceleration and drive and was doing its best to stay even.

Vigors' defeat resulted in fact from an error far more fundamental. His jockey moved too soon. In that definitive fixture, with a champion speed horse on the lead, and everyone from the horse's owner to the lowliest swipe expecting **Vigors** to win with his customary explosion, an extremely talented jockey chased the pace prematurely. He did not dare to disappoint so many by not getting there in time.

But pace is tyrannical. By moving up earlier than normal, when McHargue turned into the stretch, instead of arriving there with the Great White Tornado, the jockey arrived with a tiring horse. That horse could not simply blow by another tiring horse, was bothered, and eventually would "hang" at the wire.

To be sure, Bill Shoemaker sometimes waits and loses. This happens too in races as rich and important as the Hollywood Gold Cup. On one such occasion, a writer grabbed at Shoemaker as he hopped off the weighing scale shortly following the big race. Shoemaker's horse had been favored to win, and despite finishing well, ended a length or so short.

What happened, asked the reporter.

He didn't get there, responded Shoemaker, and, unblinkingly, walked off to the jockeys' room.

Shoemaker did not assure his interrogator he had ridden the horse properly. He did not explain that had he moved earlier, the horse might have had no energy towards the end. He did not mention mishaps in the running or problems with the footing or with other horse traffic. He merely stated the obvious, that despite best efforts by horse and jockey, things did not work out.

Major league jockeys must develop a diverse array of riding skills and competitive qualities, but none supersedes the capacity to at once (1) understand the needs, problems, capacities, and idiosyncracies of their mounts, and (2) respond in kind to the demands of races, pressures notwithstanding. At times the two purposes conflict, and cannot be happily reconciled. When this happens, the best of jockeys normally choose to maintain rapport with their mounts. To put it differently, they do what is best for the horse. Shoemaker does this, unstintingly. He loses a few races each season that way. But he wins much more frequently, when races unravel to his mount's liking or, as in the Hollywood example, when another rider, through lapse of technique or judgment, takes his horse's best race away.

Months later that 1978 season, in October, Shoemaker and **Exceller** were joined again, this time for Belmont Park's Jockey Club Gold Cup, the most prestigious race on the New York handicap calendar, and at the classic mile and one-half **Exceller's** best distance. Now **Exceller** was running for Horse-of-the-Year honors. He again was not expected to win. The track was sloppy. In a small field the class of the opposition were **Seattle Slew** and **Affirmed**.

Against these champions in the slop Shoemaker again dropped **Exceller** far behind the early pace, which was blistering fast. At one point **Exceller** appeared distanced. In the stands owner Bunker Hunt felt little hope. Halfway around the far turn **Seattle Slew** drew clear of the other frontrunners. **Affirmed**, in dulling form, proved no factor. Shoemaker and **Exceller** were 22 lengths behind. Suddenly the two began a tremendous run.

Coming from that far disadvantage in the slop with a surge along the inside rail, **Exceller** caught **Seattle Slew** in the upper stretch and passed him, seeming to draw away. Under Angel Cordero, Jr. **Seattle Slew** fought back. In turn **Exceller** responded to that, and the two fought doggedly for three-sixteenths of a mile. **Exceller** prevailed, to win by a nose. It was as gallant and precious a show of Thoroughbred class and virtuoso jockeying as any racing fan will ever see.

In the grandstand far above, Bunker Hunt, almost incredulous, knew he had experienced something special in those moments, that peaking kind of sensation we rarely feel. He would later call it the greatest racing thrill of his life.

Hollywood Gold Cup

EIGHTH RACE
Hollywood
JUNE 25, 1978

1 ¼ MILES. (1.58⅕) HOLLYWOOD GOLD CUP HANDICAP. 39th Running. Purse $350,000 guaranteed. 3-year-olds and upward. By subscription of $150 each, to accompany the nomination, $750 to pass the entry box and $2,000 additional to start, with $192,500 guaranteed to the winner, $70,000 to second, $50,000 to third, $25,000 to fourth, $8,500 to fifth and $4,000 to sixth. Weights Monday, June 19. Starters to be named through the entry box by closing time of entries. A Gold Cup of original design will be presented to the owner of the winner. Trophies will be presented to the winning trainer and jockey. Nominations closed Wednesday, June 14 with 19 nominations.

Value of race $350,000, value to winner $192,500, second $70,000, third $50,000, fourth $25,000, fifth $8,500, sixth $4,000. Mutuel pool $1,010,937.

Last Raced	Horse	Eqt.	A.Wt	PP	¼	½	¾	1	Str	Fin	Jockey	Odds $1
29May78 ^{8}Hol^{1}	Exceller		5 128	7	7	7	7	$6^{2\frac{1}{2}}$	$4^{1\frac{1}{2}}$	1^{nk}	Shoemaker W	a-1.20
29May78 ^{8}Hol^{5}	Text	b	4 118	6	4^{3}	4^{5}	$3^{\frac{1}{2}}$	2^{2}	$3^{1\frac{1}{2}}$	2^{hd}	Castaneda M	29.00
4Jun78 ^{8}Hol^{1}	Vigors	b	5 129	4	6^{3}	$6^{2\frac{1}{2}}$	5^{hd}	$3^{1\frac{1}{2}}$	$2^{\frac{1}{2}}$	3^{4}	McHargue D G	.70
14May78 ^{8}Hol^{1}	J. O. Tobin		4 128	1	$1^{2\frac{1}{2}}$	$1^{3\frac{1}{2}}$	1^{6}	1^{6}	$1^{1\frac{1}{2}}$	$4^{2\frac{1}{2}}$	Cauthen S	a-1.20
28May78 ^{5}Hol^{1}	Palton		5 114	5	$5^{\frac{1}{2}}$	5^{1}	$6^{3\frac{1}{2}}$	7	6^{2}	5^{4}	Moreno H E	96.50
4Jun78 ^{8}Hol^{2}	Mr. Redoy		4 116	2	2^{1}	$3^{1\frac{1}{2}}$	4^{4}	4^{hd}	5^{3}	6^{5}	Pincay L Jr	7.50
17Jun78 ^{8}Hol^{3}	Juan Don		4 112	3	3^{1}	2^{2}	$2^{1\frac{1}{2}}$	5^{1}	7	7	Campas R	81.80

a-Coupled: Exceller and J. O. Tobin.

OFF AT 5:59, PDT. Start good, Won driving. Time, :22⅗, :45⅖, 1:09⅕, 1:33⅗, 1:59⅕ Track fast.

$2 Mutuel Prices:				
	1-EXCELLER (a-entry)	4.40	2.60	2.10
	6-TEXT		8.60	2.10
	4-VIGORS			2.10

B. h, by Vaguely Noble—Too Bald, by Bald Eagle. Trainer Whittingham Charles. Bred by Engelhard Mrs C W (Ky).

EXCELLER showed no early speed, began his bid at the five-sixteenths pole, came around horses to the upper stretch, found an opening between horses while settling into the final furlong and closed steadily to share the lead inside the sixteenth pole then was gradually going away at the end. TEXT, taken in hand and rated to the half mile pole, closed ground while narrowing the gap on the pacemaker, responded to stiff urging through midstretch and, continuing to gain, held the edge briefly between calls just inside the sixteenth pole and kept up his bid to the end in a good try. VIGORS checked just inside the sixteenth pole then showed no early speed, caught his full stride into the far turn to loom a threat at the head of the stretch then was repeatedly floated out yet kept to his task to almost be on the lead fifty yards from the finish and hung. J. O. TOBIN showed the most speed at the outset to sprint to a long lead, drifted out when leaving the stretch turn, began to weaken steadily and had little left in the final furlong. PALTON was outrun. MR. REDOY raced within striking distance of the pacemaker in the opening half but faltered. JUAN DON appeared overmatched.

Owners— 1, Belaire Stud Ltd & Hunt; 2, Elmendorf; 3, Hawn W R; 4, Combs & El Peco Ranch & Hunt; 5, Pinetree Stable; 6, Yoder F J; 7, Lepaulo V.

Trainers— 1, Whittingham Charles; 2, Clyne Vincent; 3, Sterling Larry J; 4, Barrera Lazaro S; 5, Moreno Henry; 6, Doyle A T; 7, Johnson E Oren.

The Jockey Club Gold Cup

EIGHTH RACE
Belmont
OCTOBER 14, 1978

1 ½ MILES. (2.24) 60th Running THE JOCKEY CLUB GOLD CUP. $300,000 Added. (Third leg of fall championship series). 3-year-olds and upward at weight for age. By subscription of $200 each, which shall accompany the nomination; $1,000 to pass the entry box; $2,000 to start, with $300,000 added. The added money and all fees to be divided 60% to the winner, 22% to second, 12% to third and 6% to fourth. Weight for age. 3-year-olds, 121 lbs. Oller, 126 lbs. Starters to be named at the closing time of entries. The Jockey Club will present a Gold Cup to the owner of the winner, and trophies to the winning trainer and jockey and momentos to the grooms of the first four finishers. Closed with 14 nominations.

Value of race $321,800, value to winner $193,080, second $70,796, third $38,616, fourth $19,308. Mutuel pool $555,865, OTB pool $304,219.

Last Raced	Horse	Eqt.	A.Wt	PP	¼	½	1	1¼	Str	Fin	Jockey	Odds $1
30Sep78 ^{8}Bel^{2}	Exceller		5 126	5	5^{6}	5^{8}	4^{6}	2^{7}	$1^{\frac{1}{2}}$	1no	Shoemaker W	3.80
30Sep78 ^{8}Bel^{1}	Seattle Slew		4 126	1	$1^{\frac{1}{2}}$	1^{hd}	$1^{2\frac{1}{2}}$	1^{hd}	2^{14}	2^{14}	Cordero A Jr	.60
30Sep78 ^{8}Bel^{4}	Great Contractor	b	5 126	6	6	6	6	5^{14}	$3^{\frac{1}{2}}$	$3^{4\frac{3}{4}}$	Hernandez R	22.50
30Sep78 ^{4}Bel^{1}	One Cut Above		4 126	3	4^{7}	4^{2}	5^{7}	$4^{\frac{1}{2}}$	5^{26}	4^{nk}	Cruguet J	53.10

In his tribute to jockey Shoemaker the author argues only a truly great rider could have delivered either of the performances charted above, coming from far behind to win by the narrowest margins the 1978 Gold Cups of California and New York.

Riding Ability Defined

So the ideal rider, first of all, establishes rapport with his mount and as best he can meshes its needs and capacities with the demands of the race. Whether the occasion is a $20,000 claiming race or a definitive stakes worth several hundred thousand dollars, he rides in a way that suits his horse. Versatile runners aside, if the converse is tried, altering horses capacities to suit race demands, either by changing running styles or by pressing limits, the game is lost. The best of jockeys won't do it.

Since all of this must be accomplished within seconds, the ideal rider must develop superlative instincts and reflexes. Talent counts most. Experience helps tremendously.

Few jockeys would have completed the handicap double just detailed. A moment's impatience, a single premature move, a move too-long delayed, just of bit of time or ground lost here or there, and all is lost. None of the necessary precision can occur unless horse and jockey remain in perfect harmony throughout, even as the combustion of the action intensifies.

The ideal rider displays remarkable handling. If a horse races too fast, the jockey slows it. If it races too slow, the jockey quickens it. If the early pace is too hotly contested, the jockey snugs his horse back, away from a struggle that will doom it later. If the pace is plodding, the jockey loosens his grip, guiding the horse to the front, or towards the front, so that it might be positioned to make an effective stretch run. If trouble occurs, or traffic develops, the jockey anticipates the problems and smoothly steers his horse into the clear, while not breaking stride and losing momentum. All of this is done with the hands. Some might say the head.

Shoemaker analysts never forget to mention his hands. He is widely recognized to have the surest pair ever, light, sensitive, knowing, of the kind that invite no resistance whatsoever from horses. In fact, Shoemaker's hands are thought so talented several established trainers regularly use him to handle younger, developing horses who run rank (out of control) with their generous portions of natural speed. Speed outbursts of that kind sooner or later become self-defeating, usually sooner. Shoemaker's job is to control the horse's speed quotient, first settling it into a slower pace, and without struggling or fighting against one another, next measuring its speed out efficiently (the technique known as "rating") as the horses race through the early and middle furlongs of races, finally gathering the animal's reserves together, for a final fast run through the stretch. If the horse runs out of gas, the jockey has failed.

Other trainers use Shoemaker's hands to educate "green" horses, uneducated types that have not yet learned what to do and when to do it. One of these is the aforementioned Whittingham.

In Southern California trainer Whittingham conditions horses for some of the most prosperous, most demanding patrons of the sport, including Hunt, British soccer pools magnate Robert Sangster, Florsheim heiress Mary Jones Bradley, Howard B. Keck, Serge Fradkoff, and others, including numerous powerful racing patrons from other countries. The horses are regally-bred and targeted from the outset at stakes races.

Shoemaker routinely rides the Whittingham horses. What few understand, including many patrons he services, is the extent to which the Shoemaker touch is employed deliberately at the onset of horses' competitive seasoning programs, a critical phase of the training process. The pattern repeats itself season after season. The jockey remains content to lose overnite races with the horses while they learn the game. Later, when the horses have been prepared to deliver the big blows, Shoemaker wins the stakes titles and big monies their pedigrees and fastidious training regimens have entitled them to.

Regarding handling too, jockeys who would make it to the top in major racing absolutely must master three basic rides, and deliver with them flawlessly throughout any core season.

The first and most important is the wire-to-wire victory on the lone or fastest frontrunner. Shoemaker's magical hands are often referred to in this special context. A contending horse that can control the pace of the race by getting out in front of the others early is fully expected to win. All leading jockeys can deliver this victory consistently. Those that cannot do not become top boys.

What distinguishes Shoemaker so consistently to horsemen is the ability to complete the ride by taking the smallest of leads and least of energy from horses. He is known to keep a horse on the lead by a neck or head for six furlongs, a mile, a mile and one-eighth, or farther, eventually winning by just that margin, perhaps by more, normally after turning back successive challenges of different horses. For those who know what to look for, the frontrunning ride on a speed horse is one of the prettiest in racing. Indeed Shoemaker, in response to queries about his greatest rides, often cites his 1962 frontrunning ride on dyed-in-the-wool sprinter **Olden Times** in the mile and three-quarters San Juan Capistrano Handicap, on turf. In one of the longest and most important stakes on the American calendar, **Olden Times** needed perfect handling and rating all the way to get there first. (See the result chart which accompanies this piece.)

The second basic ride is the close, competitive finish requiring an all-out effort by the horse. A top jockey saves his horse's best for the end. He is known as a strong finisher. Indeed if he cannot finish strongly, he cannot win. Regardless of what has happened previously, horses win races only by outfinishing other horses that are contending in the late stages. Jockeys that run out of horse, or simply run too low on horsepower before the wire, do not get near the highest echelons of this sport.

And the third ride, least frequently needed nowadays, is the come-from-behind, one-run special. This requires the aforementioned patience, poise, and timing, meticulously combined. So tempting is it to move into contention earlier, even nationally-ranked riders fall below par when forced to come from farthest behind, and especially when the stakes are great. Because he does it so frequently and so seemingly effortlessly, it is my personal favorite of the Shoemaker repertoire.

Years ago, in an aborted effort to compete with the Fall championship races at Belmont Park in New York, Oak Tree at Santa Anita instituted a big-ticket race and named it the Race of Champions. For the first running, although no New York horses of consequence decided to run for the money, the gate was loaded. Shoemaker was on a Whittingham mare named **Dulcia**. She was hardly expected to beat the males.

By the time the 14 horses headed into the clubhouse turn of the mile and one-quarter race, Shoemaker had taken hold and was already at the rear, four-five lengths behind the horses directly in front of him, and 20-25 lengths behind the leaders. Down the backstretch and into the far turn, Shoemaker sat still, far in arrears.

He finally started to move. So had other horses in front of him. His mare was forced seven or eight horses wide. But she continued to move into the upper stretch and towards the wire. In a multiple horse photo, **Dulcia**, still seven-wide in the lane, won by a nose. It was a remarkable win, engineered by Shoemaker,.of the kind most jockeys, even top ones, would have let get away.

The ideal rider stays clear of trouble. Trouble can happen, or it can result from the interference of other horses and jockeys. No matter. Top jockeys normally avoid it or elude it. Their ability to do so relates strongly to the number one requisite on this list—having already established great rapport with their mount.

The ideal rider keeps his body in condition, his mind clear, and his social calendar attuned to the demands of the daily competition. If a top jockey has trouble making weight, he abstains from the table or diets in a manner that still permits him to perform at his best. He avoids arduous sessions in the sweat box and the continual vomiting of meals. If he's injured, he protects the ailment, or rests until it's satisfactorily healed.

If his family life or social life has been suffering, the top jockey does whatever he must to keep his mind on race riding during the program. Afterwards, he doesn't drink or carouse, or stay out late to help himself forget. He deals actively with personal problems as best he can, and rides on.

And by definition jockeys who sustain their careers at the highest echelons of the sport possess abounding competitive spirit, knowhow, and courage.

That Bill Shoemaker has possessed each of these talents and competitive qualities for fully 33 seasons of race riding distinguishes him from other ranking riders of the profession only by longevity. Some four dozen men dominate the national winner's circle, winning approximately 25 per cent of the available purse money, and each possesses all of the ideals. What distinguishes them from one another is the extent to which they can combine everything. That Shoemaker has remained on his mountain for the 33 years means most of all that he has combined the several talents and qualities of the champion to optimum degree. If at fifty his talent has not diminished, it's in part because his motivation and competitive spirit have not diminished, in part because his personal storms have not interfered with his work.

A Matter of Style

The Shoemaker seat and form are said to be classic, or of the best that has been traditional. That style accentuates balance over leverage, finesse over force, touch over strength, harmony more than swagger. Shoemaker is thought to belong to the sit-still school, a variety of waiting riders. In practice, that kind of rider is active yet restrained, positioned but patient, waiting instead of hustling. Horsemen like to say Shoemaker wins by half-lengths or necks when others might need the security of lengths. Horsemen like this type performance, as it saves their horses' limited energies.

All of this is true enough. And Shoemaker does take as little from horses as races demand. He is a jockey who honors purity of form and elements of style. Yet in all-out finishes Shoemaker can be highly active and rugged, flailing with the whip in a quick piercing staccato style, even as he pumps on horses with his arms, hips, and upper torso. The final charges of horse races are completed at high voltage. Even then, however, Shoemaker maintains the classic balance and harmony of form that punctuates his technique.

Like that of all masterful jockeys, the real magic of Shoemaker is that he extracts from racehorses all that they are capable of giving. In the lexicon of the game, horses run for him. If Shoemaker has an added dimension it might be the ability to get the most with the least amount of effort, again the touch in the hands.

Of style, the Shoemaker form, in the manner of Eddie Arcaro before him, and of contemporaries Jorge Velasquez, Sandy Hawley, Darrell McHargue, and Steve Cauthen, looks balanced upright, still, and posed, with a long loose hold on the reins, dependent on touch and hand signals for proper communication. If the touch works, horses act as if they want to run harder for that rider. An opposite style, low slung, highly leveraged across the horse's withers, puts horse and rider in active rhythm, of a kind that almost forces horses to respond with greater run. The style is linked to a succession of Panamanian jockeys who imported it here in high fashion, in the manner of a Braulio Baeza, Ismael Valenzuela, Laffit Pincay, Jr., or the Puerto Rican Angel Cordero, Jr. If any style sets the fashion for younger riders today, it is this model, from Panama.

Rivalries

Of Shoemaker's rivals near the pinnacle of racing, just a few have equalled or approached his achievements, even for a time. None have so endured. Shoemaker's career can be fairly imagined as running in concentric circles, as at race courses. Round and round he has competed against the best jockeys for four decades.

At first it was Eddie Arcaro, The Master, who had ridden in championship form since 1940 when Shoemaker began in 1949. Shoemaker learned in Arcaro's long shadow, and credits Arcaro with helping him develop his form and technique. By 1953 Shoemaker had established himself as Arcaro's peer, eventually succeeding him as the best of his time.

In 1953 too arrived the incomparable Bill Hartack. He set performance standards Shoemaker did not, including his winning three million in purse monies as early as 1957, and five Kentucky Derbies within 15 years. No one topped the three million until 1967, though Shoemaker fell short by only tens of thousands as early as 1958. Many argue that Hartack at his flaming best was best of his time, perhaps the best ever. But Hartack burned out suddenly, his time at the top short-lived by Shoemaker's standards.

In the mid-sixties came Braulio Baeza, all the way from Panama, as would a succession of great ones. After Shoemaker had led the money-won column for no less than 10 seasons, a standing record, with seven of those consecutive, Baeza in 1965 replaced him, and repeated with the title for four straight years. Shoemaker has not since won the ferocious money-won rivalry, though annually placing close. Now many argued Baeza was best, and that perhaps he was best of all time. After a final banner season in 1975, when he was money king again, Baeza too departed the top positions quickly, and in a way that reflected the mental pressures of the game. Baeza at his best lasted only a decade.

In the late sixties and early seventies emerged Laffit Pincay, Jr., also from Panama, and another who would be called best of his time, perhaps the best of all time. By any standard the premier jockey of the seventies, Pincay, in his strength, aggressiveness, and robust riding, proved a counterpoint to the Shoemaker finesse and touch, and by combining those talents with the handling and timing of the champion, represented the archrival to Shoemaker's preeminent position. For the first time too Shoemaker's rival as kingpin rode regularly on the Southern California circuit, and geographical closeness intensified the competition. The two battled for top mounts and domination. Both won.

During the seventies on the East coast rode Angel Cordero, Jr., peerless in some ways, the rival of any jock on all important dimensions. Another New York jockey, Jorge Velasquez, more of the Shoemaker touch and sit tradition, and as complete a rider as exists anywhere, crowded Shoemaker, Pincay, and Cordero at the top.

Then in the mid-seventies out of Canada rode Sandy Hawley, who immediately became four-time riding champion of North America, and led the jockey standings wherever he chose to ride, including Southern California. That racing has never produced a more talented rider than Hawley cannot be denied, but his ambition dulled quickly, and his position weakened.

Then something extraordinary transpired. From the mid-seventies until 1980 emerged a number of young jockeys so superlative in ability that never in its history has racing luxuriated with as many riding luminaries as remain on the scene today. Three migrated in short time to Southern California, as had Hawley, just as Bill Shoemaker was passing 45, heading towards age 50.

From Oklahoma through Florida and on to California came Darrel McHargue, national champion of 1978. Out of Maryland shot Chris McCarron, national champion of 1980, and money champion again in 1981. From the midwest more quietly arrived Eddie Delahoussaye, less glamorous and less publicized than the others—and therefore less immediately fashionable to trainers and owners who supply the mounts— but every fiber the stuff of the national champion, and who has become arguably the best off-pace finisher of the day.

If this unnatural confluence of great jockeys were not enough excitement, in 1976 a sixteen-year-old boy thundered out of Kentucky, to Chicago, to New York, compiling an apprentice record so remarkable it previously had been unapproached by anyone. He was racing's Six Million Dollar Man, America's Athlete of the Year. Not since the early Shoemaker had an apprentice jockey been such a perfect fit for a thoroughbred as was Steve Cauthen. Riding at the top in England today, Cauthen at 22 already appears to have decided on life goals other than the singular pursuit of Shoemaker's records.

These few men have been Shoemaker's peers across 33 seasons. Perhaps it will endure as the jockey's greatest tribute that as Shoemaker progressed in age from 40 to 50 jockeys Hawley, McHargue, McCarron, Delahoussaye, and for a time Cauthen, converged on Southern California racing, where Pincay was an established kingpin. If Shoemaker's riding career were poised for a fall, the arrival of five national champions would have hastened the crash. That did not happen. The point is not that Shoemaker survived the great jockey migration of the 1970's, but that he strengthened his preeminent position in that circuit's sun. No one has replaced him. It is abundantly clear by now that no one will.

That point has not been lost to younger men who now ride to beat him, or to retired peers who once upon a time did. When in May 1981 Shoemaker passed 8000 races won—an average of 250 a year for 32 years—figures unthinkable in the abstract, several jockeys commented that the milestone seemed incomprehensible, even to them. The testimonials were not of the usual trite or pat salutations, but of a tone that wanted it recorded that this man must be regarded as singular, unique to himself, his own point of reference.

Bill Hartack, now a racing official in Southern California, expressed respect and wonder at the monument Shoemaker was still erecting. It has now been 20 years since he rode at Shoemaker's level, said Hartack, trying to grasp that kind of continuity.

Younger riders Hawley and McCarron, in the prime of phenomenal careers, foreswore any hope of matching Shoemaker's lifetime achievements, while pausing to consider how it could be that one man has done this so well for so long. McHargue called him one of a kind. From New York, Angel Cordero, Jr., in a rare accolade, referred to Shoemaker as the best jockey alive. Eddie Arcaro said flatly that Shoemaker is the greatest of all time.

On the occasion of his 8000 winners Shoemaker told the press he has never set professional goals or set out to break others' records. That that kind of thing has just happened. And that furthermore he is certain his own records will be similarly toppled.

Will anybody break his records?

With inflation galloping along for so many years and race-track purses soaring at annual percentage increases that astonish even the shrewdest analysts in the industry, Shoemaker's money-won records can be considered already in jeopardy, even though he himself rides on, and nobody among today's jockeys appears likely to catch him. In 1979, Laffit Pincay, Jr.'s mounts earned $8.1-million. McCarron ended 1981 at $8.3-million. Within a few years racing will crown its first ten million a year jockey. A twenty-year-old man making ten million a year has rung up two hundred million in 20 years. Shoemaker's money marks will fall.

Will another jockey in another time win 8000 races, or more?

Very probably not.

The Public Shoemaker

Once upon a summer's afternoon in Del Mar's walking ring, little Nikki Bacharach, daughter of Burt and Angie, ran to Shoemaker as he entered and jumped upon him. He carried her a small ways, put her down, and took her hand as they walked towards the adults. The horses were delayed a bit, and owners, their guests, and horsemen fell into the customary small circles of conversation, Shoemaker talking to Nikki.

Suddenly Nikki reached for his whip. He handed it to her. In a friendly, playful manner she began to strike him with the whip, increasing her intensity with each stroke, and lashing Shoemaker across the chin and upper chest. He stook there, smiling at her, and making no gesture of defense or restraint as the little child flailed away repeatedly. She was playing. Shoemaker knew that. He played along. Soon an adult ran over, took the whip, and handed it to Shoemaker. He reached down, touched the child's shoulders, and kissed her cheek.

A genuine love of little children is one slice of Shoemaker's public personality that finds frequent expression at racetracks. It happens often during walking ring ceremonies, as the horses exit to the track. If a child calls to him, Shoemaker reacts instinctively, smiling warmly and making direct eye contact. When able, he reaches out physically to any child at any opportunity, obviously drawn to their friendliness, innocence, and affection.

With owners and trainers who employ his skills, Shoemaker remains cooperative and attentive, if seemingly detached and understated. To observe familiar trainers give him riding instructions becomes amusing. Shoemaker typically stares forwardly as the trainers talk, shaking his head in a continually affirmative motion. The mannerism has surely become a reflex action, following 35,000 races, and similar sets of instructions. Perhaps 20,000 races ago Shoemaker signed a pact with himself whereby he agrees with anything a trainer says.

Another slice of Shoemaker gets enlarged by encounters with small-time owners and their parties when at last the good horse has emerged and the world's winningest jockey has accepted the mount. During Santa Anita 1980 a three-year-old won by just plain folks in a Canadian lottery was entered in the Santa Anita Derby. The colt had won stakes races smashingly throughout the Northwest and suddenly the lucky owners were on their way to Santa Anita with a horse that belonged. It was storybook stuff, of dreams come true. Named on their Derby colt, a rather little horse called **Loto Canada**, was jockey William Shoemaker.

On Derby day in the walking ring there must have been 50 of them, from Canada, from Seattle, and from other points North. Their bright-eyed colt entered the ring and the world's leading jockey walked out to get aboard. It was a large moment in these people's lives and Shoemaker, who must have played the scene hundreds of times before, responded in the same personally gracious, friendly, and engaging manner that he always seems to have available to the occasion. Cap off, he must have shaken hands with 30 men, accepted kisses from a dozen ladies. It was a special kind of racetrack theater, half amusing, wholly touching.

With trainer Whittingham, and other associates, the byword for his relationships is professional. As a result, his working arrangements tend to be loyal and longterm. For one outstanding example among many, he has had since 1949 a handshake agreement with jockey agent Harry Silbert. As are so many business arrangements in this unbelievable field, jockey-agent agreements are typically unwritten, but they are also typically short-lived, rarely extending beyond five years. Shoemaker has never had a second agent.

Even though the trainer uses other jockeys and the jockey rides other stables' horses when it particularly suits either to do so, the Whittingham-Shoemaker axis has ruled in the Southern California stakes division since 1968, and not without severe personal tests of the two men. The worst problems usually involve owners' prerogatives, as these apply to the selection of jockeys to ride stakes horses.

Years ago Florsheim heiress Mary Jones Bradley decided she preferred that Laffit Pincay, Jr. ride her turf champion **Courgar II** in a major stakes. Shoemaker had ridden the horse regularly for two seasons, winning major titles and big money. If **Courgar II** were a turf champion for his time, Mrs. Bradley preferred to believe he was an all-time great. Whenever the horse lost, which happened in 33 of 57 races, the owner, in a great tradition of its own, concluded the jockey or trainer or the devil must have had something to do with it. Of owners who distinguish themselves as noisy and ignorant nuisances to horsemen, these exceed their worst behavior when the champion or almost-champion finally belongs to them. Few owners can experience the really top horse without blowing their cool. Unless horsemen such as Whittingham and Shoemaker can maintain theirs, the horse itself is ultimately doomed.

To be fair, these were frustrating days for Mary Jones Bradley. During **Cougar's** time Whittingham also trained the great **Ack Ack**, and that horse was Horse-of-the-Year. When turf writers inquired as to which horse was better, Whittingham would respond by saying **Ack Ack** was the best horse he had ever trained. Mrs. Bradley hoped to prove Charlie wrong on the point.

In the Santa Anita Handicap 1971, a dirt race, Mrs. Bradley insisted her turf star start, though Whittingham had not intended that. Whittingham obliged. Shoemaker rode **Ack Ack**. Pincay was named for **Cougar II**. **Ack Ack** won, but **Cougar II** ran second, finished strongly, and was beaten a short length.

The next season, for the Hollywood Gold Cup, **Ack Ack** now retired, Mrs. Bradley wanted **Cougar II** to run, but she wanted Pincay to ride. Whittingham obliged. Shoemaker took another Whittingham horse, **Kennedy Road**. The press picked up the issue and turned the race into a personal contest. What nagged at Shoemaker was that some took the important switch to indicate his career had started to slide.

As he has so often said she has, Lady Luck smiled again on Shoemaker and he won the race by a thrilling nose, one of his most personally rewarding and satisfying moments. He did not beat **Cougar II** that day, but still a third Whittingham stakes star, **Quack**. **Courgar II** ran third, beaten several lengths.

In the Hollywood walking ring that Gold Cup day the crowd booed Mrs. Bradley so persistently she turned her face to the infield and sobbed. When Shoemaker won the race, she took another lacing, from the press and fans. Despite all that, weeks later, in the Sunset Handicap, Shoemaker was back aboard **Cougar II**, and he won that big race handily. A top jockey had been snubbed, and a top trainer had been overstepped by an overanxious owner, yet the owner-trainer-jockey relationship more than survived, and endures in wonderfully good health even today.

In this context it must be recorded that jockeys even of the highest status continually pick up one another's regular mounts. When good horses lose, as often happens, in the tradition previously remarked, owners and trainers seek to make explanation or to change their strategy. The only real change is often the jockey.

From this tendency William Shoemaker has benefitted as much or more than any rider in history. That he lost the mount on **Cougar II** sometime ago under special circumstances that might have gone beyond merely bruising the ego, indeed might have threatened his sense of professional worth, is hardly an isolated event. His mere presence and availability has done the same to numerous undeserving riders for decades. His colleague and friend Don Pierce bristles still at losing to Shoemaker the mount on Kentucky Derby contender **Hill Rise**, and that was in 1964. That year Shoemaker lost the Derby to **Northern Dancer** by a head, and Pierce pointedly tells anyone who asks that he would have won with the horse.

Only months ago, in a move that had no justification whatsoever, Shoemaker was given the call on favorite **John Henry** for the Arlington Million, after archrival Pincay had ridden the horse brilliantly the entire season, winning for grateful owner Sam Rubin the 1980 turf Eclipse award and more than a million dollars. But while temporarily grounded, Pincay missed a race in New York. Shoemaker rode, and won easily, against easy opposition. When the subsequent jockey change was announced, it brought sharp indignation from Pincay agent George O'Bryan. Jockey agents are thoroughly hardened to these circumstances, but this wound went too deep. O'Bryan cried foul. He was decidedly correct. If the time ever arrives that Shoemaker is dumped from important stakes engagements, however unceremoniously, by bubbleheaded owners, he will have no room to maneuver for sympathy among those who know the game too well.

A modest, quiet, elementary man, unaffecting, unpretentious, reportedly a prankster in the jockeys' quarters, the personal Shoemaker enjoys the respect and fellowship of his riding colleagues. It is his habit to stand by them, not apart from them. This holds for the rawest recruits, not just the champions-in-arms.

When the industry calls, as has happened repeatedly in recent years, he normally responds. Various scattered racing associations (these produce race meetings) in recent years have invited Shoemaker to come to their spot of a day or night, to promote the local sport. He goes. And he rides. In Southern California the associations have attached his name to seasonal promotions or to special events. He once graced a full-sized poster—THE SHOE WANTS YOU—designed to stimulate local business. As he has reached each new plateau in his phenomenal career, racing's marketing men have not missed opportunities to tie each performance record to racetrack promotions. Shoemaker cooperates. It's mostly hype, but it plugs an industry sorely in need of a healthy hype or two.

Now that he has turned a golden fifty, all of this and more can be expected to take on heightened dimensions. Nowadays when he rides at Belmont Park or Aqueduct in New York, or Arlington Park in Chicago, or Churchill Downs in Kentucky, or Hialeah in Florida, or Oaklawn Park in Hot Springs, Ark., or The Meadowlands in New Jersey, out of town cosmopolitan centers crowded with racing's hardboots, the walking rings are circled around and around with racing people who want to see him, at least once more. There is something highly appropriate to the scenes. It's as if the people have come to feel jockey Shoemaker now represents something more than the usual, the best not only of their sport, but also of athletics.

During the inaugural Arlington Million week in Chicago that track was ablaze with all that glitters in the sport of kings today. It was a glamorous time. Everybody was there. On Saturday, the day before the million dollar race, Shoemaker was engaged to ride in the Arlington-Washington Futurity and one overnite race, the sixth. When the sixth arrived, Arlington's walking ring was suddenly alive, crowded beyond comfort with rings of people. They stood four and five rows deep. As Shoemaker walked into the circle, the Chicagoans broke into a spontaneous ovation, a highly unusual scene at racetracks. He had been there only a year before, to ride **Spectacular Bid**, in the Washington Park Stakes, but as Chicagoans remembered it, it wasn't the same. That Shoemaker at fifty had taken on a new kind of public personality was all too clear. He acknowledged the cheers and the people graciously, and took the occasion in his stride. He always does.

1953

To comprehend the Shoemaker of 1983 fully, we need reach far back, briefly, to the first of his three definitive seasons. Fully 30 years before, when 1953 started, four years of jockeying had already earned for Shoemaker a classy national reputation. Peers had judged him completely competent. Leading stakes rider Eddie Arcaro had marveled publicly at the subtlety and finesse of his skill, in 1950 calling Shoemaker the greatest apprentice of all time. Top trainers sought his services. In each of his first four years he had ranked first or second in races won or money won. He had already made it big.

Yet 1953 would alter the record, change perspectives, deepen impressions already formed.

On April 4, at Tanforan, in California, Willie Shoemaker rode six winners on the card (eight races were programmed). That might be a remarkable riding feat, as the racing manuals refer to it, but journeyman jockeys at every class track in the nation regularly ride four and five winners during an afternoon's work. Numerous apprentices, teenagers, do it. Good riders do it five or six times a season.

During 1953 Willie Shoemaker rode four or more winners on a single card 30 times.

Besides Tanforan, he was six for eight June 20 at Hollywood Park. He was six for nine at Golden Gate Fields October 10.

On the consecutive afternoons May 7 and May 8 he was five for eight. He was five for eight again, November 12.

He was four for six on March 17, May 6, and August 19. He was four for seven 11 times, four for eight nine times.

At Tanforan on the three consecutive afternoons of May 6-7-8 Shoemaker won with 14 of 22 thoroughbreds, a percentage of .64. He was 22-years-old.

Racing's divisions were well-stocked that season for the coming of television. The three-year-old division featured a popular hero, the champion **Native Dancer**, who had equalled the world record for six-and-one-half furlongs at two in 1:14 2/5 seconds (two-year-olds do not equal world records), and at three won nine of 10 races, including The Preakness and Belmont Stakes, and an unprecedented half million dollars.

Tom Fool dominated a strong older division, winning all 10 of his starts and $256,355. He was voted Horse-of-the-Year. **Porterhouse**, the only good horse making hay for his trainer Charlie Whittingham, led the two-year-olds. **Grecian Queen** was tops among three-year-old fillies.

Willie Shoemaker never sat on **Native Dancer**. He never rode **Tom Fool**. He never rode **Porterhouse**. He never rode **Grecian Queen**. Nor did Shoemaker ride 1953's best handicap mare, nor its top two-year-old filly, nor its grass champion.

During 1953 Shoemaker handled no champions. He did not win a single one of the 22 races having a gross value of $100,000. Yet Shoemaker led the national jockey standings in money-won, at $1,784,187, leading Arcaro in that prime category for the second time in his five young seasons.

Stakes monies aside, in all other riding categories Shoemaker of 1953 stood so far removed from the others any comparisons were meaningless. He won an astonishing 485 races, a world record that stood until 1973. No one in history had won even 400 races. His win percentage too was the highest of all time at .29, and he shattered a record of 723 races-won for two consecutive years that had survived since 1906-07. During 1952-53, Shoemaker won 800 races, 10 per cent of his lifetime total today.

Almost too fast he was becoming his own point of reference. Shoemaker was winning 333 races a year, with a win percentage of .24, numbers unapproached in history. The coldly factual, steadfastly uncritical **American Racing Manual** was moved to judge the riding record of Willie Shoemaker "a statistical wonder."

Million Dollar Ride

Of Shoemaker's latest triumph, victory by a nose in the inaugural Arlington Million, the ride was not spectacular perhaps, but shrewdly professional, of the kind he might dispense under classified allowance conditions in the seventh race of an afternoon at Santa Anita.

His mount was favored to win, at practically even money. When lots were drawn, **John Henry** drew post position 14, the far outside in a field traveling one mile and one-quarter over turf. Post position has incidental effects on the outcomes of races having a long run to the first turn. Horses breaking from the outside normally have ample time to secure favorable inside position before losing ground on the wider swings of the turn.

Though the run to the clubhouse turn of Arlington Park's turf course extends a quarter-mile, **John Henry** did not break from the gate sharply and had not established satisfactory forward position as the clubhouse turn approached. The favorite was expected to race on or near the lead. He did not. As the turn approached, **John Henry** was running seventh or eighth.

At this first important juncture Shoemaker did what any top rider would do as a matter of routine—though this race was hardly routine, an important point. He dropped behind the front flight and angled **John Henry** toward the inside lane, next to the rail. He got there. This saves ground, and reserves stamina, but invites traffic problems later.

Even more importantly, Shoemaker stayed put. Around the clubhouse turn, down the backstretch, and around the far turn he remained content to save the ground and energy he had decided to save. Even as other horses maneuvered into contention and into striking position while rounding the far turn, Shoemaker sat chilly, not hustling **John Henry** in premature ways at incidental points in the race.

As the horses turned into the upper stretch the lane by the rail remained blocked by two frontrunners. To get clear sailing, **John Henry** now had to move out and around. Another horse was moving forward in the lane Shoemaker needed, and the jockey was barely able to angle between horses and find room at that second and decisive juncture. Had the angle not been wide enough, **John Henry** and Shoemaker would have lost time and momentum, and surely would have been defeated. That was a risk many riders would have avoided in this race, but at cost.

Now all **John Henry** needed to do was run by two frontrunners, which presumably had weakened one another, and hold off any late comers. As Shoemaker later admitted, what looked easy enough at that point became furiously difficult. **The Bart**, loser by the thinnest nose at the finish, in the upper stretch had considerable energies stored under jockey Eddie Delahoussaye. **John Henry** would be pressured to gain six lengths and complete the final quarter mile on a soft turf in 24 seconds flat, championship demands, to win. He prevailed, barely.

Few who watched that finish called **John Henry** the winner. Even people positioned directly across from the finish line announced the longshot had won. The photo camera proved differently. **John Henry** won an unlikely head bob, and $600,000 first money. To be sure, Shoemaker brought his Lady Luck to Chicago with him for the inaugural Arlington Million. On the other hand, it took quite a good, heady ride to get there.

Importance to Racing

Shoemaker's significance to racing, the sport and industry, is not so snappily understood. The achievements and records, singular as they will remain for a time, are not the mark of the man. He has provided leadership of a sort, by example, and serves as president of the Jockey Guild, but even here he has preferred to lead by example and remains rather evenhanded, uncomplicated, and uncontroversial in relation to matters political, economic, or managerial, and affecting the sport or industry.

Beyond singular achievement, the importance of Shoemaker resides in what is now increasingly becoming a kind of public persona. It consists of the tremendous dignity and integrity which for 33 years has characterized his personal and professional conduct. Performing in a sport where personal and professional conduct directly impact the public interest, Shoemaker has done it all with grace and dignity, and without posturing.

As his time in the public domain has extended now into a fifth decade, the quiet, unassuming, dignified manner of the man has flourished magnificently for an industry still troubled by its image, and lately blackened anew by scandals involving leading jockeys at major tracks.

Now more than before Bill Shoemaker is unquestionably the man of his time in thoroughbred racing, the topic of conversations, the presence in any room, the center of the public's attention. It makes less difference to him than to racing itself. Newly remarried in 1979, the father of daughter Amanda in 1980, Shoemaker at 51 is as much the family man as he is the jockey.

When asked to assess the meaning of winning 8000 horse races, he answered, curiously, "When compared to that little girl (Amanda), they don't mean anything."

That's the short of it, I suppose. As the golden age of Bill Shoemaker continues, what makes it all the more magnificent is that it really means so much less to his personal center than his little girl in his arms.

STATISTICAL SHOE

When the American Racing Manual in 1953 referred to the prodigious five-year riding record of William Shoemaker as a "statistical wonder," the jockey's statistics had not even begun to materialize. He had won, for example, only a single purse of $100,000. Shoemaker by 1983 has won more than 190 six-figure stakes. No one else in major racing is close enough to mention.

With a lifetime win percentage of .23 and presently more than 90 million dollars in purse winnings, the Statistical Shoe is peerless, even on a list of jockeys who are all-time greats in the sport. We begin with just such a list:

LIFETIME RECORDS OF LEADING JOCKEYS

Jockey	Years Riding	Mounts	1st	2nd	3rd	Unplaced	Win P.C.	Amount
Shoemaker, W	32	34,219	'7,925	5,335	4,257	16,699	.232	$79,690,253
Longden, J. (1966)	40	32,407	²6,032	4,914	4,273	17,194	.186	24,665,800
Arcaro, E. (1961)	31	24,092	4,779	3,807	3,302	12,204	.198	30,039,543
Pincay, L. Jr.	15	19,563	³4,327	3,281	2,786	9,169	.221	55,555,590
Hartack, W.	'22	21,535	4,272	3,370	2,871	11,022	.198	26,466,758
Cordero, A. Jr.	19	'23,730	4,178	3,651	3,477	12,604	.176	55,182,847
Hawley, S.	13	16,678	⁴4,172	2,819	2,275	7,512	.250	31,185,729
Valasquez, J.	18	²22,800	3,504	3,504	3,311	11,994	.175	50,219,515
Baeza, B. (1976)	16	⁵17,239	3,140	2,730	2,422	8,947	.182	36,150,142
McCarron, C.J.	7	12,099	2,574	2,022	1,641	5,862	.212	24,965,318

WORLD'S LEADING JOCKEY
Shoemaker's Year-by-Year Record

The lifetime record of Bill Shoemaker follows:

Year	Mts.	1st	2nd	3rd	Pct.	Amt. Won
1949	1,089	219	195	147	.20	$ 458,010
1950	1,640	388 (1)	266	230	.24	844,040
1951	1,161	257	197	161	.22	1,329,890 (1)
1952	1,322	315	244	174	.24	1,049,304
1953	1,683	385 (1)	302	210	.29	1,784,187 (1)
1954	1,251	380 (1)	221	142	.30	1,876,760 (1)
1955	1,149	307	178	138	.27	1,846,884
1956	1,229	328	187	165	.27	2,113,335
1957	1,191	295	183	134	.25	2,544,782
1958	1,133	300 (1)	185	137	.26	2,961,693 (1)
1959	1,285	347 (1)	230	159	.27	2,843,155 (1)
1960	1,227	274	196	158	.22	2,123,961 (1)
1961	1,256	304	186	175	.24	2,690,819 (1)
1962	1,126	311	156	128	.28	2,916,844 (1)
1963	1,203	271	193	137	.23	2,526,925 (1)
1964	1,056	246	147	133	.23	2,649,553 (1)
1965	1,069	247	161	120	.23	†2,228,977
1966	1,037	221	158	107	.21	2,671,198
1967	1,044	244	146	113	.23	3,052,108
1968	104	19	14	11	.18	175,950
1969	454	97*	63	58	.21	†1,047,949
1970	952	219	133	106	.23	2,063,194
1971	881	195	136	104	.22	2,931,590
1972	869	172	137	111	.20	2,519,384
1973	639	139	95	73	.22	2,016,874
1974	922	160	126	108	.17	2,558,862
1975	957	215	142	124	.22	3,514,213
1976	1,035	200	154	146	.19	3,815,645
1977	975	172	149	142	.18	3,633,091
1978	1,245	271	194	156	.22	††5,231,390
1979	983	168	141	118	.17	††4,480,825
1980	1,052	159	140	132	.15	††5,188,883
1981	878	156	119	99	.18	6,122,481
(33)	35,497	8,081	5,452	4,356	.23	$85,812,731

*Includes two wins in Argentina, five wins in England, three wins in Ireland and two wins in South Africa. †Foreign earnings not included. Figures in parenthesis indicate year as national leader in races won and/or total mounts' earnings. ††Foreign earnings included.

ANNUAL LEADING JOCKEY—MONEY WON
1949-1981

Year	Jockey	Mts.	1st	2d	3d	Pct.	Amt. Won
1949	Brooks, S.	906	209	172	110	.23	1,316,817
1950	Arcaro, E.	888	195	153	144	.22	1,410,160
1951	Shoemaker, W.	1,161	257	197	161	.22	1,329,890
1952	Arcaro, E.	807	188	122	109	.23	1,859,591
1953	Shoemaker, W.	1,683	485	302	210	.29	1,784,187
1954	Shoemaker, W.	1,251	380	221	142	.30	1,876,760
1955	Arcaro, E.	820	158	126	108	.19	1,864,796
1956	Hartack, W.	1,387	347	252	184	.25	2,343,955
1957	Hartack, W.	1,238	341	208	178	.28	3,060,501
1958	Shoemaker, W.	1,133	300	185	137	.26	2,961,693
1959	Shoemaker, W.	1,285	347	230	159	.27	2,843,133
1960	Shoemaker, W.	1,227	274	196	158	.22	2,123,961
1961	Shoemaker, W.	1,256	304	186	175	.24	2,690,819
1962	Shoemaker, W.	1,126	311	156	128	.28	2,916,844
1963	Shoemaker, W.	1,203	271	193	137	.22	2,526,925
1964	Shoemaker, W.	1,056	246	147	133	.23	2,649,553
1965	Baeza, B.	1,245	270	200	201	.22	2,582,702
1966	Baeza, B.	1,341	298	222	190	.22	2,951,022
1967	Baeza, B.	1,064	256	184	127	.24	3,088,888
1968	Baeza, B.	1,089	201	184	145	.18	2,835,108
1969	Velasquez, J.	1,442	258	230	204	.18	2,542,315
1970	Pincay, L.Jr.	1,328	269	208	187	.20	2,626,526
1971	Pincay, L.Jr.	1,627	380	288	214	.23	3,784,377
1972	Pincay, L.Jr.	1,388	289	215	205	.21	3,225,827
1973	Pincay, L.Jr.	1,444	350	254	209	.24	4,093,492
1974	Pincay, L.Jr.	1,278	341	227	180	.27	4,251,060
1975	Baeza, B.	1,190	196	208	180	.16	3,674,398
1976	Cordero, A.Jr.	1,534	274	273	235	.18	4,709,500
1977	Cauthen, S.	2,075	487	345	304	.23	6,151,750
1978	McHargue, D.	1,762	375	294	263	.21	6,188,353
1979	Pincay, L.Jr.	1,708	420	302	261	.25	8,183,535
1980	McCarron, C	1,964	405	318	282	.20	7,666,100
1981	McCarron, C	1,494	326	251	207	.22	8,397,604

Years Led	Money Won
Shoemaker, W.	10
Pincay L.	6
Arcaro E.	6
Baeza B.	5
Hartack W.	2
McCarron C.	2
All Others	1

Other Singular Achievements, Shoemaker, Lifetime

Most Money Won By A Jockey, Lifetime	$90 Million-Plus
Most Races Won By A Jockey, Lifetime	8,100-Plus
Most Wins In Stakes Races, Year	46, in 1971
Highest Win Percentage, Year	.30, in 1954
Most Years Led, Races Won	5 in 1950-53-54-58-59
Most Years Led, Stakes Races Won	14, 1958-59, 1961-64, 1966-67, 1971, 1975-77, 1980-81
Most $100,000-Plus Stakes Races Won, Lifetime	190-Plus

Masterful jockeys can be compared tellingly on their money-won in stakes competition. By that standard Shoemaker and Arcaro have dominated the sport for generations. Here's a 45-year list:

Annual Stakes-Winning Jockey—Money Won
(Total Winners' Value)

Year	Jockey	Stakes Won	Total Earnings	Year	Jockey	Stakes Won	Stakes Win Val.	Year	Jockey	Stakes Won	Total Win Val.
1935	Wright, W. D.	18	$ 122,150	1951	Arcaro, E.	18	$ 531,250	1967	Shoemaker, W.	38	$1,629,874
1936	Richards, H.	14	173,470	1952	Arcaro, E.	40	1,172,404	1968	Baeza, B.	25	1,181,745
1973	Kurtsinger, C.	16	259,820	1953	Arcaro, E.	20	839,734	1969	Rotz, J. L.	20	931,565
1938	Wall, N.	19	286,170	1954	Arcaro, E.	29	895,690	1970	Rotz, J. L.	24	1,031,548
1939	Stout, J.	15	231,985	1955	Arcaro, E.	34	1,226,657	1971	Shoemaker, W.	46	1,567,295
1940	Arcaro, E.	16	170,165	1956	Hartack, W.	26	1,037,077	1972	Turcotte, R.	21	1,226,282
1941	Arcaro, E.	15	229,975	1957	Hartack, W.	43	1,718,231	1973	Turcotte, R.	18	1,087,397
1942	Woolf, G.	23	341,680	1958	Shoemaker, W.	36	1,600,503	1974	Pincay, L. Jr.	38	1,427,407
1943	Longden, J.	20	290,222	1959	Shoemaker, W.	29	1,034,422	1975	Shoemaker, W.	29	1,353,655
1944	Woolf, G.	14	338,135	1960	Ussery, R.	20	931,441	1976	Shoemaker, W.	30	1,569,960
1945	Longden, J.	24	528,220	1961	Shoemaker, W.	25	1,156,470	1977	Shoemaker, W.	30	1,496,920
1946	Arcaro, E.	21	404,380	1962	Shoemaker, W.	38	1,474,516	1978	McHargue, D.G.	37	1,662,595
1947	Dodson, D.	35	899,915	1963	Shoemaker, W.	32	996,785	1979	Pincay, L. Jr.	44	2,720,006
1948	Arcaro, E.	35	1,082,585	1964	Shoemaker, W.	34	1,243,827	1980	Shoemaker, W.	35	2,381,656
1949	Brooks, S.	26	728,335	1965	Baeza, B.	24	1,085,661	1991	Shoemaker W.		
1950	Arcaro, E.	30	689,035	1966	Shoemaker, W.	37	1,303,787				

Years Led	Stakes Winnings
Shoemaker W.	14
Arcaro E.	10
Hartack W.	2
Baeza B.	2
Pincay L.	2
All Others	2 or 1

SHOEMAKER'S RECORD OF VICTORIES
IN $100,000 STAKES

Date	Stake Track	Winner
Feb 3, 1951	Santa Anita Maturity	Great Circle
Feb 27, 1954	Santa Anita Handicap	Rejected
Mar 20, 1954	Florida Derby (GP)	Correlation
Apr 24, 1954	Wood Memorial (Jam)	Correlation
Feb 26, 1955	Santa Anita Handicap	Poona II.
May 7, 1955	Kentucky Derby (CD)	Swaps
Aug 20, 1955	American Derby (Was)	Swaps
Sep 5, 1955	Washington Park 'Cap	Jet Action
Mar 3, 1956	Santa Anita Derby	Terrang
Jly 4, 1956	American 'Cap (Hol)	Swaps
Jly 14, 1956	Hollywood Gold Cup	Swaps
Jly 25, 1956	Sunset Handicap (Hol)	Swaps
Sep 3, 1956	Washington Park 'Cap	Swaps
May 25, 1957	Californian S. (Hol)	Social Climber
Jun 15, 1957	Belmont Stakes	Gallant Man
Jly 13, 1957	Hollywood Gold Cup	Round Table
Jly 20, 1957	Westerner Stakes (Hol)	Round Table
Aug 31, 1957	American Derby (Was)	Round Table
Sep 2, 1957	Washington Park 'Cap	Pucker Up
Sep 14, 1957	U.N. 'Cap (Atl)	Round Table
Oct 12, 1957	Champagne S. (Bel)	Jewel's Reward
Nov 23, 1957	Pimlico Futurity	Jewel's Reward
Mar 1, 1958	Santa Anita Handicap	Round Table
Mar 8, 1958	Santa Anita Derby	Silky Sullivan
Mar 22, 1958	Gulfstream Park 'Cap	Round Table
Jly 12, 1958	Hollywood Gold Cup	Gallant Man
Jly 22, 1958	Sunset Handicap (Hol)	Gallant Man
Aug 2, 1958	Arlington Futurity	Restless Wind
Aug 30, 1958	Washington Park Fut'y	Restless Wind
Sep 13, 1958	U.N. 'Cap (Atl)	Clem
Sep 20, 1958	Futurity Stakes (Bel)	Intentionally
Sep 27, 1958	Woodward S. (Bel)	Clem
Oct 11, 1958	Hawthorne Gold Cup	Round Table
Nov 22, 1958	Pimlico Futurity	Intentionally
May 2, 1959	Kentucky Derby (CD)	Tomy Lee
May 30, 1959	Metropolitan 'Cap (Bel)	Sword Dancer
Jun 13, 1959	Belmont Stakes	Sword Dancer
Jun 27, 1959	'Hollywood Derby	Bagdad
Jly 25, 1959	Monmouth Handicap	Sword Dancer
Aug 22, 1959	Arlington Handicap	Round Table
Aug 29, 1959	Hopeful Stakes (Sar)	Tompion
Sep 7, 1959	Wash. Pk. 'Cap (AP)	Round Table
Sep 19, 1959	U.N. 'Cap (Atl)	Round Table
Mar 5, 1960	Santa Anita Derby	Tompion
Jun 3, 1967	Belmont Stakes (Aqu)	Damascus
Jly 24, 1967	Sunset Handicap (Hol)	Hill Clown
Aug 5, 1967	American Derby (AP)	Damascus
Sep 4, 1967	[8]Aqueduct Stakes	Damascus
Sep 9, 1967	[8]Arl.-Wash. Fut'y. 2nd Div. (AP)	Vitriolic
Sep 23, 1967	Futurity Stakes (Aqu)	Captain's Gig
Sep 30, 1967	Woodward S. (Aqu)	Damascus
Oct 28, 1967	Jky Club G. C. (Aqu)	Damascus
Sep 1, 1969	[2]Arl.-Wash. Las. S. (AP)	Clover Lane
Mar 28, 1970	Santa Anita Derby	Terlago
Apr 4, 1970	Capistrano 'Cap (SA)	Fiddle Isle [DH]
Jun 20, 1970	H'wood Pk. Inv. T. 'Cap	Fiddle Isle
Mar 13, 1971	Santa Anita Handicap	Ack Ack
Apr 10, 1971	Capistrano 'Cap (SA)	Cougar II.
May 22, 1971	California Derby (Hol)	Cougar II.
Jun 26, 1971	[6]Ford Pinto Inv. 'Cap (Hol)	Cougar II.
Jly 17, 1971	H'wood Gold Cup 'Cap	Ack Ack
Jly 24, 1971	H'wood Juv. Ch. S.	Royal Owl
Oct 30, 1971	Oak Tree Inv. S. (SA)	Cougar II
Dec 18, 1971	California Juv. S. (BM)	Royal Owl
Feb 12, 1972	[4]Strub Stakes (SA)	Unconscious
Mar 4, 1972	Margarita 'Cap (SA)	Turkish Trousers
Apr 22, 1972	California Derby (Hol)	Quack
Apr 29, 1972	Century 'Cap (Hol)	Cougar II.
May 20, 1972	Californian S. (Hol)	Cougar II.
Sep 13, 1972	Del Mar Futurity	Groshawk
Nov 1, 1972	Oak Tree Inv. S. (SA)	Cougar II.
May 5, 1973	Century 'Cap (Hol)	Cougar II.
Jun 24, 1973	H'wood G. C. Inv. 'Cap	Kennedy Road
Jly 23, 1973	Sunset Handicap (Hol)	Cougar II.
Sep 12, 1973	Del Mar Futurity	Such a Rush
Mar 30, 1974	Fantasy Stakes (OP)	Miss Musket
Apr 23, 1974	California Derby (GG)	Agitate
Jun 23, 1974	H'wood G. C. Inv. 'Cap	Tree of Knowledge
Jun 30, 1974	Swaps Stakes (Hol)	Agitate
Jly 14, 1974	H'wood Inv. Derby	Agitate
Oct 22, 1960	Gardenia Stakes (GS)	Bowl of Flowers
Jan 28, 1961	Santa Anita Maturity	Prove It
Feb 25, 1961	Santa Anita Handicap	Prove It
Mar 11, 1961	Capistrano 'Cap (SA)	Don't Alibi
Oct 7, 1961	Frizette Stakes (Aqu)	Cicada
Oct 21, 1961	Gardenia Stakes (GS)	Cicada
Nov 4, 1961	Garden State S. (GS)	Crimson Satan
Nov 18, 1961	Pimlico Futurity	Crimson Satan
Mar 10, 1962	Sn. Jn. Cap. 'Cap (SA)	Olden Times
Jun 9, 1962	Belmont Stakes	Jaipur
Sep 3, 1962	Wash. Pk. 'Cap (AP)	Prove It
Sep 8, 1962	[2]Arl. Wash. Fut'y (AP)	Candy Spots
Sep 15, 1962	Futunty Stakes (Aqu)	Never Bend
Nov 10, 1962	Garden State Stakes	Crewman
Mar 2, 1963	Santa Anita Derby	Candy Spots
Mar 30, 1963	Florida Derby (GP)	Candy Spots
May 18, 1963	Preakness S. (Pim)	Candy Spots
May 30, 1963	Jersey Derby (GS)	Candy Spots
Jly 13, 1963	American Derby (AP)	Candy Spots
Aug 3, 1963	Arlington Classic	Candy Spots
Aug 31, 1963	[2]Arl.-Wash. Las. S. (AP)	Sari's Song
Jan 25, 1964	[4]Strub S. (SA)	Gun Bow
Mar 3, 1964	Flamingo Stakes (Hia)	Northern Dancer
Mar 21, 1964	Gulfstream Park 'Cap	Gun Bow
Apr 4, 1964	Florida Derby (GP)	Northern Dancer
Jun 20, 1964	Illinois Handicap (AP)	Olden Times
Sep 12, 1964	[2]Arl.-Wash. Fut'y (AP)	Sadair
Oct 10, 1964	Frizette Stakes (Aqu)	Queen Empress
Nov 7, 1964	Gardenia Stakes (GS)	Queen Empress
Mar 6, 1965	Santa Anita Derby	Lucky Debonair
May 1, 1965	Kentucky Derby (CD)	Lucky Debonair
Jly 24, 1965	H'wood Juv. Ch.	Port Wine
Aug 7, 1965	Chicagoan Stakes (AP)	Tom Rolfe
Aug 28, 1965	Arlington Classic	Tom Rolfe
Sep 13, 1965	American Derby (AP)	Tom Rolfe
Jan 29, 1966	[4]Strub Stakes (SA)	Bold Bidder
Feb 26, 1966	Santa Anita Handicap	Lucky Debonair
Mar 3, 1966	Flamingo Stakes (Hia)	Buckpasser
Aug 6, 1966	Sapling Stakes (Mth)	Great Power
Sep 5, 1966	Aqueduct Handicap	Tom Rolfe
Sep 10, 1966	[2]Arl.-Wash. Fut'y (AP)	Diplomat Way
Feb 25, 1967	Santa Anita Handicap	Pretense
Apr 22, 1967	Wood Memorial (Aqu)	Damascus
May 20, 1967	Preakness S. (Pim)	Damascus
Oct 2, 1976	Marlboro Cup 'Cap (Bel)	Forego
Oct 24, 1976	Oak Tree Inv. S. (SA)	King Pellinore
Nov 6, 1976	Chpn. Invit'l 'Cap (SA)	King Pellinore
Nov 7, 1976	Norfolk Stakes (SA)	Habitony
Feb 13, 1977	La Canada S. (SA)	Lucie Manet
Mar 27, 1977	Santa Anita Derby	Habitony
May 30, 1977	Metropolitan 'Cap (Bel)	Forego
Jun 26, 1977	Hollywood Oaks	Glenaris
Jly 3, 1977	Swaps Stakes (Hol)	J. O. Tobin
Jly 25, 1977	Sunset Handicap (Hol)	Today 'n Tomorrow
Sep 17, 1977	Woodward 'Cap (Bel)	Forego
Oct 23, 1977	Oak Tree Invit'l S. (SA)	Crystal Water
Nov 6, 1977	Norfolk Stakes (SA)	Balzac
Apr 9, 1978	Capistrano 'Cap (SA)	Exceller
May 29, 1978	H'wood Invit'l Turf 'Cap	Exceller
Jun 25, 1978	H'wood Gold Cup 'Cap	Exceller
Jly 16, 1978	Vanity Handicap (Hol)	Afifa
Jly 24, 1978	Sunset Handicap (Hol)	Exceller
Aug 27, 1978	Longacres Mile 'Cap	Bad 'n Big
Oct 14, 1978	Jky Club G. C. S. (Bel)	Exceller
Nov 4, 1978	Yellow Ribbon S. (SA)	Amazer
Nov 5, 1978	Oak Tree Invit'l S. (SA)	Exceller
Feb 25, 1979	St. Marg. Inv. 'Cap (SA)	Sanedtki
Mar 11, 1979	Santa Susana (SA)	Caline
Jly 8, 1979	Citation Handicap (Hol)	Text
Jly 15, 1979	Vanity Handicap (Hol)	It's in the Air
Jly 21, 1979	H'wood Juv. Ch.	Parsec
Aug 25, 1979	Haskell Handicap (Mth)	Text
Sep 1, 1979	Flower Bowl 'Cap (Bel)	Pearl Necklace
Sep 8, 1979	Marlboro Cup 'Cap (Bel)	Spectacular Bid
Sep 9, 1979	Del Mar Debutante	Table Hands
Oct 18, 1979	Meadowlands Cup 'Cap	Spectacular Bid
Jan 19, 1980	San Fernando S. (SA)	Spectacular Bid
Feb 2, 1980	Strub Stakes (SA)	Spectacular Bid
Feb 18, 1980	San Luis Obispo 'Cap (SA)	Silver Eagle
Mar 2, 1980	Santa Anita Handicap	Spectacular Bid
Mar 15, 1980	San Felipe 'Cap (SA)	Raise a Man

Jly 22, 1974	Sunset Handicap (Hol)	Greco II.
Sep 11, 1974	Del Mar Futurity	Diabolo
Feb 9, 1975	Strub Stakes (SA)	Stardust Mel
Mar 9, 1975	Santa Anita Handicap	Stardust Mel
Jun 7, 1975	Belmont Stakes	Avatar
Jly 6, 1975	Vanity Handicap (Hol)	Dulcia
Oct 19, 1975	Oak Tree Invit'l S. (SA)	Top Command
Nov 1, 1975	Nat. Thoro. Ch. Inv. S. (SA)	Dulcia
Apr 17, 1976	Hollywood Derby	Crystal Water
May 31, 1976	H'wood Pk. Inv. T. 'Cap	Dahlia
Sep 6, 1976	Del Mar Handicap	Riot in Paris
Sep 18, 1976	Woodward 'Cap (Bel)	Forego
Apr 20, 1980	Native Diver 'Cap (Hol)	Replant
Apr 27, 1980	Century 'Cap (Hol)	Go West Young Man
May 18, 1980	LeRoy 'Cap (Hol)	Spectacular Bid
May 24, 1980	Golden St. Brdrs Sire S.	Rumbo
Jun 8, 1980	Californian S. (Hol)	Spectacular Bid
Jly 4, 1980	American 'Cap (AP)	Bold Tropic
Jly 19, 1980	Wash. Pk. S. (AP)	Spectacular Bid
Jly 21, 1980	Sunset Handicap (Hol)	Inkerman
Aug 16, 1980	Haskell 'Cap (Mth)	Spectacular Bid
Aug 31, 1980	Roman 'Cap (Dmr)	Queen to Conquer
Sep 13, 1980	Arl.-Wash. Lassie S.	Truly Bound
Sep 20, 1980	Woodward (Bel)	Spectacular Bid

[1]Run as the Westerner Stakes prior to 1959. [2]Arlington and Washington Park Futurities combined into one race, beginning in 1962. [3]Run as Arlington Lassie prior to 1963. [4]Run as Santa Anita Maturity prior to 1963. [5]Changed from handicap to allowance

Result Chart — Shoemaker's greatest ride

San Juan Capistrano Handicap

SEVENTH RACE
SA 12463
March 10. 1962

ABOUT 1 3-4 MILES (turf). (Royal Living, March 11, 1959, 2:45⅘, 4, 117.)
Twenty-third running SAN JUAN CAPISTRANO HANDICAP. $100,000 added. 3-year-olds and upward. By subscription of $100 each, to accompany the nomination, $250 to pass the entry box and $750 additional to start, with $100,000 added, of which $20,000 to second, $15,000 to third, and $10,000 to fourth. A gold cup will be presented to the owner of the winner. Closed with 30 nominations.
Value of race $118,000. Value to winner $73,000; second, $20,000; third, $15,000; fourth, $10,000.
Mutuel Pool, $722,816.

Index	Horses	Eq't	A	Wt	PP	¼	½	1	1½	Str	Fin	Jockeys	Owners	Odds to $1
12243SA^{3}	Olden Times		4	119	8	1^{1}	$1^{1/2}$	$1^{1/2}$	1^{h}	1^{h}	1^{nk}	W Sh'maker	R C Ellsworth	a-2.90
12439SA^{3}	Juanro		4	109	4	$4^{1/2}$	5^{1}	5^{h}	7^{2}	$6^{1/2}$	$2^{1/2}$	R Campas	Mrs M Barnes	24.50
12227SA^{1}	The Axe II.	b	4	122	7	2^{h}	3^{1}	$3^{1/2}$	2^{h}	$2^{1\frac{1}{2}}$	$3^{1/2}$	I Val'zuela	Greentree Stable	5.00
12422SA^{3}	Notable II.		7	110	15	7^{1}	$7^{1/2}$	$7^{1/2}$	$6^{1/2}$	4^{h}	$4^{1/2}$	R Neves	La Doma Cp-Rcho Rio H'do	34.10
12243SA^{1}	Physician		5	120	9	11^{2}	$12^{3\frac{1}{2}}$	$13^{1\frac{1}{2}}$	14^{2}	11^{2}	$5^{1/2}$	D Pierce	L A Boice	a-2.90
12227SA^{2}	Oink	b	5	120	13	6^{1}	8^{1}	8^{1}	9^{6}	8^{4}	$6^{1/2}$	M Ycaza	Jacnot Stable	2.80
12422SA^{1}	Prenupcial	b	6	119	5	10^{h}	$9^{3\frac{1}{2}}$	9^{2}	$5^{1/2}$	3^{1}	$7^{1\frac{1}{4}}$	A Val'zuela	Mr-Mrs M H Robineau	6.90
12422SA	Hunter's Rock		4	115	11	8^{1}	10^{3}	10^{2}	12^{8}	9^{h}	$8^{1/2}$	W Harmatz	Mrs H Obre	13.70
12415SA^{4}	Fighting Felix	b	4	109	10	5^{1}	2^{1}	2^{1}	4^{1}	$5^{1\frac{1}{2}}$	$9^{1\frac{1}{4}}$	R York	L E Hutson	f-23.60
12422SA^{2}	Dusky Damion	b	5	113	1	15	15	15	15	14^{1}	10^{2}	D Rich'son	Swiftsure Stable	40.30
12422SA^{4}	Chimorro	b	6	112	6	$13^{1\frac{1}{2}}$	$14^{3\frac{1}{2}}$	14^{4}	13^{1}	12^{h}	11no	R Mundorf	Wagner Stable	f-23.60
12243SA	Micarlo	b	6	116	2	9^{3}	6^{h}	6^{h}	3^{h}	$7^{1/2}$	$12^{2\frac{1}{2}}$	J Leonard	Elmendorf	19.30
12230SA^{1}	Vinci		4	112	14	3^{h}	$4^{1/2}$	4^{1}	8^{h}	$10^{1/2}$	$13^{1/2}$	H Moreno	R Lowe	52.00
12407SA	Queen America	b	6	108	12	$12^{1/2}$	$11^{1/2}$	11^{2}	$10^{1/2}$	13^{1}	$14^{1\frac{1}{2}}$	G Taniguchi	Beaty-Dorney	f-23.60
12406SA^{4}	Lustrous Hope	b	5	116	3	14^{4}	13^{2}	12^{1}	11^{2}	15	15	J Longden	Alberta Ranch Ltd	10.00

a-Coupled, Olden Times and Physician. f-Mutuel field.

Time, 2:53. Track soft.

$2 Mutuel Prices:			
1-OLDEN TIMES (a-Entry)	7.80	5.00	3.80
5-JUANRO		13.40	7.20
7-THE AXE II.			5.20

B. c, by Relic—Djenne, by Djebel. Trainer, M. A. Tenney. Bred by R. C. Ellsworth.

IN GATE—5:03. OFF AT 5:03½ PACIFIC STANDARD TIME. Start good. Won driving.

OLDEN TIMES was sent to the front at once under clever rating, saved all possible ground throughout, shook off THE AXE II. in midstretch and, continuing on gamely to the wire, held JUANRO safe. JUANRO was a sharp factor from the beginning but encountered traffic troubles on the backstretch, came wide to find clear racing room, then cut to the rail for the final drive and was not far away in a good effort. THE AXE II. was in hand early while racing forwardly, made a strong bid from the far turn but could not sustain it and hung in the final sixteenth. NOTABLE II., always within striking distance, moved up boldly a quarter out but could not improve position in the run to the wire. PHYSICIAN, badly outrun early, came very fast through the stretch but the bid was too late to be effective. FIGHTING FELIX was through when the real racing began. OINK was forced wide on the final turn. VINCI was steadied out of close quarters entering the backstretch. MICARLO raced only spottily. QUEEN AMERICA lacked a rally. LUSTROUS HOPE was very wide entering the stretch but was not in contention at the time. Overweight—Fighting Felix, 3 pounds.

Bill Shoemaker's greatest ride? The jockey himself often selects his wire-to-wire 1962 victory by a neck on the sprinter **Olden Times** in Santa Anita's famous San Juan Capistrano Handicap, run over 1 3/4-miles of "soft" turf.

Never leading even by a length after the quarter-mile, and turning back successive challenges by four horses at various points of call, Shoemaker takes **Olden Times** all the way, in the style that has established his "hands" as the finest pair of all times.

BIBLIOGRAPHY

Ainslie, Tom. *Ainslie's Complete Guide to Thoroughbred Racing,* Simon and Schuster, New York, 1979.

Ainslie, Tom. *Ainslie's Encyclopedia of Thoroughbred Handicapping,* William Morrow and Company, Inc., New York, 1980.

Beyer, Andrew. *Picking Winners.* Houghton Mifflin Company, Boston, Mass., 1975.

Beyer, Andrew. *The Winning Horseplayer.* Houghton Mifflin Company, Boston, 1983.

Cramer, Mark. "Jockey Angle: dropping to win." *American Turf Monthly,* Amerpub, New York, December 1981, pp. 6-7.

Davidowitz, Steven. *Betting Thoroughbreds.* E. P. Dutton, New York, 1977.

Davis, Fred. *Probability Computation.* Millwood Publications, New York, 1974.

Davis, Fred. *Thoroughbred Racing: Percentages and Probabilities.* Millwood Publications, New York, 1974.

Dowst, Robert Saunders. *Profits on Horses.* Morrow Company, New York, 1937.

Fabricand, Burton. *Horse Sense.* David McKay Company, Inc., New York, 1965.

Gaines, Milt. *The Tote Board Is Alive and Well.* GBC Press, Las Vegas, Nevada, 1981.

Jones, Gordon. *Smart Money.* Karman Communications, Huntington Beach, Ca., 1977.

Kuck, Henry. *Situation Handicapping.* Woodside Associates, New York, 1981.

Ledbetter, Bonnie and Ainslie, Tom. *The Body Language of Horses.* William Morrow and Company, Inc., New York, 1980.

Mahl, Huey. *Money Management.* A technical paper, presented at Sports Tyme Handicapping Seminar, Dunes Hotel & Country Club, Las Vegas, Nevada, December 12-13, 1979.

Meyer, John. *"The T.I.S. Pace Report," The National Railbird Review,* Vol. II, Nos. 8 and 9, San Clemente, CA. 1981.

Quinn, James. *The Handicapper's Condition Book.* GBC Press, Las Vegas, Nevada, 1981.

Quinn, James. *Quinn's International Stakes Catalogue.* Foothills Publications, Arcadia, Ca., 1983.

Quirin, William. *Winning at the Races: Computer Discoveries in Thoroughbred Handicapping.* William Morrow and Company, Inc., New York, 1979.

Roman, Steven A. "Dosage: A Practical Approach," *Daily Racing Form,* "Bloodlines" column, Spring, 1981.

Scott, William L. *How Will Your Horse Run Today?* Amicus Press, Baltimore, 1984.

Scott, William L. *Investing at the Racetrack.* Simon and Schuster, New York, 1982.

Selvidge, James. *Hold Your Horses.* Jacada Publications, Seattle, Washington, 1974.

Selvidge, James. *Hold Your Horses Quarterly,* Vols. 1 & 2, (Various), Jacada Publications, Seattle, Washington, 1979-81.

THE WORLD'S FINEST LIBRARY
OF GAMING BOOKS

THE FAMOUS FACT BOOKS

	Retail Price
_____ THE FACTS OF BACCARAT *by Walter Nolan*	$ 4.95
_____ THE FACTS OF BLACK JACK *by Walter Nolan*	$ 4.95
_____ THE FACTS OF CRAPS *by Walter Nolan*	$ 4.95
_____ THE FACTS OF KENO *by Walter Nolan*	$ 4.95
_____ THE FACTS OF ROULETTE *by Walter Nolan*	$ 4.95
_____ THE FACTS OF SLOTS *by Walter Nolan*	$ 4.95

BACCARAT

_____ BACCARAT DECISIONS *by Huey Mahl*	$ 5.00
_____ BACCARAT FAIR AND FOUL *by Professor Hoffman*	$ 5.00
_____ FACTS OF BACCARAT *by Walter Nolan*	$ 4.95

BLACK JACK

_____ BASIC BLACKJACK BETTING *by Charles Einstein*	$ 6.95
_____ FACTS OF BLACKJACK *by Walter Nolan*	$ 4.95
_____ HOW TO WIN AT BLACKJACK *by Charles Einstein*	$ 7.95

GAMBLING LORE

_____ BE A WINNER *by The Gaming Council*	$ 5.00
_____ CARD SHARPERS *by Robert Houdin*	$ 9.95
_____ GAMBLING AND GAMBLING DEVICES *by John Quinn*	$15.00
_____ GAMBLING KNOW-HOW *by Irv Sutton*	$ 5.00
_____ HANDBOOK OF PERCENTAGES *by Charles Shampaign*	$ 5.00
_____ RIGHT WAY TO DO WRONG *by Harry Houdini*	$ 5.95
_____ RICH UNCLE FROM FIJI *by M. P. Adams*	$ 5.00
_____ SHARPS AND FLATS *by John Nevil*	$12.95
_____ TAKING THE EDGE *by Martin Allen*	$ 5.00
_____ THREE CARD MONTE *by John Scarne and Audley Walsh*	$ 5.00
_____ TWENTY YEARS A FAKIR *by James Weldon*	$ 7.95

GAMES

_____ GIN RUMMY *by George Monkland*	$ 6.95
_____ HOW TO WIN AT GIN RUMMY *by Harold Hart*	$ 5.00
_____ KEY TO CRIBBAGE *by William Green*	$ 6.95
_____ ODD TRICKS (BRIDGE) *by Travis White*	$ 5.95
_____ PLAY BACKGAMMON TONIGHT *by Dave Thompson*	$ 5.00

MAGIC

_____ CARD CONTROL *by Arthur Buckley*	$ 9.95
_____ EXPERT AT THE CARD TABLE *by W. W. Erdnase*	$ 8.95
_____ LITTLE SECRETS *by Frank Bonville*	$ 5.00
_____ MASTER KEY AND RUN-UP SYSTEMS *by Anonymous*	$ 5.95
_____ HOW TO MEMORIZE A DECK IN 5 MINUTES *by Charles Edwards*	$ 5.95

cut

_____ PRINCIPLES AND DECEPTIONS
      by Arthur Buckley $ 9.95
_____ SPOTLIGHT ON THE CARD SHARP
      by Scaife $ 5.00

MISCELLANEOUS

_____ CRAPS LINE DECISIONS *by Huey Mahl* $ 5.00
_____ CROSSBET II (sports betting) *by Huey Mahl* $ 5.00
_____ KENO HANDBOOK *by Jim Claussen* $ 5.95
_____ HOW TO SELECT YOUR BEST BETS
      by Dean Wiley $ 7.95
_____ UNDERSTANDING GAMBLING SYSTEMS
      by Dean Wiley $ 7.95

POKER

_____ HOLD 'EM POKER *by David Sklansky* $ 7.95
_____ HOW TO WIN AT STUD POKER
      by James Wickstead $ 7.95
_____ PLAY WINNING POKER *by Jack King* $ 6.95
_____ POKER BY HARDISON *by Theo Hardison* $ 5.00
_____ POKER POKER *by Philip Dangel* $12.95
_____ SKLANSKY ON RAZZ *by David Sklansky* $ 5.00
_____ STUD POKER BLUE BOOK *by George Fisher* $ 5.00

RACING

_____ AVERAGE PURSE TABLES *by Huey Mahl* $ 5.00
_____ DOWST REVISITED *by Ron Thacker* $ 5.00
_____ HOW THEY RAN *by Huey Mahl* $ 5.00
_____ THE BEST OF THOROUGHBRED
      HANDICAPPING *by James Quinn* $12.95
_____ MORE BLUE RIBBON SYSTEMS
      by C. P. Editorial Staff $ 6.95
_____ 150 BLUE RIBBON WINNING SYSTEMS
      by C. P. Editorial Staff $ 6.95
_____ PARI-MUTUEL BETTING *by James Hillis* $ 5.00
_____ RACE IS PACE *by Huey Mahl* $ 6.95
_____ RACING MAXIMS AND METHODS OF
      PITTSBURGH PHIL *by Edward Cole* $ 7.95
_____ 25 WAYS TO BEAT THE HORSES *by Walter Gibson* $ 7.95

ROULETTE

_____ FACTS OF ROULETTE *by Walter Nolan* $ 4.95
_____ ROULETTE BY THE DOZENS
      by Allan Ackerman $ 5.00
_____ ROULETTE BY THE NUMBERS
      by Huey Mahl $ 5.00
_____ ROULETTE ROUGE ET NOIR
      by Allan Ackerman $ 5.00

NOTE: All books are softcover editions.

AVAILABLE AT BETTER RETAIL OUTLETS.

To Order by Mail use the order form above or enclose a list of the title(s) being ordered. Include a check or money order for the retail price of each title plus $1.00 per book for postage and handling.
Send order to: CASINO PRESS, INC., Dept. F-84, 128 E. 56th Street, New York, N. Y. 10022. Allow 3 weeks for delivery.

cut